GOV
P9-BZR-244
3 1611 00102 7868

DNO
OAT
LO-12
8-18-8

DATE DUE

3-26-02	11:50	2629	
JUN 05 2008			

Demco, Inc. 38-293

School Wars

Barbara B. Gaddy
T. William Hall
Robert J. Marzano

. . . .

School Wars

Resolving Our Conflicts Over Religion and Values

Jossey-Bass Publishers
San Francisco

GOVERNORS STATE UNIVERSITY
UNIVERSITY PARK
IL 60466

LA 217.2 .G33 1990

Gaddy, Barbara B., 1953-

School wars

325393

Copyright © 1996 by Jossey-Bass Inc., Publishers, 350 Sansome Street, San Francisco, California 94104.

All rights reserved. No part of this publication may be reproduced, stored in a retrieval system, or transmitted, in any form or by any means, electronic, mechanical, photocopying, recording, or otherwise, without the prior written permission of the publisher.

Substantial discounts on bulk quantities of Jossey-Bass books are available to corporations, professional associations, and other organizations. For details and discount information, contact the special sales department at Jossey-Bass Inc., Publishers (415) 433–1740; Fax (800) 605–2665.

For sales outside the United States, please contact your local Simon & Schuster International office.

Manufactured in the United States of America on Lyons Falls Pathfinder Tradebook. This paper is acid-free and 100 percent totally chlorine-free.

Library of Congress Cataloging-in-Publication Data

Gaddy, Barbara B., date.
School wars: resolving our conflicts over religion and values / Barbara B. Gaddy, T. William Hall, Robert J. Marzano. — 1st ed.
p. cm.
Includes bibliographical references (p.) and index.
ISBN 0–7879–0236–5 (alk. paper)
1. Public schools — Unites States. 2. Educational change — United States. 3. Politics and education — United States. 4. Christianity and politics — United States. 5. Humanism — United States. 6. Religion in the public schools — United States. I. Hall, T. William (Thomas William), date. II Marzano, Robert J. III. Title.
LA217.2.G33 1996
371'.01'0973 — dc20

96–3995
CIP

HB Printing 10 9 8 7 6 5 4 3 2 1 FIRST EDITION

Contents

Preface

A conflict is being played out in the public schools today. At the heart of the conflict are collisions among different views of the world held by politically active fundamentalist Christians and others on the spectrum, including mainline Christians, liberals, and humanists. These world views are made up of people's most basic assumptions about life. These assumptions define their values, their sense of right and wrong, and their definitions and standards of justice. The stakes in this struggle are high because the school environment is viewed as the place where the knowledge, historical perspectives, and values that are the basis for our culture are passed from one generation to the next. The stakes are even higher for parents, especially those who believe that schools are promoting values—perhaps religious values—that are antithetical to their own. Certainly, the public schools have never been completely free of controversies over what children should be taught. Yet, in recent years these controversies have become more passionate, focused, and polarized. All too often the result is gridlock.

This book clarifies the major issues and central players in conflicts over elements of educational reform. Specifically, our focus is on the concerns and criticisms of those conservative Christians who are most vocally, forcefully, and politically involved in these conflicts. Our aim is to clarify the nature of the current public school controversies.

Obviously, world views are not neat categories; individuals embrace assumptions and beliefs from a broad continuum. Yet, certain beliefs and values shared by the broad groups involved in the debate can be articulated. Understanding these commonly held beliefs and values is vitally important.

It is equally important that the principles of school reform be understood by a broader population than is currently familiar with them. Wider awareness of the impact of public education and other converging factors has resulted in increased attention being paid to the public schools. Societal problems, a perception of declining academic achievement and test scores, and the school reform movement have contributed to increased debate over what—and how—children should learn. Confusion and misinformation exist, compounding and further inflaming controversies over the education of the nation's children. Thus, in this book we articulate the basic research and fundamental concepts upon which much school reform is based.

In Part One, we describe the players involved in these controversies and provide a historical perspective for understanding how the conflicts arose. In Part Two, we discuss the reforms, literature, and curricula that are being contested and, more importantly, why they are being contested. In Part Three, we explore the differing religious and philosophical world views of those involved in the conflict. We also discuss the relationship between government and religion in the context of the First Amendment's religious liberty clauses. In Part Four, we recommend solutions to the conflicts raised throughout the book. These proposals include teaching about religion, values education, parent-teacher cooperation, the development of school policies, and a model for communities to live and work productively amid conflicting beliefs. Appendix A provides background, detailing key court cases related to battles over educational materials, as well as cases that articulated important constitutional principles regarding the delicate balance between the rights of students and the responsibility of school board authorities. In

Appendix B we provide a list of resources for readers who might want to learn more or get involved with the issues raised in this book.

Complete agreement by all people on every issue cannot be expected. Nevertheless, it is worth hoping that an increasing number of people will seek to understand the deeply held convictions of others while preserving political and religious liberties. Then, cooperation, even accommodation, can be sought so that institutions that serve the public may benefit everyone. Some individuals and groups are already making attempts at communication, understanding, and reconciliation. However, a great deal of work still needs to be done. Our hope is that this book will contribute to more productive future interactions among the school administrators, teachers, parents, religious leaders, and community members involved in the debate.

Denver, Colorado
January 1996

Barbara B. Gaddy
T. William Hall
Robert J. Marzano

The Authors

Barbara B. Gaddy, an editor and communications specialist, is a senior associate with Mid-Continent Regional Educational Laboratory. She earned her B.S. degree (1975) in marketing management from Miami University and her M.A. degree (1992) in mass communications from the University of Denver, where her research focused on litigation concerning public school books and materials. Gaddy is a member of the Executive Committee of the Colorado Language Arts Society, an affiliate of the National Council of Teachers of English. She is also president of the board of the Ricks Center for Gifted Children at the University of Denver.

T. William Hall is professor emeritus of Syracuse University, having served as professor of religion for nineteen years and as chair of the Department of Religion for eight years. He earned his B.A. degree (1943) in history at Kansas Wesleyan University, his Th.M. degree (1946) from the Iliff School of Theology, and his Ph.D. degree (1956) in the philosophy of religion from Boston University. Before joining the Syracuse University faculty, he served on faculties at the University of Denver, Stephens College, Kansas Wesleyan University, and Pittsburg (Kansas) State College. Hall is an ordained minister in the United Methodist Church.

Throughout his professional career, Hall has been interested in public education, with a special concern for the transmission of values and objective teaching about religion. In the 1950s, he participated in the nationwide Teacher Education and Religion Project sponsored by the American Association of Colleges for Teacher Education. He also has served on a special task force on Religion and Public Education for the American Academy of Religion.

In addition to publishing book reviews and scholarly articles, Hall has edited a textbook, *Introduction to the Study of Religion* (1978), and was coauthor of *Religion: An Introduction* (1985, with Pilgrim and Cavanagh).

Robert J. Marzano is deputy director for training and development at the Mid-Continent Regional Educational Laboratory (McREL) in Aurora, Colorado. He earned his B.A. degree (1968) in English at Iona College, his M.Ed. degree (1971) in reading and language arts at Seattle University, and his Ph.D. degree (1974) in curriculum and instruction at the University of Washington, Seattle. Prior to joining the staff at McREL, he was an associate professor at the University of Colorado.

Marzano has developed numerous programs and practices, used in K-12 classrooms, that translate current research and theory in cognition into instructional methods. During his twenty-eight years in education, he has authored more than ten books and one hundred articles and chapters in books on such topics as reading and writing instruction, thinking skills, performance assessment, curriculum design and school reform.

During the 1960s, Marzano spent four years in New York State as a monk with the Christian Brothers of Ireland.

School Wars

Part I

The Challenge to Public Education

1

The Current Conflict

This scenario is based on actual events and characterizes the dynamics and conflicting views at play in communities across this country.

The lead article in the local newspaper read, "Local School Accused of Fostering a New Religion." It went on to explain that a war was raging in the local school district—not a war of bullets, but a war of ideas. On one side was a highly vocal and aggressive group of community members who were convinced that the changes the school district was trying to make were actually a thinly veiled attempt to promote a new satanically based religion. On the other side were teachers, administrators, and community members who had planned to systematically make significant changes in the district over the next few years. They saw the attempts of the community group as the first step toward undoing two years' worth of work to upgrade their educational system. How had things gotten to this point?

Two years earlier, district teachers and administrators had decided that drastic changes had to be made in the local educational system. They reached this conclusion after reading national reports such as *A Nation at Risk*, written by a presidentially sponsored commission, which stated that American education must change to meet the demands of a changing society and a changing marketplace. The school system, which had worked well in the past, simply was not going to make it in the world of the future. Over a one-and-a-half-year period, 150 teachers, administrators, and parents from the community studied every report they could get their hands on. What type of curriculum was needed to prepare students for the future? What changes should be made in testing practices, instructional practices, scheduling, and report cards? They talked to people from other districts who were engaged in the same basic efforts. They were committed to leaving no stone unturned. Finally, they developed a strategic plan that detailed every proposed change along with a starting date and an ending date. The plan was submitted to and passed by the district's school board.

It was only after the strategic plan had been accepted by the school board that the community group began asking questions. In the beginning, they presented themselves as interested parents and community members who simply wanted to review the proposed changes in the educational system. However, somewhere along the way the tone and function of the group changed radically. They became a formal entity calling themselves Concerned Citizens for Educational Change, or CCEC. Their initial requests for information gradually turned into a demand to be involved in any meetings that dealt with decisions about district policy. They even asked to be at any meetings of two or more teachers who were discussing curriculum or instruction, asserting that such meetings affected educational policy and should therefore be monitored by community members.

At first, all of their requests were granted by district administrators and teachers. However, members of the group began showing up at any and every meeting. Their presence at these meetings was often highly disruptive. They not only asked questions regarding the rationale for proposed changes but demanded to see the research and theory supporting those changes. Although district teachers and administrators tried to provide the requested information, these efforts soon began taking up a significant amount of time for district personnel. Additionally, it seemed as though the questions asked by CCEC were not answered by the information provided by the district. They always asked new questions and needed more documentation. Finally, district personnel began saying no to what they considered inordinate requests for documentation.

About a week before one of the first changes specified by the strategic plan was to be implemented, the members of CCEC sponsored a speaker from out of state to make a presentation to a local conservative church. No one from the school district was invited. The speaker, who worked for a national self-proclaimed "conservative Christian organization" whose stated purpose was to bring Christianity back to public education, explained to a packed house that schools and districts across the country were involved in a plot to take over the hearts and minds of American children. This plot permeated education and had roots that reached as far as the White House. Knowingly or unknowingly, the American educational system had become part of Satan's attempt to destroy Christianity. In effect, the attempts to reform American education were part of the efforts of the Antichrist to take over the world, and the local school district had fallen into his trap. If they were allowed to continue, the proposed changes would lead to indoctrination of all schoolchildren into a new anti-Christian religion. Members of the church were captivated by the presentation. Many of them had read books from their local Christian bookstores that presented the same odious scenario of a satanically based plot to take over American education. And here it was, happening in their own school district—in their own backyard. Members of CCEC urged the crowd to take action.

It just so happened that a school board meeting was scheduled for the next evening. CCEC members provided directions to the meeting and even helped to establish a system whereby those who did not have rides could get them from others who were going. On the night of the school board meeting, most board members were shocked to find three hundred people in attendance; usually fewer than ten community members were present at such meetings. Also present were television cameras from local stations and reporters from the local press who had been told by CCEC members that "big news" would be made at the board meeting. One school board member was not at all surprised at the turnout, however. She had been apprised of CCEC's intentions since the early formation of the group and was highly sympathetic to their charges. She, too, had read many books and articles about the satanic conspiracy permeating education. She and the group had determined early on in their efforts that they would wait for the right moment to overturn the district's strategic plan. Now was the right moment.

The meeting soon resembled a mob scene. Accusations were presented and sometimes shouted out. Attempts by board members and district personnel to explain their decisions and proposed changes were drowned out by boos and jeers. Finally, the angry crowd demanded that the planned changes be tabled indefinitely. Completely overwhelmed by the accusations of the group and the force of their demands, the school board acquiesced. They voted to discontinue the strategic plan indefinitely, until further studies could be completed. It seemed the prudent and safe thing to do. Better to hold off on the proposed changes than risk a heated conflict. The media representatives were, for all practical purposes, delighted. They had their promised story. A battle was certainly raging in the public schools.

A System in Gridlock

With variations in intensity, in the major actors, and in minor issues, this scenario is occurring in school districts all across the country. America's educational system is in the midst of not only a financial crisis but a crisis of its character and direction. At issue are not simply the educational merits of specific programs but the nature of the allegedly religious and political agendas underlying them.

Challenges to materials and practices in the public schools have occurred for decades. In recent years, however, the number of challenges has dramatically increased. One group that monitors such challenges reports, for example, that the 1993–94 school year saw 462 challenges to remove or restrict public school instructional materials, literature, library materials, activities, or programs. These

462 challenges in forty-six states across the nation represented the largest single school-year total in the previous decade.[1]

The character of challenges in recent years has also changed dramatically. Whereas the challenges were once isolated incidents, they now appear to be the design of a movement of dedicated, influential, and at times extreme Christian fundamentalists. People and groups involved with this movement have become increasingly vocal, active, and effective in opposing public school materials and teaching methods. Specifically, these critics assert that public schools are conveying a relativistic value system to children and an incorrect view of history and science, that certain teaching methods undermine parental and religious authority and patriotism, and that textbooks do not give sufficient weight to the impact of religious beliefs on American history. Their most serious allegations are that public schools are performing psychological experiments on children, undermining Christianity, and indoctrinating students into a variety of "religions," including secularism, humanism, New Age religions, Eastern religions, mysticism, and worse, Satanism. The result of these liberal, secular, and experimental programs, they believe, is declining church participation, illiteracy, immorality, increased teenage pregnancies, and a greater interest in the occult.

Much of this opposition has been generated by organizations that are loosely affiliated with each other. These include Phyllis Schlafly's Eagle Forum, Pat Robertson's Christian Coalition and American Center for Law and Justice, Citizens for Excellence in Education (CEE), and Mel and Norma Gabler's Educational Research Analysts. Their challenges cut a broad swath. In addition to history and science textbooks, these groups have objected to self-esteem programs and sex education materials, as well as general teaching methods including role playing, journaling, and open-ended discussions designed to foster imagination and critical thinking.

Allegedly liberal and secular curricular materials are being protested through a number of avenues, with numerous challenges occurring at the classroom level. Protests also are lodged through the formal reconsideration policies—which spell out procedures for handling complaints about materials and programs—that are in place in many school districts. In addition, the courts have been the site of challenges based on the grounds that some curricular materials promote a variety of belief systems akin to religions and thus violate the First Amendment's mandate of separation of church and state.

Several groups are countering these criticisms, attempting to stem the tide of attacks on public education. These groups include the National Education Association, the Freedom to Read Foundation, the American Library Association, the National Coalition Against Censorship, the American Civil Liberties Union, People For the American Way (PFAW), and the National Council of Teachers of English (NCTE). Perhaps the most active and visible of these groups is PFAW. Headed by television producer Norman Lear, PFAW was established in 1980 to combat the "intolerance of the 'Religious Right'" and to monitor increasing "censorship" activities.[2] PFAW has defended numerous school districts around the country in court battles over educational materials and instructional practices.[3]

PFAW and like-minded organizations argue that public schools should prepare students to participate effectively in America's democratic and diverse society by giving them access to a variety of ideas, encouraging them to think for themselves, and promoting tolerance and acceptance of diversity.[4] They maintain that teachers are the best judges of appropriate textbooks and curricular materials and that new public school programs and practices are based on sound educational principles, backed by years of research. These organizations also allege that Christian "extremists" have a hidden agenda to take over the public schools and that their efforts to bring public school educational materials in line with sectarian religious beliefs violate the principle of separation of church and state. Those who oppose efforts to eliminate or restrict educational materials see such efforts as direct assaults on students' freedom to learn. According to Rebecca Sargent, a member of the Redondo Beach, California, school board, which battled over a controversial literature series called *Impressions*, these efforts are "pure and simple censorship."[5]

In battles over public school materials and practices, fears run high. Groups opposing efforts to restrict books and materials are fearful that ideological zealots will take over the schools in an attempt to indoctrinate children with narrow, sectarian views that are intolerant of diversity and hostile to intellectual freedom and critical thinking. Christian fundamentalists, on the other hand, are fearful that their children's religious faith is being undermined because, they believe, the majority of educational materials currently in use in public schools promote an anti-Christian view of the world. They argue that the so-called marketplace of ideas, supposedly in place in the public schools, excludes the voices and ideas of conservative Christians.

The perspectives of the groups involved in public school battles often are diametrically opposed. In fact, these groups are extremely polarized on nearly every issue. For example, "liberals" argue that the separation of church and state is a constitutional mandate that must be followed in the schools. "Conservatives," particularly fundamentalists, argue that public schools have become hostile to traditional religions; some believe that alternative religions are being promoted in the schools. These critics accuse educators of religious persecution and suppression of students' and teachers' religious freedoms. Organizations opposed to efforts to restrict or eliminate educational materials or instructional practices cry "censorship." School critics maintain that they do not advocate censorship but, instead, better textbook selections and an emphasis on the basics.

Differences in convictions are central to a democratic society. However, when polarization of diverse beliefs becomes extreme, institutions such as the public schools cease to function well as servants of the public. This condition of crisis, when found in the national government, is called gridlock, and it makes governance ineffective. Public education is facing a similar crisis; effectively dealing with this crisis is of paramount importance.

Historical Perspectives

Controversy over children's educational programs and practices is not new. For over two millennia, people have asked: What educational materials should our children be exposed to? What, specifically, should we teach our children, and how? Should certain topics or facts be withheld from children? Twenty-four hundred years ago, Plato commented on the subject in *The Republic*: "And shall we just carelessly allow children to hear any casual tales which may be devised by casual persons, and receive into their minds ideas for the most part the very opposite of those which we should wish them to have when they are grown up? We cannot. Then the first thing will be to establish a censorship of the writers of fiction, and let the censors receive any tale of fiction which is good, and reject the bad."[6]

Books and curricular materials used in the United States have been challenged since the beginning of the common schools in the nineteenth century.[7] The allegedly religious nature of materials has most often been at the heart of the controversy. In the early nineteenth century, schools were private or religious institutions. However, a host of social, economic, and philosophical factors converged during this time, and the common school movement was born. One of the most significant influences on the development of public schools was immigration. The Industrial Revolution had brought urbanization and, along with it, poverty, slums, and poor factory conditions. Compounding these problems were the large numbers of newcomers now competing for jobs. These converging factors resulted in increasing pressures for public education in two significant ways.

First, social reformers argued that a strong, free public education system would help to provide a common ground for assimilating diverse peoples into American culture. This argument looked more and more appealing to the general population as people feared that the varied backgrounds, customs, and beliefs of European immigrants would upset American society. As historian S. Alexander

Rippa notes, this "mass influx from Europe created new social tensions in the United States. . . . Old religious arguments flared anew as natives and aliens clashed in daily human relations." Free public education also became the cry of labor leaders, who saw equal educational opportunity as a way to relieve the social inequities so apparent in the often-abusive factory system.[8]

Second, the philosophy of humanitarianism, an Enlightenment idea flourishing anew through the voice of Ralph Waldo Emerson, provided impetus for the movement for free public education. Rippa writes that "Emerson's speeches and writings gave it new strength and conviction, inspiring one of the greatest reform movements in American history."[9] Humanitarianism spoke to what Emerson called the "infinite worthiness in man," that is, the idea that each human being is part of the divine, and thus inherently good and perfectible. This philosophy converged with workers' desires for betterment, lending further momentum to the cause of public education.[10]

Not everyone approved of the movement to establish free public schools. Some argued that factory workers were destined to remain poor and uneducated. Others believed that education was the responsibility of the family, not the public. Still others spoke to the deep religious prejudices and fears in American society, arguing that public education would conflict with religious schools.[11] However, in spite of its detractors, free public education in the form of common schools established a strong foothold in American society.

Although common schools offered free public education to all children regardless of social class or religious belief, they were not free from all religious influence. On the contrary, Horace Mann, one of the educational leaders of the time, believed in the importance of "inculcat[ing] all Christian morals."[12] Although Mann was deeply opposed to religious dogma, he thought it was vital to use the Bible to teach moral values, but in a nonsectarian way. Because of his nonsectarian (though decidedly Protestant) stance, Mann was denounced by certain religious leaders as an atheist who was undermining the Bible.[13]

In the nineteenth century, public school use of the Bible in a purportedly nonsectarian way also led to controversy. Although Mann may have considered public school Bible use to be nonsectarian and thus appropriate, Catholics disagreed. For example, in Boston, Massachusetts, Roman Catholics were upset by the use of Protestant versions of the Bible and textbooks that had a distinctly Protestant bias. Subsequently, Catholics took over the school committee; Protestants were upset and demanded the nonsectarian teaching of basic Christian principles. The controversy finally ended when a political solution was reached, returning control of the school committee to the Protestants. In the ensuing years, the number of privately funded Catholic schools increased, largely in response to concerns about Protestant curricula.[14]

Several factors in the late 1800s contributed to continued conflict over religion in the public schools. The event that most inflamed this conflict was the publication of Charles Darwin's *The Origin of Species* in 1859. Rippa describes this as "a momentous turning point in the history of ideas."[15] Darwinism set forth the theory of evolutionary change, which profoundly affected not only the study of biology and the process of scientific inquiry, but other fields of study as well. Darwinian ideas were especially applicable to sociology, psychology, and education. Scholars, philosophers, and scientists began to view the world, and people, as evolving and changing rather than fixed and immutable. It is hardly a leap to conclude that if human beings and their environment are constantly changing, then ideas and beliefs must also be changing. This philosophy conflicted with the heart of traditional theology and offended most Christian fundamentalists.[16] Opposition to the teaching of evolution in the public schools in the succeeding years led to the famous *Scopes* "monkey" trial in Tennessee in 1927. (See Chapter Two for a discussion of the *Scopes* trial.)

Darwinism had a significant effect on John Dewey, probably the most influential educator of the time. Dewey wrote several books in the early decades of the twentieth century detailing his philosophy of education, which emphasized the evolving *process* of learning. He believed that traditional education, which emphasized passive absorption and recitation of largely unimportant bits of information, was out of touch with the practical and philosophical changes occurring in society and, therefore, was a waste of a child's life. In Dewey's view, true learning took place through living—through active, practical, self-directed engagement with the subject matter.[17]

Changes in society were occurring rapidly, including greater questioning of the absolute and unchanging nature of morals and values. Yet Darwinian ideas of evolution were only part of the reason for these changes. The increasingly diverse population that resulted from mass immigration greatly affected American culture. Immigrants were "Americanized," true, but American culture was also changed by this massive influx of new people and new ideas.[18] In discussing the secularization of public education, writer Steven Lee notes, "The teaching of traditional Christian morality declined as society's concepts of morality became more diverse. Industrialization depleted the role of the family as a morally unifying force, and mass immigration introduced concepts of morality that conflicted with the formerly predominant Protestant view. . . . In order to accommodate an increasingly diverse constituency, public education began to emphasize open inquiry as opposed to teaching set religious values."[19]

In the mid-twentieth century, public education was again dramatically altered by societal changes that reached an apex in the turbulent era of the 1960s. The civil rights movement was an impetus for the Supreme Court to order the desegregation of public schools. The women's movement, along with the civil rights movement, contributed to changing ideas about lifestyles and traditional concepts of the family. This led to increasing pressure to eliminate racial and sexual stereotypes from textbooks. Further, the Vietnam

War and the Watergate scandal eroded the public's confidence in government.[20]

Other changes occurred during the 1960s in the educational process itself, changes that are the basis of many of the current challenges to public school materials and practices. Federal funds were made available to schools to finance change and innovation. As a result, innovations such as open classrooms, team teaching, new math, individualized instruction, and alternative curricula appeared in American public schools. Educators began to emphasize thinking and decision-making skills rather than simply teaching facts. Textbooks themselves also changed and became more realistic, supplanting the "idealistic" literature previously used. These new books began to deal with new topics that reflected the lifestyle and attitude changes occurring in society, topics that included real-life family problems such as divorce and living on welfare; working mothers; death and dying; the changing roles of men and women; the lifestyles and practices of different ethnic groups; and formerly taboo adolescent subjects such as pregnancy, abortion, and homosexuality. The language in these books also became more graphic; street language began to be used to make the stories seem more "real." Not coincidentally, attacks on the public schools escalated.[21]

The 1960s were also an important turning point for public education because of Supreme Court cases that seemed to redefine the relationship between government and religion. School-sponsored prayer and Bible reading were declared unconstitutional and a state statute barring the teaching of evolution was struck down.[22] Although many applauded changes that occurred in public education during the mid-twentieth century, others firmly believed that public education was on a disastrous course of secularization.

In sum, the history of public education is filled with conflict over what children should learn and how they should be taught. Controversies over religion, values, morals, and ideologies have often been at the heart of the matter and have escalated in recent years.

What is occurring is a clash of the most basic assumptions through which different people see the world, assumptions that define our values, our sense of right and wrong, our standards and definitions of justice—our view of the world. The stakes are high because people view the public schools as the place where the knowledge, historical perspectives, and values that are the basis for our culture are passed from one generation to the next. But whose values? Whose perspectives? Sharp differences between values, beliefs, and priorities—in short, differences in world views—are making it difficult for teaching and learning to take place. Pressures on both sides are creating a crisis in education hitherto unknown in this country.

2

School Critics: Who Are They?

Many conservative Christian groups and individuals have common concerns about public education. Yet, only a handful of groups have been at the forefront of public school controversies.

Leaders of the Pack

The most prominent of the groups and individuals involved in public school issues are Citizens for Excellence in Education (CEE), Phyllis Schlafly's Eagle Forum, Pat Robertson and his Christian Coalition, Mel and Norma Gabler of Educational Research Analysts, and the Reverend Jerry Falwell.

Citizens for Excellence in Education

Historically, the most proactive of these groups has been CEE, an affiliate of the National Association of Christian Educators (NACE). CEE's founder and president, Robert Simonds, has also held the position of chair of the Southern California chapter of the National Association of Evangelicals. Additionally, Simonds was a member of President Ronald Reagan's Task Force to Implement the National Commission on Excellence in Education's Report, *A Nation at Risk*. Finally, he has served as national chair of the Education Sphere of the Congress on the Christian World View.[1]

In 1985, Simonds stated that the purpose of CEE was to "inform and educate people on [political] candidates' positions, including training for candidates." At that time Simonds stated that CEE worked closely with the Eagle Forum, Beverly LaHaye's Concerned Women for America, Coalition for Christians in Government, the Freedom Council, and many pro-life groups, which Simonds described as a coalition operating as a "formidable force in any community."[2]

Proclaiming itself as a "voice of reason," CEE maintains that its mission is to bring "moral sanity" back to the public schools.[3] To accomplish this goal, CEE encourages parents and community members to become involved in the public schools, and sells a Public School Awareness (PSA) kit to help them. The kit contains a copy of Simonds's book *How to Elect Christians to Public Office*. The kit also contains a set of audiotaped interviews with Simonds that give instructions on how to set up a church-sponsored PSA committee. On the first tape, "What a PSA Committee Is and Can Do," Simonds proclaims that "schools belong to the community." A PSA committee's involvement in schools is justified, he says, because polls show that 75 to 85 percent of communities across the country claim to be Christian.[4]

Simonds writes a monthly *President's Report,* in which he speaks to "traditionalist Christians," detailing CEE's concerns and accomplishments. CEE's stated goals include establishing a CEE chapter in every one of the nation's 15,700 school districts and having Christian parents gain a majority influence on every local school board. Simonds reported that 220 PSA committees were organized across the country in the six-month period prior to March 1991; by January 1995, the number had grown to 1,700.[5]

As far as can be discerned from its publications, NACE/CEE is an independent corporate entity that is not formally affiliated with any Christian denomination. However, within many of NACE/CEE's publications, frequent references are made to cooperation with like-minded individuals and organizations. Five individuals whose organizations appear particularly closely tied to NACE/CEE in philosophy, purpose, and strategies are Pat Robertson, Jerry Falwell, Phyllis Schlafly, and Mel and Norma Gabler. In *How to Elect Christians to Public Office*, Simonds refers to Pat Robertson as a "modern day prophet,"[6] and the work of Mel and Norma Gabler, a Texas couple who founded Educational Research Analysts, is featured prominently in the materials distributed by NACE/CEE. All of these individuals and their organizations have been explicitly acknowledged by NACE/CEE as laborers in the same cause.

Phyllis Schlafly's Eagle Forum

The Eagle Forum was founded in 1972 by Phyllis Schlafly. According to author Jonathon Green, who keeps track of censorship controversies in the public schools, the Forum "opposes anything anti-family, anti-God, anti-religion, anti-children, anti-life (i.e., abortion) and anti-American defense."[7] The Eagle Forum's two major publications, *The Phyllis Schlafly Report*, begun in 1967, and the *Education Reporter*, begun in 1985, are distributed nationally.

Schlafly was appointed by President Reagan as a member of the Commission on the Bicentennial of the United States Constitution. Additionally, she is the author of thirteen books, the most famous of which is *Child Abuse in the Classroom* (1984), which Schlafly calls "the basic tool to explain the problem of how children's values are often manipulated and damaged by classroom courses."[8] The book contains selected excerpts from the Official Transcript of Proceedings before the U.S. Department of Education in the matter of the proposed regulations to implement the Protection of Pupil Rights Amendment, also known as the Hatch Amendment. For fourteen years Schlafly was named in *Good Housekeeping*'s annual list of the ten most-admired women in America.[9]

Pat Robertson and the Christian Coalition

As a result of his bid for the presidency in 1988, Pat Robertson is perhaps the best-known figure of those involved in public school challenges. His Christian Broadcasting Network (CBN) has been in existence since 1960, when it had the call letters WYAH-TV and reached only a few hundred miles. Robertson is the host of the nationwide television show "The 700 Club," which reportedly reaches eighty-four other countries around the world.[10]

In 1977, Robertson founded CBN University, which later became Regent University. The institution declares itself to be a "Christian University . . . possessing America's only accredited, Bible-based law school."[11] In 1986, it was estimated that Robertson was seen in 16.3 million homes and reached 27 million Americans each month. In 1987, it was estimated that Robertson's network controlled nearly a quarter of a billion dollars a year and that his "700 Club" television program received four million prayer calls, using 4,500 volunteers manning telephones in sixty counseling centers.[12] Since that time, one can safely speculate that Robertson's popularity and influence have increased because of the exposure he received during his bid for the presidency. This is evidenced by the fact that in a week-long telethon in January 1995 entitled "Rebuilding the Wall," Robertson's 700 Club organization col-lected more than two million dollars in pledges *per month* for his ministry.

Robertson also created the Christian Coalition, which has been involved in promoting particular candidates for school board races and for other local and state-level elective positions across the country. One example of the Coalition's success in such races was the 1990 elections in San Diego, California. Critics charged, however, that Coalition-supported candidates kept the full extent of their views and agendas hidden from the public. Yet, according to a 1992 *Los Angeles Times* article, the Christian Coalition's executive director made no apologies for such tactics: "Stealth was a big factor in San Diego's success. But that's just good strategy. It's like guerilla warfare. If you reveal your location, all it does [is] allow your opponent to improve his artillery bearings. It's better to move quietly, with stealth, under cover of night."[13]

In May 1995, the Christian Coalition broke into the national spotlight with the presentation of its Contract with the American Family, in which it called for the return of American education to parents. Calling the contract "a bold agenda for Congress intended to strengthen families and restore common-sense values," the Christian Coalition claims that the contract's provisions are supported by 60 to 90 percent of Americans.[14] Robertson also established the American Center for Law and Justice (ACLJ), which has been actively involved in defending student-led prayer in public schools.

Robertson's zeal and energy apparently come from his belief that he has been ordained by God for a holy mission. Referencing a March 1988 *Los Angeles Times* article detailing Robertson's claims, author John Dart writes that Robertson believed he received a prophecy from God in 1968, which was delivered through Harold Bredesen, a close associate. Bredesen, Dart reports, "laid his hand on Robertson's head and spoke as though God were speaking . . . ," telling Robertson, "I have called you to usher in the coming of My Son." According to Dart, Robertson reiterated the prophecy in a 1982 letter to supporters, declaring, "God has assigned to CBN, in these last days, a ministry of John the Baptist—to prepare the way for Jesus' second coming." Robertson also repeated the prophecy at a televised gathering in Dallas in December 1984, the same month he was interviewed for a *Saturday Evening Post* cover story introducing him as a potential 1988 Republican presidential candidate. Dart writes that, speaking at the Dallas gathering, "Robertson drew a mental picture of a crime-free society in which Christians would be 'taking dominion' and reaping the wealth of non-believers. This dominion was only several years away, and the changes would include the election of a 'spirit-filled President' and 'judges speaking in tongues from the bench.'"[15]

The Gablers

Mel and Norma Gabler, founders of Educational Research Analysts, fulfill a key role in the eyes of fundamentalist critics of the public schools. Because these critics are deeply concerned about ideas children are exposed to in schools, scrutinizing textbooks and curricular materials is viewed as vitally important research. The Gablers' organization, founded in 1961, is located in Longview, Texas, and is one of the most active organizations in the United States in questioning and evaluating public school instructional materials. The Gablers claim to have "the world's largest textbook review library."[16] They were initially alone in their attack on American public education, but they have been joined by a host of individuals and organizations.

The Gablers spend a great deal of time evaluating each book in detail and have thousands of reviews on file. Where reviews are not available, the Gablers recommend that parents conduct their own personal review. Claiming that most textbooks in use reflect the ideology that children are "tools for social change," they advise parents to review textbooks page by page, line by line, in order to identify specific objections and to locate subtle biases. The Gablers detail a long list of things to look for during the review process, including content that "emphasizes the morbid and depressing over the positive," "censors absolute values," "promotes changing values," "dwells on the affective (feelings), not the cognitive (academics)," "marginalizes Christians or Christianity," "teaches the occult," or "stresses [the] faults of America's founding fathers."[17]

The Gablers produce a semiannual newsletter that is sent to contributors, as well as handbooks on specialized areas of concern in education, including humanism, acceptable sex education programs, values clarification, phonics, and creation science.[18] In the 1990 *Encyclopedia of Censorship*, Jonathon Green describes the Gablers as "the most prominent of America's self-appointed citizen censors." Green reports that the Gablers and their staff use a mailing list of twelve thousand people to inform parents about materials they consider to be harmful.[19]

Jerry Falwell and the Moral Majority

Although Jerry Falwell's Moral Majority was disbanded in 1986, the organization was a significant coalescing force for fundamentalist Christians concerned about the quality and secular tone of public schools. Created by Falwell in 1979, the Moral Majority at one time was reported to have seventy-two thousand ministers and four million dedicated lay members. The Moral Majority has described itself as a "political movement dedicated to convincing morally conservative Americans that it is their duty to register and vote for candidates who agree with their moral principles."[20] In their book *Prime Time Preachers*, Jeffrey Hadden and Charles Swann describe Falwell as "a self-proclaimed fundamentalist" who has explicitly stated his opposition to liberalism, sex education in school, and the Equal Rights Amendment. They describe Falwell's message as "a call to return to an America . . . that was guided by biblically inspired moral principles and that knew not the agony of moral ambiguity."[21]

Focus on the Family

Focus on the Family, headquartered in Colorado Springs, Colorado, is included here because it is increasingly linked by its critics to attacks on public school materials and practices. Focus is a nonprofit, worldwide organization. Its founder and president is James Dobson. Dobson is not a minister or evangelist but a psychologist, and the author of several books on child rearing and family relations, including *Dare to Discipline*, which has sold more than two million copies.

According to its literature, Focus on the Family is "dedicated to strengthening the home."[22] Dobson states that Focus stands for the ideal of the permanence of the marital situation, the value of bearing and raising children, the worth of every individual person, and Christian principles, including love for Jesus Christ. It is a member of the National Religious Broadcasters, the Evangelical Christian

Publishers Association, and the Evangelical Council for Financial Accountability.[23] It publishes several magazines, including *Citizen* and *Teachers in Focus*. The organization has created numerous community projects and programs designed to strengthen the family.

Opinions vary widely about this influential organization. From time to time, Focus reviews specific public school programs that it finds particularly objectionable. However, the organization is not aggressively involved in attacks on public school materials, centering its attention primarily on the wider issue of what it calls the "civil war of values." During an interview in April 1993 on KVOR-AM, a Colorado Springs radio station, Dobson declared that he is a supporter of the public school system: "I taught school for three years. I have a great love for schoolteachers. They work hard. They're under a lot of pressure. In some ways, they can't win. They take the children who come from all kinds of homes. They get blamed for the things that the kids do. The SAT scores are falling. I've got to tell you, if schools did everything perfectly, those SAT scores would still be falling because families are disintegrating and that influences learning. So I'm a strong supporter of public school teachers. I've been there. I know the pressures that are on them."[24]

People For the American Way (PFAW) has aggressively and publicly attacked Dobson, demanding that he "come out of his closet" and reveal the true "political" purpose of Focus on the Family.[25] Mike Hudson, director of PFAW's Boulder, Colorado, office, launched the opening of this regional office with a press conference and a fourteen-page attack on Focus, charging that it has a secret "extremist political agenda" that is "cloaked in the rhetoric of family values."[26] Hudson also accused Focus of political activities because the organization ran numerous full-page ads in newspapers around the state of Colorado titled "In Defense of a Little Virginity," during the time that the Jefferson County, Colorado, school board was considering the adoption of its new explicit sex education program.[27]

Focus on the Family responded to these criticisms with newspaper editorials, a press release, and what it called a "point-counterpoint refutation" of the error-filled PFAW attack. Tom Minnery, vice president of public policy for Focus, said that the organization's purposes are hardly covert, declaring, "We're as obvious as the Statue of Liberty." Minnery cited an audience of three million listeners for its daily radio show and five million recipients of its publications.[28] In 1994, representatives from Focus on the Family spoke at educational conferences around the country. Minnery stated that, unlike other organizations, Focus is not intent on 'taking over' school boards or destroying public education.

In addition to the efforts of CEE, the Eagle Forum, Pat Robertson and his Christian Coalition, and the Gablers, a rapidly growing literature base of books and pamphlets supports the general principles of politically active fundamentalists. Most of these books are common fare in Christian bookstores and some are marketed and distributed through NACE/CEE. Among the more popular writers in this genre are Randall Baer, Dave Hunt, Jay Adams, Eric Buehrer, Texe Marrs, James Kennedy, Constance Cumbey, Johanna Michaelsen, and Joseph Kennedy.

In sum, although numerous authors have written books expressing the concerns of public school critics, only a handful of organizations have been at the forefront of the battle over public school materials and practices. However, other national groups—as well as scores of local and statewide groups—have formed in communities across the country to protest one aspect or another of public education. Although these groups and their viewpoints span a broad range, some appear to resonate with the ideas of the critics discussed in this chapter. Many of the groups reported to be involved in or producing materials that were used in challenges to public school materials and practices during the 1991–92, 1992–93, 1993–94, and 1994–95 school years are listed in Exhibit 2.1, along with the states where they have reportedly been active.

Exhibit 2.1. Groups Associated with Challenges to Public School Materials and Practices, 1991–1995.

Alabama Family Alliance (Ala.)
American Family Association (Alaska, Fla., Ill., Md., N.C., Tex.)
American Parents Association (S.C., Va.)
Arkansas Family Council (Ark.)
Back to Basics (Calif.)
Chesapeake Research Institute (Md.)
Christian Advocates Serving Evangelism (Tex.)
Christian Civil Liberties Union (Wis.)
Christian Coalition (Ala., Calif., Md., N.J., Pa., S.C., Wis.)
Christian Legal Society (Pa.)
Citizens Acting for Responsible Education (C.A.R.E.) (Md.)
Citizens Advocating Responsible Education (CARE) (N.J., N.Y.)
Citizens for an Abstinence-Directive Curriculum (Minn.)
Citizens for Academic Excellence (Oreg.)
Citizens for Better Books (Calif.)
Citizens for Classroom Decency (Mich.)
Citizens for Common Sense in Schools (Utah)
Citizens for Quality Education (C.Q.E.) (Mich., Calif.)
Citizens for Responsible Education (Mass.)
Citizens United for Responsible Education (CURE) (Md., Ind.)
Coalition for Back to Basics in Education (Del.)
Coalition of Concerned Citizens of Clay County (Fla.)
Community Impact Council (Tex.)
Concerned Christians of Concord (N.H.)
Concerned Citizens (W.Va.)
Concerned Citizens for Excellence in Education (N.C.)
Concerned Citizens for the Constitution (Ind.)
Concerned Citizens of Bedford (N.H.)
Concerned Citizens of Florida (Fla.)
Concerned Citizens of Washington Township (N.J.)
Concerned Citizens Viewpoint (Mass.)
Concerned Dover Citizens (N.H.)

Exhibit 2.1. Groups Associated with Challenges to Public School Materials and Practices, 1991–1995, cont'd.

Concerned Parents About Curriculum (N.J.)
Concerned Parents Coalition (Wash.)
Concerned Parents for Academics (Oreg.)
Concerned Parents for Better Education (Ga.)
Concerned Parents for Education (Pa.)
Concerned Parents for Educational Accountability (N.Y.)
Concerned Parents of Citrus County (Fla.)
Concerned Parents of Fulton County (Ga.)
Concerned Women of America (Ind., Md., Pa., Tenn.)
D.A.D.S. Foundation (Calif.)
Education Policy Council (S.D.)
Families Restoring Excellence in Education (Okla.)
Family Action Coalition of Tennessee (Mo., Tenn., Va.)
Family Defense Council (N.Y.)
Family Research Council (Ala., Calif., Minn., N.C., Wash.)
Free World Research (Iowa)
Guilford Citizens for Responsible Sex Education (N.C.)
Gwinnett County Citizens for Educational Excellence (Ga.)
Hamilton Parents Coalition (Ohio)
Heritage Education and Review Organization (H.E.R.O.) (Ga.)
Impact New Mexico (N.M.)
Indiana Family Institute (Ind., Ohio, Pa., Wis.)
Kansas Education Watch Network (Kans.)
Liberty and Justice For All (Fla.)
The Light House Project (Ill.)
Lyndon LaRouche Organization (Pa.)
Maryland Coalition of Concerned Parents (Md.)
Michigan Alliance for Families (Mich.)
Minnesota Berean League (Minn.)
Minnesota Family Council (Colo.)
Mission America (Md.)
Moms in Touch (Colo., Ohio, Wis.)

Exhibit 2.1. Groups Associated with Challenges to Public School Materials and Practices, 1991–1995, cont'd.

National Monitor of Education (Calif.)
Nevada Concerned Citizens (Nev.)
The New Age Movement Exposed (Ind.)
Oklahomans for Quality Education (Okla.)
Oregon Citizens Alliance (Oreg.)
Parents Against Control—They're Our Children (Calif.)
Parents Against D.A.R.E. (Colo.)
Parents' Education Awareness Forum (PEAF) (Mich.)
Parents Evaluating and Reviewing Curriculum (PERC) (Ind.)
Parents for Academic Excellence (Oreg.)
Parents for Back to Basics (Calif.)
Parents Opposed to Propaganda in Schools (POPS) (Fla.)
Parents Raising Educational Standards in Schools (Wis.)
Parents Resisting Outcome Based Education (PROBE) (Md.)
Parents Who Care/Parents Do Care (Ariz.)
Pennsylvania Coalition for Academic Excellence (Pa.)
Phronesis Group (Wash.)
Public Rejection of Outcome Based Education (PROBE) (Md.)
Public Schools Awareness Committee (Fla.)
Putting Children First (N.C.)
Rutherford Institute (Ala., Calif., Fla., Hawaii, Idaho, N.Y., Ohio, Pa., Tex.)
Schiller Institute (Md.)
Seminole [County] Christian Coalition (Fla.)
Stop Promoting Homosexuality Hawaii (Hawaii)
The Support Group (Ind.)
Target the Basics (Wis.)
Texas Council for Family Values (Tex.)
Traditional Values Coalition (Calif.)
U.S. Justice Foundation (Calif.)
Washington Alliance of Families (Wash.)
Watchman Fellowship (Ala., S.C.)

Exhibit 2.1. Groups Associated with Challenges to Public School Materials and Practices, 1991–1995, cont'd.

Watchman Foundation (Ala., Fla., Ind., Mo., Ohio, Tex., Va.)
We Care About Curriculum (Colo.)
William Coulson's Research Council on Ethnopsychology (Tex.)
Wyoming Insight (Wyo.)

Source: Compiled from People For the American Way's annual state-by-state reports, *Attacks on the Freedom to Learn: 1991–1992, 1992–1993, 1993–1994,* and *1994–1995*; and from the American Library Association's bimonthly *Newsletter on Intellectual Freedom,* Jan. 1993–May 1995 (J. F. Krug, ed.).

The Role of Fundamentalism

At their core, the challenges to public education are intimately tied to the Christian fundamentalist movement. Understanding Christian fundamentalism, then, greatly enhances one's understanding of the crisis in American education. Christian fundamentalism grew out of evangelicalism in the early part of the 1900s. According to history scholar Jaroslov Pelikan, the term *fundamentalism* first appeared in 1910 when a group of American Protestant laymen published a series of twelve small books bearing the overall title *The Fundamentals: A Testimony of the Truth.*[29] *The Fundamentals* defended the inerrant, literal word of God as passed down through the Bible and sharply criticized liberal thinking, including that of modernist Protestants, Roman Catholics, and members of other Christian sects such as Mormons. *The Fundamentals* served as a rallying point for Protestant conservatives[30] and gave legitimacy to a movement that had been developing within American Protestantism during the 1800s. In the decade following the publication of *The Fundamentals*, the division between conservative and liberal Protestants widened. In 1919, the World's Christian Fundamentals Association was formed, marking the beginning of fundamentalism as a distinct movement within evangelicalism.[31]

Although there is no fundamentalist creed, Stewart Grant Cole, the first historian of the movement, identified the Five Points that have informally become the defining beliefs of fundamentalism. They are "the Inerrancy of the Scriptures, the Deity of Christ, his Virgin birth, the Substitutionary Atonement of Christ, and his physical Resurrection and coming bodily Return to earth."[32]

The rise of fundamentalism can be characterized as a revolution against modernism—the forces that caused rapid cultural changes in American society. In addition to a literal view of the Bible, fundamentalist beliefs encompassed an opposition to intellectualism and an emphasis on superpatriotism, individual piety, and conservative lifestyles. Fundamentalists vehemently opposed the teaching of evolution in the schools, seeming to view it as a prime example of modernism at its worst. Indeed, in the early 1900s several fundamentalist organizations were formed specifically to battle evolution. They sponsored rallies and lobbied state legislatures to prevent it from being taught in the public schools. However, although antievolution laws were introduced in twenty state legislatures, most failed to pass. A few succeeded, notably in Tennessee and Arkansas.[33]

In 1927, Tennessee's statute was challenged in the now-famous *Scopes* "monkey" case.[34] John Scopes taught high school physics rather than biology. Although he doubted that he had violated the state's antievolution law, he had once led a review class for the biology final exam using an assigned textbook that emphasized evolution. On that basis, he agreed to participate with the American Civil Liberties Union (ACLU) in a test case of the antievolution statute.

The ACLU assembled a team of defense attorneys from around the country who tried to raise objections to the statute, in part on the grounds that the statute infringed on individual freedom. The prosecution argued that the statute did not abridge individual freedom because it only applied to teachers in the public school system—an institution the state had a right to control. Scopes was convicted under the statute.[35]

The case was appealed to the Tennessee Supreme Court. The court overturned the conviction on a technicality, but it upheld the constitutionality of the antievolutionary statute. On a national level, American public sentiment was clearly proevolutionary. The press had a field day ridiculing and humiliating the fundamentalists for their actions and statements at the trial. As a result of the court's ruling, however, the power of the states to establish sectarian policies continued without constitutional restraint.[36]

Although many viewed the 1927 *Scopes* case as a defeat for fundamentalism, the movement was far from dead. The negative publicity fundamentalists received after the *Scopes* trial had the effect of arousing and strengthening the extremist element of the movement. During the 1930s and 1940s, subscriptions to fundamentalist publications increased dramatically, as did enrollments at fundamentalist colleges and Bible institutes. Fundamentalists also capitalized on the new medium of radio, and religious programs multiplied.[37]

In the 1950s, fundamentalists again rallied around one major theme—anti-Communism—and, as in the 1920s, attacked the public schools. They objected to sex education courses, for example, viewing them as evidence of a Communist plan to undermine American morality. Many conservative Christians were critical of the fundamentalists' tactics, however, which further emphasized widening divisions in Protestantism.[38]

In the 1960s and 1970s, fundamentalism continued to flourish. The number of Christian bookstores and magazines grew rapidly, and Christian radio and television shows were established. During this time, the number of fundamentalist Christian schools also expanded, spurred in part by the teaching of evolution and by the changing content of public school textbooks.[39] In the mid 1970s, highly charged controversies over textbooks took place in Kanawha County, West Virginia, and in Warsaw, Indiana. Citizens and school board members were polarized over whether certain books violated students' privacy and undermined religious and cultural values. In both instances, extreme emotions were inflamed. In Kanawha

County, a fundamentalist minister called on people to pray for the death of three school board members. In Warsaw, a group of senior citizens publicly burned copies of a controversial textbook.[40] (See Appendix A for a more detailed account of these two incidents.) These controversies seemed to set the stage for continued challenges to library and educational materials. In the years following these two incidents, book banning and attempted book banning increased dramatically. According to the Office for Intellectual Freedom of the American Library Association, some three hundred incidents of attempted "censorship" were reported during 1977–78, more than at any time in the preceding twenty-five years.[41]

During this time, some fundamentalists dropped their separatist philosophy and became involved in national political issues. The impetus for this might have been provided, in part, by local political controversies like the one in Kanawha County. In 1976, fundamentalists joined evangelicals in backing Jimmy Carter for president. Three years later, Jerry Falwell founded the Moral Majority, creating one of the first politically active fundamentalist organizations.[42]

3

The Great Conspiracy: Secular Humanism and the New Age

Criticisms leveled at public education by politically active fundamentalist critics are numerous and span the entire educational process. However, one theme seems to dominate their literature: that public schools are under the influence of a secular, liberal "religion" and are participating in a conspiracy to alter society by modifying children and their thinking.[1] In 1993, Robert L. Simonds, president of Citizens for Excellence in Education, wrote, "Every day Christian children all across America are quietly sitting in their public school chairs while, unbeknownst to either the church, their parents, or the children themselves, they are being subjected to a subtle but systematic mind-altering and faith-destroying curriculum."[2]

This conspiracy theory is a thread that runs through much of the criticisms leveled at the schools and at American society as a whole. Pat Robertson asserts that "secularism has focused intently on the overt de-Christianizing of America." Robertson further declares:

> This plundering of traditional morality and Christian values was never accidental. It has been a deliberate and methodical assault on the tenets of society . . . and has proliferated from the classrooms to the courtrooms, and from the newsrooms to the living rooms of America. More and more, it even comes from the pulpits of America.

> The end has not just been to supplant Christian values with humanism, but to weaken American sovereignty and supplant it with a one world socialist government. . . .
>
> The great irony of this situation is that the very men and women we have entrusted to educate and challenge our children have been the corrupters.[3]

This conspiracy, it is alleged, seeks to subvert Christian values through often-subtle means within public education. For example, as early as the 1960s, the Gablers opposed what was then the "new math" curriculum because, they claimed, it could undermine faith in absolute values, leading to relativistic thinking. Testifying before the Texas textbook hearings, the Gablers asserted: "On a moral basis there is fear that such abstract teaching to young minds will tend to destroy the student's belief in absolutes—to believe that nothing is concrete. This could be instrumental in helping erode their faith in other absolutes such as Christian faith."[4]

The effort to subvert absolute values, it is asserted, is also evident in the types of reading materials to which students are exposed. In a controversy that reached the courts in 1987, parents testified that a compulsory basic reading series imparted an overall philosophy that was contrary to and, in fact, denigrated their religious beliefs. In requesting alternative reading materials, these parents stated that it was a violation of their religious beliefs to allow their children to read the books in the series and, thus, that their rights to free exercise of religion were burdened. By way of example, one parent pointed to a poem that described imagination as a vehicle for seeing things that are not visible to the physical eye. She stated her belief that it is an "occult practice" for children to use their imagination beyond the boundaries of the Scriptures.[5] (See Appendix A for a detailed discussion of this case, *Mozert* v. *Hawkins County*.)

The So-Called Religion of Secular Humanism

What appears most objectionable to fundamentalist critics is their perception that Christianity not only has been deemphasized in American culture but has been supplanted by a rival religion, variously described as an Eastern religion, satanism, the occult, witchcraft, secular humanism, and the New Age religion. This, they assert, is particularly evident in public education. For example, Carl Sommer, in *Schools in Crisis*, asserts that "children are compelled to accept a religion contrary to their beliefs, students are trained in an environment that is hostile toward theistic religion and prayer, the rights and liberties of the majority who believe in God are violated since they are forced to sustain a religion in which they do not believe in a tax-supported school, and schools are financing and establishing a religion in violation of the First Amendment."[6]

Similarly, the Gablers write: "Would it shock you to know that a 'new' religion is being taught in textbooks today—a religion that is hostile to the Judeo-Christian principles upon which American liberty is founded?"[7]

Battling the so-called religion of secular humanism has long been the fundamentalist critic's pledge. Proclaimed definitions of secular humanism vary, but all focus on the rejection of God. Writer Randall Baer describes it as "the belief that man is divine in nature."[8] Similarly, Douglas Groothuis calls it a world view that focuses on "the glory of humanity, to the exclusion of the glory of God."[9] Jerry Falwell has described secular humanism as the new American religion, replacing the Bible.[10] Other definitions given to secular humanism include "a religion dedicated to . . . opposing or showing hostility to Christianity" and a religion that believes that "man is God and rejects Biblical standards of living."[11] Advocates of these views frequently point to a footnote in the 1961 *Torcaso* Supreme Court decision that includes secular humanism as an example of religions that should be protected by the First Amendment's free exercise clause.

The terms *secular humanism* and *humanism* are often used interchangeably. Mel and Norma Gabler say that what is particularly dangerous about humanists is that they will stop at little to achieve their goals. In their book *What Are They Teaching Our Children?*, the Gablers declare, "Humanists are aggressive and evangelistic. They are adept at tearing down traditional faith, even if it means permitting the occult to enter the classroom. They are skillful at pouring their anti-God dogmas into the void."[12] Although the Gablers' book was written in 1985, it is still widely read and is marketed by their organization, Educational Research Analysts, and included by CEE in its PSA kits.

Conspiracy theorists believe that virtually every sector of American society has been infiltrated by secular humanists in a great conspiracy. Tim LaHaye, once a board member of the Moral Majority and a prominent fundamentalist spokesman, claimed at one point that 272,000 humanists in America controlled the national media, government, and education, with the ultimate goal of controlling the hearts and minds of the American people.[13]

Fundamentalists believe that the so-called religion of secular humanism has completely invaded the public school educational system in violation of the First Amendment's establishment clause. They believe that secular humanist textbooks, teachers, and curricula are anti-Christian and anti-God. Critics claim that, after exposure to secular humanism, their children no longer believe in God.[14]

Apparently, Senator Jesse Helms has given his support to the fundamentalists in battling secular humanism. In his introduction to Homer Duncan's book *Secular Humanism: The Most Dangerous Religion in America*, Helms states, "When the U.S. Supreme Court prohibited children from participating in voluntary prayers in public schools, the conclusion is inescapable that the Supreme Court not only violated the right of free exercise of religion for all Americans; it also established a national religion in the United States—the religion of secular humanism."[15]

A Deliberate Plan

Key to an understanding of the complaints about American public education that are leveled by many of those who share the fundamentalist world view is an understanding of their criticisms and interpretations of the path of American history during the twentieth century. A particularly instructive source is *The New Millennium*, by Pat Robertson—as previously noted, a televangelist, leader of the Christian Coalition, and recognized "prophet" for some fundamentalist and conservative Christians.[16]

Robertson argues that a powerful group of liberal intellectuals undertook a deliberate plan in the early part of the twentieth century to "undermine and to disassemble the entire fabric of Western society." In fact, he states, "Hard core Marxists . . . had been organizing the United States since 1918." As Robertson sees it, for many Americans the Depression of the 1930s represented the failure of capitalism. The resulting despair many people experienced left them vulnerable to the influence of the "anti-Christian thinking" of educational leader John Dewey, whom Robertson describes as a "powerful atheist and communist sympathizer." Robertson asserts that American economic and foreign policy in the mid-twentieth century sprang from an attitude that was formed "in the classroom, in academia, in the think tanks, and only then in the newsrooms."[17]

Asserting a similar interpretation of the early twentieth century, the Gablers argue that secular humanists have drawn America away from its Christian heritage. Although the roots of humanism can be traced back to the Renaissance, the Gablers maintain that it was the liberal intellectuals of the early 1900s who established a foothold for secular humanism in America: "Liberal theologians, for example, used the methods of German 'higher criticism' to attack the authority and authenticity of the Bible. American universities advocated Darwin's theory of evolution. Within so-called intellectual circles it became fashionable to reject theism and the Bible for the 'natural' belief that man must be his own savior. This set the stage for Humanists to seize the helm in public education."[18]

Those sharing a fundamentalist world view contend that Dewey's grounding in Darwinism translated into the belief that truth is not eternal and that this belief has become ingrained in the basic public school philosophy. In short, these fundamentalist critics fear that values and concepts once accepted as absolute and unchanging—parental authority, unquestioned loyalty to the United States, faith in a supernatural God, the six-day creation of the world by God, and innate gender differences—are now being undermined by the underlying philosophy of public education.

The Gablers share Robertson's criticism of John Dewey, claiming that it was Dewey's influence that led the modern American educational system to embrace secular humanism and work against Christianity. In their book *What Are They Teaching Our Children?*, the Gablers describe what they assert to be Dewey's beliefs: "A declared atheist who sometimes used religious terminology, Dewey was a Hegelian, holding that truth always is in process; it never is eternally fixed. Morals changed, he believed, as society changed. Students should, therefore, be taught to adjust socially and ethically to change as it occurs. Change and adjust, change and adjust. That was Dewey's theme."[19]

Robertson argues that liberals also have greatly influenced the court system and that a deliberate rewriting of the Constitution took place as a result. It was out of this liberal, secular viewpoint that the Supreme Court decided the cases of the 1960s that further separated government from religion and "virtually destroyed neighborhood schools."[20]

Other Christian leaders point to the early 1960s as a significant turning point away from God. At a 1980 mass prayer meeting in Washington, D.C., William R. Bright, founder and president of Campus Crusade for Christ International, described "a series of plagues" that beset America including the assassination of President John F. Kennedy, the acceleration of the Vietnam War, the sweeping use of drugs, the Watergate scandal, increasing crime, teenage pregnancies, and economic difficulties. "We've turned from God," Bright declared, "and God is chastening us. . . . This is God's doing."[21]

Robertson echoes Bright's chronicle and interpretation of this era in American history, arguing that the path of American history that followed the U.S. Supreme Court decisions of the early 1960s, beginning with the assassination of President Kennedy in 1963, was "not coincidence" and that America is now experiencing the "wrath of God." Robertson firmly asserts that America has lost its moral underpinning, which has led to a degeneration of society. He maintains that virtually every problem in society, including crime, the deficit, the escalating divorce rate and suicide rate, the epidemic of drug use, and the collapse of the savings and loan industry in the 1980s, has come about because Christian and biblical standards have been removed from American national life and replaced by secular humanism. In Robertson's view, the public schools have been particularly affected by the disastrous course of American history in the twentieth century.[22]

The New Age Religion

Critics of secular humanism claim that within the last decade or so the efforts of the secular humanists have taken on a new form, that of a religion called the New Age. Pat Robertson, for example, maintains that the transition from secular humanism to the New Age was quite natural because the New Age was the perfect expression of an anti-Christian world view: "The promises of the New Age are so radical and subversive of everything Christ taught us, it seems to be tailor-made for a secular elite looking for a philosophy."[23]

Fundamentalists argue that whereas the religious orientation of secular humanism was hidden, the New Age has overt religious characteristics. As Texe Marrs, author of a number of particularly dramatic books on the New Age conspiracy, explains: "The New Age Movement has undeniably taken on the definite form of a religion, complete with an agreed-upon body of doctrine, printed scripture, a pattern of worship and ritual, a functioning group of ministers and lay leaders, and an effective outreach program carried out by an active core of proselytizing believers."[24]

The basis for the New Age religion, Dave Hunt asserts, is Hinduism, which Hunt describes as "ancient occultism." Hunt, author of a best-selling book criticizing the New Age movement, writes that the core beliefs of Hinduism have been accepted today by educated people across the societal spectrum, including scientists, physicians, psychologists, educators, politicians, and business leaders. The underlying Hindu philosophy of the New Age movement—that the individual soul is equivalent to the universal soul—professes an openness to all religions. Yet, Hunt asserts, the movement is participating in a "carefully calculated undermining of Judeo-Christian beliefs." The Eastern-based religion of the New Age movement, he argues, is the Antichrist's religion—bent on rejecting the Judeo-Christian God and declaring that "Self is God."[25]

In addition to being a well-organized religion, the New Age movement, most fundamentalists believe, has the distinction of including many members who do not realize that they are members. For example, Hunt explains, "Many New Agers are scarcely aware of the full implication of their involvement in the movement. And because the movement is more an organism than an organization, many people would vehemently deny that they are involved at all."[26]

This quality, it is thought, renders the New Age movement an insidious and expanding force that cuts across all strata of society. Exhibit 3.1 lists a few of the individuals, organizations, movies, and publications that various authors allege to be directly or indirectly

Exhibit 3.1. Individuals, Organizations, Movies, and Publications Allegedly Involved with the New Age.

Individuals

Ken Blanchard (Marrs, p. 333)
Ellen Burstyn (Marrs, p. 260)
Leo Buscaglia (Hunt, p. 184; Marrs, p. 333)
Joseph Campbell (Michaelsen, p. 225)
Lewis Carroll (Marrs, p. 275)
John Denver (Marrs, p. 332)
Linda Evans (Marrs, p. xv)
Matthew Fox (Cumbey, p. 151)
Sigmund Freud (Hunt, p. 108)
Erich Fromm (Cumbey, p. 132)
Buckminster Fuller (Cumbey, pp. 130, 152)
Teri Garr (Marrs, p. 260)
George Gurdjieff (Cumbey, p. 55)
Willis Harman (Hunt, p. 184)
Hermann Hesse (Cumbey, p. 132)
L. Ron Hubbard (Robertson, p. 77; Marrs, p. 286)
Aldous Huxley (Cumbey, p. 155)
Gerald Jampolsky (Michaelsen, p. 143)
Carl Jung (Michaelson, p. 36)
Madeleine L'Engle (Marrs, p. 275)
C. S. Lewis (Marrs, p. 274)
Jayne Mansfield (Marrs, p. xvi)
Abraham Maslow (Cumbey, p. 132)
Edgar Mitchell (Hunt, p. 184)
Ashley Montague (Marrs, p. 270)
Robert Muller (Baer, p. 81)
M. Scott Peck (Marrs, p. 155)
Senator Claiborne Pell (Robertson, p. 79)
U.N. Secretary General Javier Perez de Cuellar (Marrs, p. 144)
Prince Philip (Marrs, p. 144)

Exhibit 3.1. Individuals, Organizations, Movies, and Publications Allegedly Involved with the New Age, cont'd.

Bertrand Russell (Buehrer, p. 62)
Pierre Teilhard De Chardin (Cumbey, p. 55)
Alvin Toffler (Cumbey, p. 152)
Ted Turner (Marrs, p. 333)
H. G. Wells (Cumbey, p. 55; Hunt, pp. 49–50)
William Butler Yeats (Marrs, p. 270)

Organizations
Alcoholics Anonymous (Marrs, p. 29)
American Civil Liberties Union (Marrs, p. 66)
Amway Corporation (Marrs, p. 333)
Association of Humanistic Psychology (Marrs, p. 26)
AT&T (Cumbey, p. 131; Marrs, p. 25)
Atari Corporation (Marrs, p. 224)
Blue Cross and Blue Shield Association (Cumbey, p. 131)
Buffalo, New York, Public Schools (Marrs, p. xi)
Campbell Soup Company (Marrs, p. 223)
Carnegie Endowment (Marrs, p. 66)
Catholic Church (Cumbey, p. 147)
Chicago Police Department (Michaelsen, p. 57)
Christian Science (Marrs, p. 94)
Chrysler Corporation (Cumbey, p. 131)
Church of Jesus Christ of Latter-Day Saints (Marrs, p. 254)
EST/The Forum (Cumbey, p. 126; Hunt, p. 248; Marrs, p. 26)
Ford Motor Company (Robertson, p. 80)
Freemasons (Marrs, p. 199)
General Motors Corporation (Cumbey, p. 131; Marrs, p. 25)
City Government of Houston (Marrs, p. xi)
The Hunger Project (Cumbey, p. 133; Marrs, p. 66)
IBM (Marrs, p. 25)
Institute of Noetic Sciences (Hunt, p. 184)

Exhibit 3.1. Individuals, Organizations, Movies, and Publications Allegedly Involved with the New Age, cont'd.

Jehovah's Witnesses (Marrs, p. 226; Robertson, p. 83)
Lifespring (Hunt, p. 179)
Lockheed Corporation (Marrs, p. xi)
Mainline Protestant denominations, particularly Episcopalians and United Methodists (Cumbey, p. 39)
McDonnell Douglas Corporation (Marrs, p. 223)
Minneapolis and New York City governments (Marrs, pp. xi–xii)
Mobil Corporation (Marrs, p. 224)
Montessori Schools (Marrs, p. 249)
National Aeronautics and Space Administration (Marrs, p. 333)
National Broadcasting Company (Marrs, p. 223)
National Institutes of Mental Health (Cumbey, p. 130)
National Organization for Women (Marrs, p. 66)
Pillsbury (Marrs, p. 223)
Planned Parenthood (Marrs, p. 66)
Polaroid Corporation (Robertson, p. 80)
Princeton University (Marrs, p. 148)
Procter & Gamble Company (Robertson, p. 80)
Rockefeller Foundation (Marrs, p. 66)
Rockwell International Corporation (Marrs, p. 223)
St. James Church, London (Marrs, p. 281)
San Jose Public Libraries (Marrs, p. xii)
Science of Mind (Marrs, p. 94)
Scientology (Dianetics) (Marrs, p. 286)
Silva Method (Silva Mind Control) (Marrs, p. 296)
Social Security Administration (Marrs, p. 223)
Southern Edison (Marrs, p. xi)
Stanford University Graduate School of Business (Marrs, pp. 25–26)
Swedenborgian Church of the New Jerusalem (Marrs, p. xii)
UFO cults and societies (Marrs, p. 321)

Exhibit 3.1. Individuals, Organizations, Movies, and Publications Allegedly Involved with the New Age, cont'd.

Unification Church (Marrs, p. 325)
United Nations Educational, Scientific, and Cultural Organization (UNESCO) (Marrs, p. 66)
U.S. Army, Navy, and Air Force (Groothuis, p. 161)
U.S. Department of Defense (Cumbey, p. 129)
U.S. Department of Labor (Marrs, p. xi)
Unity Church (Marrs, p. 328)
University of Michigan (Marrs, p. 148)
University of Texas (Marrs, p. 148)
Westinghouse Electric Corporation (Robertson, p. 80)
Worldwide Church of God (Robertson, p. 83)
Yale University (Marrs, p. 148)

Books, Movies, and Television Programs
Battlestar Galactica (Robertson, p. 78)
Close Encounters of the Third Kind (Robertson, p. 78)
Cocoon (Baer, p. 155)
A Course in Miracles (Cumbey, p. 126)
E.T., The Extra-Terrestrial (Baer, p. 155)
Jonathan Livingston Seagull (Baer, p. 81)
She-ra (Michaelsen, p. 220)
The Smurfs (Michaelsen, p. 224)
Star Trek—The Motion Picture (Robertson, p. 78)
Star Wars (Michaelsen, p. 224)
Superman I (Baer, p. 155)

Sources: Baer, 1989; Buehrer, 1990; Cumbey, 1983; Groothuis, 1986; Hunt, 1983; Marrs, 1990; Michaelsen, 1989; Robertson, 1990.

involved with and influenced by the New Age movement even though they might not be aware of this fact. Similarly, Exhibit 3.2 lists some practices and convictions that allegedly are directly or indirectly associated with the New Age, or will be specifically used by those involved with the New Age to spread its agenda.

The most frightening aspect of the New Age movement to fundamentalists is that it is perceived to be directly linked to the Antichrist. Dave Hunt declares that the New Age's "denial that Jesus is the Christ is the primary identification of the spirit of the Antichrist."[27] Texe Marrs paints the most vivid picture of what he considers to be the ultimate goal of the New Age movement in his book *Dark Secrets of the New Age:*

> The New Age appears to be the instrument that Satan will use to catapult his Antichrist to power. Once he is firmly entrenched, he will unite all cults and religions into one: the New Age World Religion. When Christians refuse to be initiated into this Satanic religious system, they will be dealt with very harshly. Many will be put to death. The New Age is working hard today to set up an environment of hatred toward Christians and what they stand for, so the public mood will be ready when the Antichrist begins his brutal anti-Christian programs.[28]

In her book *The Hidden Dangers of the Rainbow,* Constance Cumbey explains how she believes the New Age will effect its domination of the world. She claims that the New Age has its own messiah called Lord Maitreya, whose followers "are now in the last stage of the New Age scheme to take the world for Lucifer."[29] To guide them, New Agers have a plan. Again, Cumbey provides some detail:

Exhibit 3.2. Practices Alleged to Have a New Age Link.

Acupuncture (Baer, p. 32)
Aerobics classes (Baer, p. 31)
Alternative medicine (Hunt, p. 76)
Biofeedback (Cumbey, p. 130; Hunt, p. 120)
Bodywork (Cumbey, p. 130)
Color therapy (Marrs, p. 38)
Creative visualization (Hunt, p. 120)
Ending world hunger (Marrs, p. xii)
Evolution (spiritual) (Marrs, p. 32)
Extrasensory perception (Marrs, p. 224; Robertson, p. 81)
Firewalking (Baer, p. 110)
Globalism (Marrs, p. 37)
Holistic health (Marrs, p. 37)
Human potential movement (Marrs, p. 335)
Hypnosis (Cumbey, p. 184; Marrs, p. 37)
Information revolution (Groothuis, p. 31)
Jewish kabala (Marrs, p. 50)
Jungian archetypes (Marrs, p. 38)
Magic (Marrs, p. 37)
Native American religious ceremonies (Marrs, p. 262)
Nature worship (Marrs, p. 61)
Networking and interconnectedness (Groothuis, p. 32; Hunt, p. 62)
One-world government (Groothuis, p. 127)
Positive thinking (Hunt, p. 120)
Possibility thinking (Hunt, p. 120)
Protect the environment campaign (Marrs, p. xii)
Psychology (Hunt, p. 248)
Reflexology (Hunt, p. 75)
Religious pluralism (Groothuis, p. 44)
Save the whales campaign (Marrs, p. xii)
Scientism (Groothuis, p. 42)
Stress management (Baer, p. 32)
Transcendental Meditation (Cumbey, p. 130)

Exhibit 3.2. Practices Alleged to Have a New Age Link, cont'd.

Unidentified flying objects (belief in) (Baer, p. 146)
Unity consciousness (Hunt, p. 65)
Vegetarianism (Marrs, p. 67)
Visualization (Marrs, p. 70; Michaelsen, p. 109)
Women's movement (Hunt, p. 68)
World peace efforts (Marrs, p. xii)
Yoga (Marrs, p. 37; Baer, p. 113)
Zen (Cumbey, p. 130)

Sources: Baer, 1989; Buehrer, 1990; Cumbey, 1983; Groothuis, 1986; Hunt, 1983; Marrs, 1990; Michaelsen, 1989; Robertson, 1990.

What is The Plan?

It includes the installation of a New World "Messiah," the implementation of a new world government and new world religion under Maitreya.

They have numerous political, social and economic goals, including the following:

- A universal credit card system.
- A world food authority which would control the world's food supply.
- A universal tax.
- A universal draft.

But there is more to The Plan—they intend to utterly root out people who believe the Bible and worship God and to completely stamp out Christianity.

They have stated that they plan to outlaw all present religious practices and symbols of orthodox Jews and Christians. The Movement is working quickly and efficiently to execute its scheme to take control of the world for Maitreya.[30]

Numerous fundamentalist writers declare that the New Age has infiltrated public education. One book dedicated to exposing this infiltration is Johanna Michaelsen's *Like Lambs to the Slaughter*. In the book's foreword, Hal Lindsey writes, "*Like Lambs to the Slaughter* is an epic book. . . . Most Americans have no idea of the extent to which the New Age occult evangelists have infiltrated our public school systems."[31] Michaelsen proclaims that children are the "key targets" of New Agers and that educators are knowingly and unknowingly part of this occult plan. In a chapter entitled "Your Teacher the Occultist?" Michaelsen writes that such allegedly New Age practices as numerology, contacting one's spirit guide, and astral projection "have become the raging vogue in public schools in every state and in virtually every community around the country."[32]

The Gablers, Robertson, and other like-minded individuals see the National Education Association (NEA) as the chief culprit in replacing moral values with secular humanism and New Age influences in the public school. Specifically, they contend that the NEA is a radical, leftist, secular, anti-Christian organization bent on altering children and society.[33] The PSA kit published by CEE states, "Yes, every public school is actually teaching the doctrines of an atheist ideology,"[34] and the Gablers allege that the schools are performing psychological and behavioral experiments on children.[35] In his book *The New Millennium*, Robertson warns, "The prime thrust of the NEA curricula is to wean children away from loyalty to 'the outdated religious superstitions,' loyalty to the family, loyalty to the United States, and belief in free market economics, and then to introduce them to socialism and world citizenship. *The actual education of the young is a totally secondary issue* [emphasis in original]."[36]

CEE's Simonds charges the NEA teacher unions with allowing pornography into the classroom, asserting that these groups reflect the philosophy of the American Civil Liberties Union (ACLU) of "promot[ing] policies that support NO limit on what is available to children in the classroom, including porno."[37] The Gablers accuse the NEA of profiting from "functional illiteracy" in children and treating children as "wards of the state."[38] In the introduction to her book *Child Abuse in the Classroom*, Phyllis Schlafly charges that "schools have alienated children from their parents."[39]

For the fundamentalist critics cited above, objections to programs and practices are not based on their educational merit, that is, their ability to produce measurable results. Rather, their objections are based on the assertion that these practices are part of a secular humanist, New Age religious movement. In his book *The New Age Masquerade*, Eric Buehrer states quite explicitly that objections to the programs he lists should be on religious grounds and not on educational merit:

> Look beyond the program's stated goal. The stated purpose may be to build self-esteem, cope with stress, boost memory and creativity, or enhance affective development. So what? If occult means are used to achieve these goals, the means are unacceptable no matter how noble the end result. . . . [These practices] offer a religious option to someone who is searching. I think you will have a hard time fighting such programs if you argue that they do not work. Rather, you should argue that they are religious because they deal with the nature of ultimate reality and how human values respond to that reality.[40]

By definition, then, such programs are evil even if they produce positive effects on learning.

A list of educational programs, individuals, and organizations that are considered to be associated with secular humanism or the New Age is presented in Exhibit 3.3. Additionally, Exhibit 3.4 lists educational practices that have been identified as being especially linked to secular humanism or the New Age.

Exhibit 3.3. Educators and Programs with an Alleged New Age Link.

American Association of School Administrators (Buehrer, p. 126)
American Federation of Teachers (Buehrer, p. 126)
Lee Anderson (Buehrer, p. 54)
Wendell Bell (Buehrer, p. 43)
Biological Sciences Curriculum Studies (Gabler and Gabler, p. 143)
William Boyer (Buehrer, p. 116)
Paul F. Brandwein (Gabler and Gabler, p. 120)
Irving H. Buchen (Buehrer, p. 61)
Jack Canfield (Michaelsen, p. 88)
Gordon Cawelti (Buehrer, p. 74)
Center for Teaching International Relations, University of Denver (Buehrer, p. 127)
Barbara Clark (Hunt, p. 80)
Danforth Foundation (Buehrer, p. 127)
John Dewey (Gabler and Gabler, p. 26)
Linda L. Faltenstein (Buehrer, p. 42)
Global R.E.A.C.H. (Respecting Our Ethnic and Cultural Heritage) (Buehrer, p. 19)
John Goodlad (Buehrer, p. 57)
Richard Gross (Buehrer, p. 53)
Anna Rose Hawkes (Buehrer, p. 53)
Gay Hendricks (Hunt, p. 80)
Bruce Joyce (Buehrer, p. 38)
Edith King (Buehrer, p. 58)
M. Frances Klein (Buehrer, p. 43)
Paula Klimek (Michaelsen, p. 88)
Richard MacLeod (Buehrer, p. 54)
Man: A Course of Study (Gabler and Gabler, p. 123)
Montessori schools (Michaelsen, p. 116)
National Council for Social Studies (Buehrer, p. 116)
National Education Association (Gabler and Gabler, p. 28)
Alexander Nicholson (Buehrer, p. 38)

Exhibit 3.3. Educators and Programs with an Alleged New Age Link, cont'd.

Northwest Regional Educational Laboratory (Buehrer, p. 129)
Parent-Teachers Association (Buehrer, p. 126)
Project 2000 (Buehrer, p. 19)
Thomas B. Roberts (Buehrer, p. 88)
SIECUS (Gabler and Gabler, p. 72)
Dorothy Sisk (Michaelsen, p. 49)
Tactics for Thinking (Buehrer, p. 84)
Kenneth A. Tye (Buehrer, p. 43)
Welcome to Planet Earth (Buehrer, p. 19)
Western Washington University (Michaelsen, p. 35)
World Core Curriculum (Buehrer, p. 19)

Source: Buehrer, 1990; Gabler and Gabler, 1985; Hunt, 1983; Michaelsen, 1989.

Exhibit 3.4. Educational Practices with an Alleged New Age Link.

Centering exercises (Michaelsen, p. 92)
Creative visualization (Buehrer, p. 89)
Cultural awareness (Buehrer, p. 17)
Cultural fairs (Buehrer, p. 39)
Cultural relativity (Buehrer, p. 137; Gabler and Gabler, p. 102)
Death education activities (Buehrer, p. 128)
Deep breathing exercises (Michaelsen, p. 97)
Designing an international postage stamp (Buehrer, p. 60)
Dream journals (Buehrer, p. 88)
Emphasizing communication over grammar skills (Gabler and Gabler, p. 107)
Focusing activities (Buehrer, p. 91)
Futurism (Buehrer, p. 17)
Guided fantasies (Buehrer, p. 91)
Guided imagery (Hunt, p. 80)

Exhibit 3.4. Educational Practices with an Alleged New Age Link, cont'd.

Having students discuss values or issues over which they disagree with their parents (Buehrer, p. 145)
Having students write about situations in which they would not be willing to die for their country (Buehrer, p. 46)
International studies (Buehrer, p. 17)
Intuition activities (Buehrer, p. 88)
Left brain/right brain theory (Michaelsen, p. 117)
Meditation techniques (Buehrer, p. 4)
Multicultural international education (Buehrer, p. 19)
Problem-solving exercises lacking fixed ethical norms (Gabler and Gabler, p. 118)
Relaxation exercises (Michaelsen, p. 93)
Role playing (Gabler and Gabler, p. 91)
Teaching about population control (Buehrer, p. 147)
Thinking skills programs (Michaelsen, p. 111)
Tolerating ambiguity (Buehrer, p. 132)
Transpersonal education (Michaelsen, p. 40)
Values clarification (Michaelsen, p. 54)
Whole brain learning (Buehrer, p. 102)
Writing a new constitution for a perfect society (Buehrer, p. 61)

Source: Buehrer, 1990; Gabler and Gabler, 1985; Hunt, 1983; Michaelsen, 1989.

Although charges of conspiracy are rampant in much of the fundamentalist literature, not all writers subscribe to the theory. One case in point is Douglas Groothuis, author of *Unmasking the New Age*. Groothuis writes that "conspiracy theories of all shapes, styles and sizes have been crisscrossing the planet throughout history. . . . Any group that has transnational allegiances . . . has been targeted as the elite conspirators plotting world takeover. New Age conspiracy charges simply transfer this thinking into a more modern context."[41] Conspiracy theory advocates often highlight the emphasis on "networking," but Groothuis writes that networking is nothing new. It is simply "linking ideas and people together for greater influence and creativity."[42] Groothuis opines that an emphasis on a conspiratorial slant is needless and misses the point. The important point is that the New Age has had a tremendous influence on American culture. He writes, "The New Age movement is better viewed as a world-view shift than a unified global conspiracy. This is not to minimize its influence but to recognize it as an intellectual, spiritual and cultural force to be reckoned with in all sobriety."[43]

4

Strategies and Tactics

Given the low opinion of public education held by fundamentalists, it is no wonder that they have developed specific strategies to influence the educational system.

Pulling the Alarm

One strategy is to paint dire pictures of the future if public education is not altered. To illustrate, consider a December 1992 fund-raising letter from CEE president Robert Simonds, the text of which was reprinted in the April 1993 issue of the *American School Board Journal*. In the letter, readers are warned that the recent election of a liberal president may lead to liberal legislative bills dealing with education, bills that must be stopped. One proposed program that is particularly alarming to Simonds is the Parents as Teachers program (PAT). Of so-called liberal legislation for programs such as PAT, Simonds writes:

> These are all deadly proposals that could remove children from any home a social worker ('parent educator') considered 'at-risk' or 'dysfunctional' (meaning 'Christian'—or 'politically incorrect').
>
> In practical terms, if these bills targeting 'at-risk' families are passed, it means if you spank a child, are

> over-weight, of low intelligence or have a low income, etc. . . . a sheriff and social worker may come to your home in a state van and drive away with your children."[1]

In fact, according to authors Ann-Maureen Pliska and Judith McQuaide, CEE markets a video called "The New World Order," which depicts this kind of frightening scene. In the video, a Christian student, labeled "at risk" and targeted for special services, "is taken away as uniformed guards restrain the parent, who struggles to save her daughter from the clutches of the state."[2]

The Stretch Technique

Another technique used by fundamentalist groups is sending "stretch letters" to school board members. According to Janet L. Jones, the "stretch" technique is often used in relationship to the federal Protection of Pupil Rights Amendment.[3] The amendment, more commonly known as the Hatch Amendment, gives parents the right to inspect classroom materials or teacher's manuals used in connection with "research or experimentation" projects, that is, "programs designed to explore or develop new or unproven teaching methods or techniques."[4]

Jones explains that the letter typically begins by reminding school board members that parents have the right to ensure that their children's moral values are not undermined by schools. The parent then requests that his or her child participate in no school activities or programs that involve, among other things, values clarification activities, sex education, alcohol and drug education, instruction in nuclear war or globalism, or discussions concerning the occult or the supernatural.

The letter ends by warning that in accordance with the Hatch Amendment, federal funds can be withheld or terminated if parental requests are not honored. Jones explains that these letters misrepresent the intention of the Hatch Amendment, which applies only to very specific and limited kinds of research or experimentation programs funded through the Department of Education: "The federal statute . . . applies only to research or experimentation programs or projects and to psychological and psychiatric testing, examination, and treatments whose primary purpose is to delve into one or more of seven areas: political affiliations; potentially embarrassing psychological problems; sexual behavior; anti-social or self-incriminating behavior; criticism of family members; privileged communications, such as those with lawyers or physicians; and family income."[5] Although the stretch letter was most widely used in the early 1980s, it is still a tool used by public school critics.

Taking Legal Action

Some strategies are much more structured and long term in nature. In the mid 1980s in particular, challengers took their complaints to the courts but were largely unsuccessful. In two secular humanism cases, *Mozert* v. *Hawkins County Board of Education*, 1987, Sixth Circuit Court of Appeals and *Smith* v. *Board of School Commissioners of Mobile County*, 1987, Eleventh Circuit Court of Appeals, plaintiffs were initially successful at the district court level but unsuccessful at the appellate court level. (These and other relevant public school cases are covered in depth in Appendix A.)

Infiltrating the School Board

Another long-term strategy used to effect change is to elect sympathetic school board members. Strategies used by CEE, for example, show the extent of the group's organization and planning. One of CEE's main tools is the PSA committee, whose "central function is to keep [the] congregation aware of local public school issues."[6] The working document of a PSA committee is the PSA kit, which articulately explains philosophy and leads parents through a step-by-step process for effectively influencing local schools. The kit contains six audiocassettes, a workbook and manual, Parent Action Guides, and reports about specific aspects of public education. Included in the kit is a copy of Simonds's book *How to Elect Christians to Public Office* and the Gablers' book *What Are They Teaching Our Children?*[7] Those who purchase the kit also receive a monthly *President's Report* from Simonds, the quarterly *Education Newsline*, and frequent bulletins about specific educational issues.

The publication that appears to be the centerpiece of the PSA kit is *How to Elect Christians to Public Office*, by Robert Simonds, published in 1985. Although this book, like the PSA manual, contains some explicit techniques to be used within education and politics, the book also establishes the philosophical basis of NACE/CEE's efforts. It begins by acknowledging several individuals, including Tim LaHaye, Jerry Falwell, Pat Robertson, and "many others [who] have taught us all to live in a world of spiritual and political reality."[8] Following the assertion that America is a Christian nation that has been seduced by the New Age humanist religion, the book reminds members of CEE and like-minded organizations that their task is to take over or "reclaim" America, returning it to its rightful, Bible-believing perspective. Simonds makes a number of explicit references to this:

> A new day has dawned! We pray for your understanding and use of this manual in reclaiming America to our heritage. . . .
>
> God's plan is to have His church in a "Front Line" ministry mode. Front Line ministers are those who are the daily "change agents" in society—evangelism at its best. . . .
>
> Government, from the President on down, should be as permeated with Christians as it now is with secularists. . . . The "gift" of "government" is clearly one of the gifts listed in I Corinthians 12:28 KJV.[9]

With this backdrop of philosophy, Simonds encourages the mobilization of evangelical churches across the country, noting that the evangelical voting bloc "is now the largest single group in America (as of 1984 Presidential elections)."[10] He then says that with the help of local pastors, all members of the local evangelical churches should be registered to vote. A detailed discussion ensues, explaining that all those who are inclined to vote "favorably" on selected issues within a community should be identified and the name, address, telephone numbers, and other pertinent information on each identified individual recorded on a three-by-five-inch card. On election day, PSA committee members are encouraged to go to the polling place and make sure that favorable voters actually vote. PSA members should give any identified voters who have not arrived by the end of the day a reminder phone call and, if necessary, help them get to the polling place.[11]

Simonds has a clear vision of what school government should be like: "We need strong school board members who know right from wrong. The Bible, being the only true source on right and wrong, should be the guide of board members. Only godly Christians can truly qualify for this critically important position."[12] It could perhaps be argued that CEE no longer holds to this view of appropriate school board membership. This statement appeared in a book published a decade ago, and Simonds has recently been actively involved in reconciliation efforts with leading educators (see Chapter Fourteen). Nonetheless, *How to Elect Christians to Public Office* continues to be promoted and sold by CEE.

In the six audiotapes that come as part of the PSA kit, Simonds warns listeners that "there is a lot of demonic activity going on" in the public schools and that schools are persecuting Christians.[13] The bulk of the workbook is devoted to describing a five-step process with the acronym AWARE, which stands for Assess, Write, Analyze, Report, and Energize.

Within the Assess step of the AWARE process, committee

members are told to call the local school district superintendent's office and get the names and addresses of school board members. They are also told to "get to know a board member's assumptions when dealing with an issue. . . . By assessing his assumptions you will know how to address the issue and win your cause." Finally, committee members are instructed to scrutinize each board member and rate them on a scale of 1 to 10 in terms of the "degree to which the board member seems conservative."[14]

Within the Write step of the process, members are instructed to articulate clear, written goals for the committee and its involvement in local public schools. This might include, for example, the PSA committee's vision for the schools over a number of years and identification of key issues needing immediate attention. Members are encouraged to "think about what you really want to see happen. . . . Do you want to have someone elected to the school board?"[15]

During the Analyze stage of the process, PSA committee members are encouraged to evaluate their goals. An important aspect of this effort is keeping church pastors and elders informed and seeking their guidance, because the "committee is under [their] authority."[16]

The Report phase of the process focuses on publicizing what the PSA committee has learned and enrolling others into the committee if possible. As an aid to this effort, NACE/CEE provides camera-ready bulletins on a regular basis—bulletins that address areas of concern and identify specific individuals and programs within education that are alleged to be part of the New Age.

Finally, in the Energize stage, members are directed to engage in Christian action designed to maximize change in the schools. One of the main ways committee members are instructed to get involved is by scrutinizing new programs. Parents and volunteers from church are encouraged to become part of the school's selection committee. Then, members are advised to obtain additional feedback on the programs' materials from the Gablers, who "do a fine job of research for the Christian community."[17]

In *How to Elect Christians to Public Office*, Simonds warns supporters not to alarm people with too overt a stance: "Communicate in an 'upbeat,' winning way. Avoid saying 'kooky' things that may cause a backlash effect."[18] Simonds explains that even CEE's name was selected to appear moderate: "The name Citizens for Excellence in Education was adopted because it is a 'friendly' name to the school board. No one is against *citizens*, or *excellence*, or *education*."[19]

Apparently, the process outlined here has been quite effective for NACE/CEE in reaching its goals. For example, Simonds reported that in 1989—the first year CEE focused on school board elections—CEE helped parents elect a mere 250 conservative school board members. However, after several years of increasing success in school board elections, CEE reportedly helped elect 7,153 board members in 1993 alone.[20]

The national Christian Coalition similarly offers seminars to teach people how to be elected to school boards. The first of these seminars was offered in Atlanta in 1995, and the Coalition plans to eventually present them in all fifty states. According to the Colorado Springs–based Citizens Project, these seminars coincide with an overriding goal articulated by the Coalition's executive director Ralph Reed, who said, "I honestly believe that in my lifetime we will see a country once again governed by Christians. What Christians have got to do is take back this country, one precinct at a time, one neighborhood at a time, and one state at a time."[21]

Opposition Efforts

Perhaps as a result of their great success, groups such as the Christian Coalition and CEE are beginning to meet with some strong opposition. One of the most active groups battling their efforts is People For the American Way (PFAW), founded by television producer Norman Lear. PFAW has defended numerous school districts around the country in court battles over educational materials. It also has published *Protecting the Freedom to Learn*, a citizen's guide

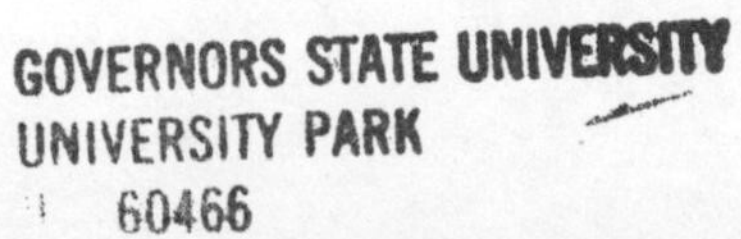
GOVERNORS STATE UNIVERSITY
UNIVERSITY PARK
60466

whose purpose is to make communities aware of censorship problems and to give advice on how to organize anticensorship campaigns and community alliances and develop written materials review policies. PFAW has found that when solid, democratic reconsideration procedures are in place—and followed—in schools, groups have less success removing or restricting educational materials.[22]

PFAW publishes an annual state-by-state report, *Attacks on the Freedom to Learn*, which documents challenges to public school materials and practices across the United States. PFAW argues that challenges by "Religious Right" political groups are nothing less than an opportunity to gain control of the public schools and to make their "narrow sectarian perspective" the standard for all instruction in public schools, which PFAW views as a clear violation of the First Amendment's establishment clause: "These attacks on the freedom to learn have created a climate of intolerance in which sectarian beliefs have become an ideological litmus test for education. Such efforts undermine the American traditions of individual liberty and church-state separation."[23]

As head of PFAW, Norman Lear has become a visible and outspoken defender of the "freedom to learn." As a result, he has been the focus of numerous personal attacks. Although some of these critics have characterized him as an "atheist," Lear professes a reverence for a "Supreme Being."[24] He also has stated that he believes that values should be taught in the public schools. At a conference on Values, Pluralism and Public Education in April 1987, Lear spoke about the need to transmit values in the public schools. He advocated instilling in students a commitment to tolerate, respect, and celebrate the diversity that is an inherent part of America. He also expressed his belief that schools should instill societal and moral values such as compassion, fairness, generosity, and brotherly love.[25]

PFAW maintains that it concurs with assertions that textbooks have ignored the contribution of beliefs and values to history. In 1987, PFAW mounted an extensive textbook review in conjunction with the Alabama textbook case *Smith* v. *Board of School Commissioners of Mobile County*, concluding, "The texts too often are static descriptions of dynamic processes, ignoring questions of belief and value at the heart of people's 'lives and fortunes and sacred honor.'"[26]

However, PFAW argues that charges that educational materials are promoting secular humanism, the New Age, and the occult are purposefully misleading and vague. In *Protecting the Freedom to Learn*, published by PFAW, Donna Hulsizer argues that

> the language of censorship is used without any attempt at precision. Its very vagueness—one educator compared defining secular humanism to 'nailing jello to a tree'—is its great virtue. Its terms are broad enough to encompass most any subject and are used to challenge any materials, methods, and ideas found objectionable. Like Humpty Dumpty in *Alice's Adventures in Wonderland*, those who adopt this language apparently believe that a word means 'just what I choose it to mean—neither more nor less.' Finally, these terms have a single purpose: to oppose teaching children to think critically and independently, to understand and tolerate different views and beliefs, and to appreciate the diversity of our society.[27]

In response to "Religious Right" organizations that are working to elect like-minded school board members, PFAW's Action Fund introduced its school board project shortly before the fall 1994 elections. The goal of the project is to educate people about the importance of public education and about the Religious Right's "agenda" for public schools. The project was initially launched in Texas and California because of the impact that educational policy decisions emanating from these states can have on the rest of the country.[28]

PFAW positions itself as a group dedicated to protecting constitutional liberties and as an advocate of tolerance and respect for diversity. Yet it appears that it, too, would have its readers believe that only one "true" perspective exists—a liberal one.

For example, PFAW severely criticized a 1993 school board election in Colorado, linking opposition candidates to the "Religious Right." PFAW's criticism led the *Rocky Mountain News* (a Denver-based newspaper) to editorialize that the school board race had become a search for "gremlins from the 'religious right'" and to pointedly retort that "religious folk have as much right as atheists and agnostics to participate in the political process."[29] The national media became involved during a December 1993 episode of NBC's "Today." During the show, PFAW's late president, Arthur Kropp, faced Terri Rayburn, a newly elected Jefferson County, Colorado, school board member who supported a back-to-basics approach. Kropp charged that Rayburn was hiding her true conservative Christian and political views and her affiliation with a "major religious-right organizer." Although Rayburn declared her opposition to prayer in the schools and the teaching of creationism, the words "Christian school board member" flashed on the screen while she spoke.[30] This incident illustrates that liberals and media organizations claiming openness may also be guilty of intolerance and even false assumptions and accusations.

Part II

School Reforms Under Attack

5

The State of Public Education

What exactly do those who share a fundamentalist world view object to in American education? How do they try to influence public education? In the next chapters we will consider both of these issues. First, however, it is important to put these issues in the context of the massive changes occurring in public education.

The Basics of School Reform

The conventional wisdom of the 1990s has been that American education is in a state of serious disrepair. Certainly a number of well-known politically active fundamentalist groups use this assumption as the platform from which to launch their attacks on public education. For example, Robert Simonds, president of Citizens for Excellence in Education, one of the most vocal critics of public education, writes that although "literally billions of dollars" have been invested in school reform, "SAT scores leveled for three years and then began a creep downward again. . . . Children will be denied a prosperous future because of the continuing decline in academic achievement."[1] Similarly, Phyllis Schlafly claims that "despite a decade of increased spending on schools, reforms and reorganizations, the academic performance of American school children is going down, not up."[2]

Just how bad *is* American education? Shouldn't this question be dealt with seriously before massive reform is undertaken? A growing number of researchers believe that the current wave of educational reform is based more on assumptions than on sound information. Education policy analyst Clark Kern writes, "Seldom in the course of policymaking in the U.S. have so many firm convictions held by so many been based on so little convincing proof."[3]

The Case Against Public Education

In the early 1980s, American education was issued the most comprehensive and drastic challenge of its 150-year history. In his book *Schoolhouse Politics: Lessons from the Sputnik Era,* Peter Dow explains:

> In 1983 educators and the general public were treated to the largest outpouring of criticism of the nation's schools in history, eclipsing even the complaints of the early 1950s. Nearly fifty reports totaling more than six thousand pages voiced a new wave of national concern about the troubled state of American education. They spoke of the fragmented state of the school curriculum, the failure to define any coherent, accepted body of learning, the excessive emphasis on teaching isolated facts, and the lack of attention to higher order skills and concepts. They called for more individualism of instruction, the development of a closer relationship between teachers and students, and methods that encourage the active participation of the student in the learning process.[4]

One report in particular gained considerable publicity. Without a doubt, *A Nation at Risk,* issued by the National Commission on Excellence in Education, was considered by many as final proof that education had indeed devolved to a state of disrepair. For all practical purposes, this state of distress was seen as a mandate to make sweeping changes in public education or to eliminate the entire system. The report noted that "the educational foundations of our society are presently being eroded by a rising tide of mediocrity that threatens our very future as a nation and a people." It also claimed that "we have, in effect, been committing an act of unthinking, unilateral disarmament."[5]

For the most part, the report initially went unchallenged. However, within a few years, education researchers began looking at the data more carefully. Since then, distinctly different conclusions have been reached about the state of American education by some of the best researchers in the country. In particular, a series of studies now known as *The Sandia Report* was conducted by the Sandia National Laboratories.[6] The Sandia scientists, as well as a number of independent researchers, have concluded that many of the charges against American public education are unfounded. Much of this perspective has been synthesized and summarized by David Berliner, past president of the prestigious American Educational Research Association. Here we consider three of these charges. (For a detailed discussion, see Berliner, 1992; Berliner and Biddle, 1995).

1. *Today's students are not as intelligent as students of the past.* Charges that today's American youth are not as intelligent as students from past generations come from many sources. According to Berliner, this charge has been "repeated by politicians, news commentators, editorial writers, [and] deans of colleges of education."[7]

In his book *The Manufactured Crisis*, Berliner presents the research findings of psychologist James R. Flynn that reveal a very different scenario. Flynn's research results indicate that intelligence test scores in the United States have, in fact, significantly increased. Specifically, Flynn's data illustrate that since 1932 the mean IQ of white Americans aged two to seventy-five has risen about three-tenths of a point per year.[8] Berliner adds: "In the United States, today's youth probably average about 15 IQ points higher than did their grandparents and 7.5 points higher than did their parents on the Stanford-Binet and Wechsler tests [the best-known IQ tests]. . . .The number of students expected to have IQs of 130 or more—a typical cut-off point for defining giftedness in many school districts throughout the nation—is now about *seven* times greater than it was for the generation now retiring from leadership positions in the country and often complaining about the poor performance of today's youth."[9]

As further evidence that the general aptitude of American students has not declined, Berliner offers the fact that the number of students taking the Advanced Placement test for college credit increased 255 percent between 1978, when 90,000 students took the test, and 1990, when 324,000 students took the test. This increase in numbers was accompanied by an increase in representation by diverse ethnic groups. For example, between 1978 and 1990, the percentage of African Americans taking the test doubled and the percentage of Hispanic students taking the test quadrupled.[10]

2. *The Scholastic Aptitude Test has shown a marked decrease over the last twenty-five years as a result of the failure of American education.* Virtually anyone who wishes to build a case against the current public education system highlights the well-publicized decline in scores on the Scholastic Aptitude Test (SAT) over the last few decades. For example, in their book *What Do Our 17-Year-Olds Know?* Ravitch and Finn write: "The most widely publicized score decline was that of the Scholastic Aptitude Test, which more than a million students take annually as part of the college entry process. The revelation in 1975 that the national average had fallen precipitously over a ten-year period stirred a public furor. . . . [It] aroused public concern about the quality of education; it alerted the media to education issues as no other single indicator had done."[11]

Hirsch makes the same claim in his condemnation of the American educational system: "It is well known that verbal SAT scores have declined dramatically in the past fifteen years."[12] Finally, William Bennett highlights the decline in his book *The De-Valuing of America:* "The public schools sustained yet another blow when the College Board revealed in 1975 that scores on the Scholastic

Aptitude Test (SAT), taken each year by more than a million high school seniors, had declined steadily since 1964. More than any other single factor, the public's concern about the score decline touched off loud calls for instruction in 'the basics' of reading, writing, and arithmetic."[13]

Again, Berliner offers a very different perspective, although he readily acknowledges that there has indeed been a decline in average SAT scores since 1965. Considering the issue from a statistical viewpoint, Berliner notes that a decline in test scores must be interpreted in the context of the range of possible scores. That is, a decline of 10 points means one thing if the total possible points are 100, and it means something quite different if the total possible points are 500. Relative to the decline in SAT scores, Berliner explains that the figures actually represent only a 3.3 percent decline in raw score total or about five fewer items answered correctly over twenty-five years. He further maintains, "The explanation for this loss is simple and should fill educators with great pride, not shame. Why? Because much greater numbers of students in the bottom sixty percent of their class have been taking the test since the 1960s."[14]

According to Berliner, educators have become more effective at inspiring students from rural areas and from commonly underrepresented minority groups to seek advanced degrees. As more students have sought college educations, the number of students taking the SAT has increased dramatically. The Sandia researchers described this same phenomenon:

> The data . . . indicate that the median class rank of SAT test takers in 1971 was the 79th percentile (or top 21 percent of the class). In 1989, the median class rank was the 73rd percentile. The reason for the drop in SAT scores is due to this decline, i.e., to the fact that more of our youth take the entrance exams.
>
> (Note that the drop from 79th to 73rd percentile is not trivial. The 79th percentile average rank would be

> achieved if the entire top 42 percent of a class took the exam. To lower the median rank to the 73rd percentile, the portion of the class between the 58th and 46th percentiles would have to be added to the group taking the test. It would be a surprise if this change did not significantly lower the test results.)[15]

Another major factor one must consider when analyzing SAT scores is that performance on the SAT has actually increased since 1975. Figure 5.1 illustrates the growth in SAT scores for various student groups. Additionally, the Sandia researchers note that the scores of "traditional" SAT test takers—those who rank at the top of the class—have increased significantly since 1975. The researchers further assert, "This illustrates again that average SAT scores are declining because a more diverse, lower performing group of test takers is being added to the traditional pool of test takers. This improving performance among the 'traditional' test takers is even more impressive in light of informal conversations with ETS analysts (developers of the SAT) that indicate that the SAT is getting more difficult."[16]

Probably the most striking illustration of the real meaning of the reported decline in SAT scores is the Sandia comparison of a matched group of students (same gender and class rank) from 1975 and 1990. Figure 5.2 shows the real improvement in SAT scores during this fifteen-year period. The Sandia researchers describe this graph as follows: "The solid line shows the performance of the students who actually took the exam each year. In contrast, the dashed line represents the year-by-year performance if the actual SAT scores obtained are weighted so that the population of students taking the test is adjusted to match the 1975 test takers."[17]

In summary, the much-publicized decline in SAT scores might be the result of dramatic changes in the types of students taking the examination, indicating that American education is getting better

Figure 5.1. Average SAT Subpopulation Scores: 1975 and 1990.

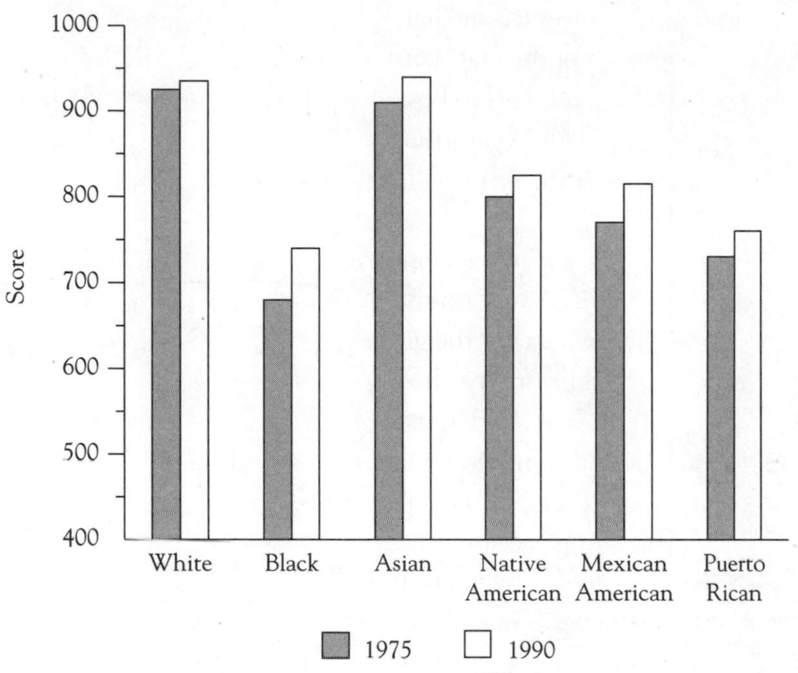

Source: Carson, Huelskamp, and Woodall, 1991, p. 41. Used with permission.

at inspiring both more students and students with more varied backgrounds to seek advanced degrees.

3. *American students simply do not know as much as students from past generations.* The common perception that American students of today do not know as much as students from past generations is certainly a theme in many books proclaiming the demise of public education. Perhaps the most widely read book based on this assertion is Ravitch and Finn's *What Do Our 17-Year-Olds Know?* In an attempt to determine the knowledge of American students in history and literature, Ravitch and Finn constructed test items that covered specific information within these domains. Following are examples of the information they tested:

Figure 5.2. SAT Scores of 1975 Test Takers.

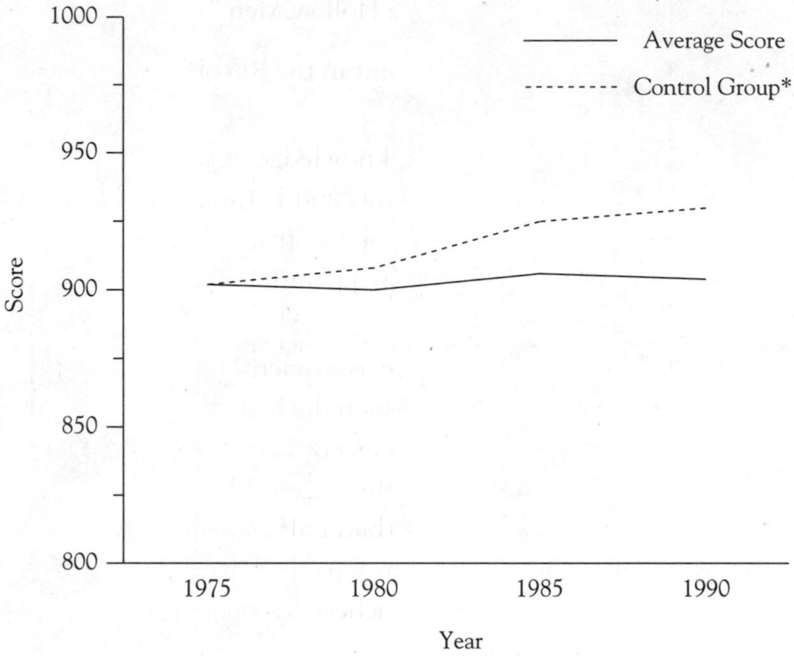

*Same gender and class rank mix as 1975

Source: Carson, Huelskamp, and Woodall, 1991, p. 47. Used with permission.

"Friends, Romans, countrymen . . ." is from *Julius Caesar.*

The invention of the cotton gin stimulated the plantation economy in the South.

Edgar Allan Poe wrote the poems "Annabel Lee" and "The Raven."

The Stamp Act of 1765 was an attempt by the English to tax the colonies.

In Greek mythology Atlas has to support the heavens on his shoulders.

Woodrow Wilson appealed for American entry into the League of Nations.

T. S. Eliot wrote "The Waste Land," "The Love Song of J. Alfred Prufrock," and "The Hollow Men."

Valley Forge was the lowest point in the Revolutionary War.[18]

The test designed to measure knowledge of this information consisted of 262 items—141 in history and 121 in literature. In all, 7,812 eleventh-grade students took the test. Ravitch and Finn report that the results were quite disappointing:

> On the history portion of the assessment, the national average is 54.5 percent correct; on the literature portion, the national average is 51.8 percent correct. Observers looking for the bright side might suggest that the proverbial glass is half full, rather than half empty. Another way of characterizing these results, however, is in the terms traditionally used by teachers: a score of less than 60 percent is failing.[19]

This is the interpretation chosen by Ravitch and Finn. They concluded that "if there were such a thing as a national report card for those studying American history and literature, then we would have to say that this nationally representative sample of eleventh grade students earns failing marks in both subjects."

Of course this interpretation made national headlines, which usually were accompanied by little or no analysis of the study. However, those who have analyzed Ravitch and Finn's data have reached quite different conclusions. For example, researcher Dale Whittington of the University of Akron argues that the test results were difficult, if not impossible, to interpret inasmuch as the test had never been given to any reference group. Without a reference group of similar students from past generations or even adults of today, there is no way of knowing whether the scores of 54.5 and 51.8 represented a gain or a loss in general knowledge. Ravitch and

Finn simply assumed that students should know all the items on the test. As Whittington reports:

> In other words, the study provided no indication whether 17-year-olds in the mid-1980s knew any more or less than anyone else living in the United States today. Nor can the test's results tell us how much 17-year-olds of the mid-80s knew compared to 17-year-olds of the past. The study's validity rested solely on the author's judgment that (a) all the questions in their test represented basic information about history, geography, and literature; (b) all students should have been instructed in the content covered by this test and have it permanently ingrained in their memory; (c) a test of factual knowledge, while not ideal, could adequately determine what America's 17-year-olds have and have not learned about history and literature; and (d) in order to "pass" the test, students needed to answer 60 percent of its questions correctly.[20]

In addition, Whittington sought out history and social studies tests administered from 1915 to the present and equated them as accurately as possible with the Ravitch and Finn test. As reported by Berliner, Whittington found that students in the Ravitch and Finn study were less knowledgeable than students from the past on about one-third of the items and scored better than past generations on about one-third of the items. Berliner concluded, "When compared to historical records, the data in Ravitch and Finn's study do not support their charge that today's seventeen-year-olds know less than they ever did."[21]

Berliner also examined the research on standardized tests to address the charge that American students today do not know as much as their counterparts from past generations. He explained that one must consider the norming procedures of standardized tests if one is to accurately interpret increases or decreases in scores. Standardized tests are renormed about every seven years; over one generation, a standardized test might be renormed about three times. Renorming means that the test makers recalculate the percentile scores, making it harder to obtain a given percentile rank. Analyzing such commonly used standardized tests as the California Test of Basic Skills, the Iowa Test of Basic Skills, and the Metropolitan Achievement Test, Berliner presented evidence that student performance on standardized tests has actually *increased:* "That means that today's youth is scoring about one standard deviation higher than their parents did when they took the test. We can estimate that around eighty-five percent of today's public school students score higher on standardized tests of achievement than their average parent did. But the high-jump bar keeps getting higher, and it takes a higher jump today than it did around 1965 to hit the fiftieth percentile."[22]

Perhaps the public education system is not in the dire straits described in the popular press and in the writings of many conservative Christian groups, although it undoubtedly could benefit from substantive changes. What are some of the changes public education should make?

Our National Educational Goals

One of the most obvious reform efforts public education can benefit from is to set clear national goals. The United States as a nation has never established clear learning goals, even though the need is self-evident. Our highly decentralized governmental structures in education, specifically public school districts, can set educational policy virtually free from state or federal control. In other words, school districts are relatively independent entities that establish their own goals. Ironically, nearly every country with which American education is unfavorably compared has well-articulated national educational goals as well as a highly centralized governance structure. A report by the National Education Goals Panel notes that "most countries embody their content standards in curriculum guides issued by the ministries of education, or their equivalents."[23]

Recognizing the importance and usefulness of national educational goals, President George Bush called for their establishment during his tenure in the Oval Office. The president's wishes were realized in February 1990 when the nation's governors met in a historic education summit in Charlottesville, Virginia, to establish educational goals for the 1990s. The summit had a well-defined intent: "to establish clear, national performance goals, goals that will make us internationally competitive."[24] Those goals are reproduced in Exhibit 5.1.

Exhibit 5.1. National Educational Goals.

Goal 1	By the year 2000, all children in America will start school ready to learn.
Goal 2	By the year 2000, the high school graduation rate will have increased at least 90 percent.
Goal 3	By the year 2000, American students will leave grades four, eight, and twelve having demonstrated competency over challenging subject matter including English, mathematics, science, history, and geography, and every school in America will ensure that all students learn to use their minds well, so they may be prepared for responsible citizenship, further learning, and productive employment in our modern economy.
Goal 4	By the year 2000, American students will be first in the world in achievement in science and mathematics.
Goal 5	By the year 2000, every adult American will be literate and will possess the knowledge and skills necessary to compete in a global economy and exercise the rights and responsibilities of citizenship.
Goal 6	By the year 2000, every school in America will be free of drugs and violence and will offer a disciplined environment conducive to learning.

Source: National Education Goals Panel, *Handbook for Local Goals Reports: Building a Community of Learners*, Washington, D.C.: National Education Goals Panel, Jan. 1993, pp. xii–xiii.

The establishment of general goals at a national level resulted in efforts to identify what students should know and be able to do within specific content areas. Goals are being established in virtually every content area.[25] For example, the National Council of Teachers of Mathematics, the professional organization for mathematics teachers, has identified thirteen goals for mathematics education:[26]

1. Enhance mathematical problem solving
2. Enhance communication in mathematics
3. Enhance mathematics reasoning
4. Enhance connections between mathematics concepts
5. Enhance understanding of functions
6. Enhance understanding and use of algebra
7. Enhance understanding of geometry from a synthetic perspective
8. Enhance understanding of geometry from an algebraic perspective
9. Enhance understanding and use of trigonometry
10. Enhance understanding and use of statistics
11. Enhance understanding and use of probability
12. Enhance understanding and use of discrete mathematics
13. Enhance a basic understanding of calculus

Similar efforts to identify learning goals in geography, history, civics, language arts, physical education, science, social studies, dance, music, theater, and the visual arts are being undertaken by the professional organizations for these content areas. For a list of documents where these various learning goals can be found, see Appendix B at the end of this book.

In summary, one might say that for the first time in the history of American education, explicit educational goals have been identified similar to those set forth in countries whose educational accomplishments we wish to emulate. At its core, the reform movement in education is driven by these goals. Coinciding with this national emphasis on explicit goals are advances in our understanding of the nature of learning. Many of the specific changes in the educational reform movement are grounded in these advances.

Advances in Learning Theory

Almost paradoxically, it was not until the 1960s that psychology began to seriously consider the internal workings of the brain as people learn. Until then, psychologists considered the mind a sealed "black box" that could not be studied. This approach to the study of human learning was referred to as *behaviorism*. Psychologist John Anderson explains that from its beginnings in 1921 the behaviorist tradition all but eliminated any serious inquiry into the cognitive processes underlying learning.[27] Behaviorism dominated psychology for over forty years.

With the advent of cognitive psychology in the 1960s, psychologists began to study the underlying processes in learning. Since then, researchers in cognitive psychology and the related fields of artificial intelligence and cognitive science have created an explosion of knowledge about learning that has resulted in a number of principles on which educators today base many of their reform efforts. In this section, we consider five learning principles from cognitive psychology that are integral to the school reform movement.

It is important to note that current educational reforms are built on many learning principles other than the five we present here. We have selected these five because they are the basis for many of the programs and practices objected to by critics of public education. We discuss these programs and practices in Chapters Six and Seven.

Enhancing Students' Self-Perceptions

One of the most consistent findings in the research on learning is that a student's attitudes and perceptions play a key role in the learning process. Of central importance are the attitudes and perceptions that deal with acceptance. Specifically, a tremendous amount of research has demonstrated that students must feel accepted if they are to learn most effectively.[28] This includes feeling accepted by the teacher and by peers; a student who has a negative perception of his or her acceptance will be distracted from the learning process. Learning is not a simple matter of acquiring new knowledge and skills and teaching is not a simple matter of presenting information. Consequently, some efforts at educational reform focus on developing a healthy sense of self in students.

A number of educators[29] have developed techniques and strategies for enhancing students' perceptions of acceptance. Some of these strategies are indirect, such as responding to students' questions and answers in a manner that signals acceptance. Others are overt, such as explicitly making positive comments to students or encouraging them to express positive opinions about themselves. Most of these techniques are aimed at developing a healthy sense of self—a perception on the part of students that they are worthy of acceptance by teachers and peers.

Deep Processing as an Aid to Internalization

Learning involves much more than understanding information. To learn, information or skills must be internalized. For example, you might understand some basic facts and principles about sharks after reading an article about them, but this information is not very useful unless it can be recalled and used at a different time. Deep processing facilitates internalization. Once information has been internalized, it can be recalled and used at a later date.

Psychologists explain this phenomenon of deep processing as one of making elaborative connections. In elaboration, an individual makes many and varied links between new and old information. According to psychologists,[30] one of the most powerful ways to elaborate on information is to imagine the mental pictures and physical sensations associated with the information. For example, to aid in the learning of information about sharks, you might create detailed mental pictures of the various types of sharks—white sharks, blue sharks, hammerhead sharks—and imagine specific characteristics of each. You might picture the white shark as being large, with retractable jaws, or imagine the hammerhead, with its strange, wide-set eyes, swimming in a large school as is its habit.

The use of imagery is also important in acquiring new skills. For example, when first learning how to hit a golf ball, you might review or "rehearse" the process in your mind, imagining in vivid detail your stance, your hand position, and your swing. This type of mental rehearsal through imagery has been shown to greatly enhance the learning of both mental and physical skills. It is commonly used by professional athletes and by those in professions in which high performance is expected.[31] Because deep-processing techniques using imagery and mental rehearsal have been shown to greatly enhance the learning of both information and skills, many schools and districts incorporate their use into their reform efforts.

The Whole Language Approach to Reading

The ability to read has long been considered fundamental to the success of a technological society. Some economists and economic historians contend that a 40 percent literacy rate is necessary but not sufficient for initiating or maintaining economic development.[32] Those who cannot read are placed at a serious disadvantage in our society. They face years of repeated failure in school, inasmuch as almost all knowledge imparted in school is dependent on the ability to read, as well as encountering serious problems in obtaining a driver's license, navigating in their physical environment, learning a skill, or obtaining a job. In addition, they suffer the social stigma of being different. Reading instruction, then, is a critical component of our educational system.

In general, two approaches have been proposed for reading instruction: the *skills approach* and the *whole language approach*. The debate over which approach is best probably reached its peak in the late 1960s and early 1970s, although the roots of the debate can be traced back to the turn of the century.[33]

The skills approach was developed as a result of a particular view of reading. Reading specialists David Pearson and Diane Stephens explain that reading was viewed as a simple process of translating letters on a printed page into sounds. The reader then listened to the sounds and translated these into words.[34] The mechanics of that process were thought to progress from the smallest element to the largest element. For example, skills theorist researcher Phillip Gough describes reading as a process of adding up the meaning of pieces. As words are recognized, the meaning of phrases and sentences are gradually understood. As more and more sentences are understood, the meaning of a paragraph is understood, and so on. The central feature of this description of reading is that meaning is gradually built from the bottom up. The reader begins with nothing and keeps adding pieces until she or he finally builds the whole.[35]

In keeping with this perspective, learning to read from the skills position is conceived of as mastery of a set of discrete skills, where a student masters first one skill, then another. Of course, the skills that should be mastered first are those that relate directly to the first steps of the reading process: recognizing letters and letter-sound relationships. The skills to be mastered within a skills approach typically include recognizing letters, recognizing letter-sound relationships, using phonics rules, breaking words into syllables, figuring out words from context, figuring out words using word parts, recognizing sentence patterns, asking and answering literal questions, and asking and answering inferential questions.

This bottom-up, skills-oriented approach to reading instruction persisted until about 1970, when two major publications caught the eye and the fancy of educators. In 1967 Kenneth Goodman presented a paper at the annual meeting of the American Educational Research Association. This paper drastically changed the perception of educators regarding the nature of the reading process and, consequently, the nature of literacy development. Instead of a precise process of using skills in a bottom-up fashion, Goodman characterized reading as a much more imprecise, meaning-driven activity. He referred to it as a "psycholinguistic guessing game," and said, "Effective reading does not result from precise perception and identification of all elements, but from skill in selecting the fewest, most productive cues necessary to produce guesses which are right the first time."[36]

Based on this theory of reading as driven by meaning, Goodman hypothesized a very different reading process from that articulated by Gough. Where the process described by Gough is bottom-up, with understanding driven by recognizing the smallest parts first, the reading process, as described by Goodman, is driven from the top down. Understanding by readers of what will probably be in the text determines where they look, what they look for, and what they perceive.

Goodman provided a different perspective of the reading process; Frank Smith provided a different perspective of the process of learning to read. Reading researchers David Pearson and Diane Stephens describe Frank Smith's contributions in the following way: "Smith's revolutionary ideas were first presented in 1971 in a book entitled *Understanding Reading*. In this seminal text, Smith argued that reading was not something we were *taught*, but rather was something one *learned* to do. . . . One learned to read from reading. The implication, which Smith made explicit, was that the 'function of teachers is not so much to teach reading as to help children read.'"[37]

From the principles outlined by Smith and Goodman, educators reasoned that reading and writing should be taught in a holistic manner, as opposed to teaching specific skills in a linear fashion. This general philosophy became known as the *whole language* approach. Kenneth Goodman outlined the basic tenets of whole language in his text *What's Whole in Whole Language?*:

- Language learning is easy when it's whole, real, and relevant; when it makes sense and is functional. . . .
- Language is both personal and social. It's driven from inside the need to communicate and shaped from the outside toward the norms of the society. . . .

- Language is learned as pupils learn *through* language and *about* language, all simultaneously in the context of authentic speech and literacy events. There is no sequence of skills in language development. . . .
- Language development is empowering; the learner "owns" the process, makes the decisions about when to use it, what for and with what results. . . .
- Language learning is learning how to mean—how to make sense of the world in the context of how our parents, families, and cultures make sense of it. . . .
- In a word, language development is a holistic personal social achievement. . . .[38]

Since Goodman's original description of whole language, many translations and applications of his basic tenets have been made, including those by Lucy Calkins, Nancy Atwell, Donald Graves, and Jane Hansen.[39] However, all of them preserve the holistic nature of Goodman's philosophy.

Many reform efforts have tried to incorporate aspects of a whole language approach, although most also maintain aspects of the skills approach. This "integrated" approach has the strongest research base. Specifically, current research indicates that the most effective way to teach reading is to emphasize the holistic process of reading as suggested by the whole language advocates, but also to ensure that students have a strong grounding in phonics as emphasized by the skills proponents.[40]

Applying Knowledge

Although it has probably been known and used for centuries, the principle that applying knowledge creates a deep type of learning was highlighted by French psychologist Jean Piaget. Piaget called this type of learning "accommodation." Stated in basic terms, this means that it is one thing to know facts and principles about sharks, but it is quite another to use that knowledge to solve a problem regarding sharks. The application of the knowledge is the true test of its utility.

Unfortunately, U.S. students do not do well when asked to apply information. This was illustrated by a 1990 report by the National Assessment of Educational Progress (NAEP), a federally funded organization whose purpose is to assess the competency of U.S. students in core content areas. The report stated: "On an analytic task that asked students to compare food on the frontier (based on information presented) and today's food (based on their own knowledge), just 16 percent of students at grade 8 and 27 percent at grade 12 provided an adequate or better response."[41]

Another graphic illustration of the difficulties students have when applying information is illustrated by the following mathematics problem:

> Treena won a 7-day scholarship worth $1,000 to the Pro-Shot Basketball Camp. Round-trip travel expenses to the camp are $335 by air or $125 by train. At the camp she must choose between a week of individual instruction at $60 per day or a week of group instruction at $40 per day. Treena's food and other expenses are fixed at $45 per day. If she does not plan to spend any money other than the scholarship, what are all the choices of travel and instruction plans that she could afford to make. Explain your reasoning.[42]

When NAEP presented this problem to eighth-graders from across the country, the following percentages of students provided adequate or better-than-adequate responses: nation, 4 percent; white, 5 percent; black, 0 percent; Hispanic, 1 percent; male, 2 percent; female, 6 percent.[43] Quite obviously, these results indicate an inability to use knowledge in practical ways. In other words, although American students do well when asked to recall or recognize information, they do not do well when asked to apply it.

In response to this shortcoming, educators have developed programs that require students to apply their knowledge. These programs are usually referred to as "thinking skills" programs. For example, the Association for Supervision and Curriculum Development publishes a thinking skills program that involves thirteen reasoning processes. Each process relates to a specific set of questions that are answered as the process is executed (see Table 5.1). As students ask and answer these questions about the content they are studying, they must quite naturally put their knowledge to use.

Many thinking skills programs exist that articulate other processes.[44] Virtually all of these have as their central purpose providing students with practice in various mental processes that require them to use what they know. An emphasis on enhancing thinking is not new to educators. Indeed, educational philosopher John Dewey emphasized this nearly eighty years ago when he said, "The sole direct path to enduring improvement in the methods of instruction and learning consists in centering upon the conditions which exact, promote and test thinking."[45] This same sentiment was expressed in 1961 by the National Education Association: "Thus in the general area of the development of the ability to think, there is a field for new research of the greatest importance. It is essential that those who have responsibility for management and policy determination in education commit themselves to expansion of such research and to the application of the fruits of this research."[46]

In recent years, calls for enhancement of thinking skills in American students have even come from the halls of Congress.[47] In response to this long history, many school reform efforts implicitly or explicitly attempt to enhance thinking and reasoning to enable students to use the knowledge they acquire.

Preparing for Success in a Diverse World

It was not long ago that aptitude was considered a single trait.[48] Conventional wisdom proclaimed that those who possessed high aptitude or intelligence could do well at whatever task they desired, but those with low aptitude or intelligence were doomed to poor

Table 5.1. Questions Related to Knowledge Application Cognitive Processes.

Questions	*Reasoning Process*
How are these alike? How are they different?	Comparing
What groups can you put things into? What are the rules governing membership in these groups?	Classifying
What conclusions or generalizations can you draw from this, and what support do you have for these conclusions? What is the probability of this happening, and what support do you have for this conclusion?	Induction
What has to be true given the validity of this principle? What is the proof that this must be true?	Deduction
What's wrong with this? What specific errors have been made? How can it be fixed?	Error analysis
What is the support for this argument? What are the limitations of this argument?	Constructing support
What is the general pattern of information here? Where else does this apply? How can the information be represented in another way (graphically, symbolically)?	Abstracting
What do you think about this issue? On what do you base your opinion? What is another way of looking at the issue?	Analyzing perspectives
What or who would be the best or worst? Which one has the most or least?	Decision making

Table 5.1. Questions Related to Knowledge Application Cognitive Processes, cont'd.

Questions	*Reasoning Process*
What are the defining characteristics? Why or how did this happen? What would have happened if . . . ?	Definitional, historical, and projective investigation
How can you overcome this obstacle? Given these conditions, what should you do to accomplish the goal?	Problem solving
What do you observe? How can you explain it? What can you predict from it?	Experimental inquiry
How can this be improved? What new thing is needed here?	Invention

Source: Marzano, Pickering, and McTighe, 1993. Copyright by Mid-Continent Regional Educational Laboratory. Adapted with permission.

performance. One way of thinking about this perspective is the "horsepower theory" of aptitude or intelligence. Some people are born with a great deal of horsepower, others with a moderate amount, and still others with very little. Those born with a great deal of horsepower will most likely do quite well at whatever task they are assigned; those with little horsepower will not.

This "single trait" theory of aptitude and intelligence persisted until the late 1970s, when psychologists began producing research and theory indicating that aptitude and intelligence were situational. For example, psychologist Robert Sternberg illustrated that these traits could only be discussed in relation to a specific situation. Because a person exhibits aptitude or intelligence in one setting does not necessarily mean that he or she will do so in another setting, and preparing for success in one setting may require the acquisition of an entirely different set of skills than would be required to prepare for success in another setting.

This new perspective suggests that schools should help students develop skills and abilities in more than the traditional academic subjects, such as mathematics, science, and history, if the students are to be adequately prepared for success in a diverse world. Realizing this, organizations such as the U.S. Department of Labor and the National Society of Trainers and Developers (NSTD) have attempted to identify the nonacademic skills and abilities that should be enhanced as part of a truly comprehensive education. Many school reform efforts have attempted to incorporate these nonacademic skills and abilities into their curricular designs. Following are some of the nonacademic skills and abilities identified by the Department of Labor and the NSTD:

- Demonstrates respect for others while working in a group
- Identifies and deals with causes of conflict in a group
- Engages in active listening
- Effectively resolves conflict with opponents
- Establishes guidelines and rules for negotiating
- Displays politeness with others
- Acknowledges the strengths of others
- Enlists others in working toward group goals
- Works well with different genders or ethnic groups
- Sets explicit long-term goals
- Manages progress toward goals
- Identifies and capitalizes on personal strengths[49]

In summary, the current efforts at school reform are based on explicit educational goals established in 1990 by the nation's governors and on a number of principles of learning, five of which we have briefly described in this section.

6

School Improvement Initiatives

In addition to the general attack on public education based on the great conspiracy theory, certain specific programs and practices are frequently targeted. Those most challenged include outcome-based education, the whole language approach, thinking skills programs, imagery techniques, self-esteem programs, the teaching of evolution, global education and multiculturalism, and sex education. We will consider these initiatives in the following chapters.

Outcome-Based Education

Outcome-based education, or OBE, as it is commonly called, is perhaps the most popular target of attacks. It is so prominent a target of attack that two of the largest educational journals devoted entire issues in 1994 to the controversy over outcome-based education. The title of the March 1994 issue of *Educational Leadership*, with a circulation of 185,000, was "The Challenge of Outcome-Based Education," and the title of the September 1994 issue of the journal *School Administrator* was "Outcomes: The Dirtiest Word in School Reform."

Perhaps one of the reasons OBE is so vulnerable to attack is that it means so many different things to so many different people. Most educators think of outcome-based education as a simple matter of articulating learning goals, as educational reporter John O'Neil notes: "At one level, outcome-based education is the simple principle that decisions about curriculum and instruction should be driven by the outcomes we'd like children to display at the end of their educational experiences."[1]

Grant Wiggins, director of programs for the Center on Learning, Assessment, and School Structure, explains that OBE is "a simple matter of making sure that you're clear on what teaching should accomplish . . . and adjusting your teaching and assessing as necessary to accomplish what you set out to accomplish."[2] In its most basic form, then, OBE is a simple concept: identify what you want students to learn and then make sure that the curriculum, teaching, and assessment are designed to produce the intended learning (that is, the intended outcome). From this perspective, one can conclude that OBE is quite compatible with the educational goals established by the nation's governors in 1990. (See Chapter Five.) It is simply an attempt to be explicit about what students should know and be able to do.

Unfortunately, a number of brands of OBE have been developed, and therein lies at least part of the problem. Three of the various brands have been articulated by William Spady. In 1988, Spady, who is credited with coining the term *outcome-based education*, made a distinction between three different types of OBE: *traditional*, *transitional*, and *transformational*.[3]

Traditional OBE involves identifying learning outcomes in traditional content areas such as mathematics, science, and history. Transitional OBE involves identifying learning outcomes both in traditional content areas and in nontraditional content areas like those in Exhibit 6.1. These outcomes are sometimes referred to as lifelong learning outcomes. Exhibit 6.1 contains sample lifelong learning outcomes developed by the Aurora Public Schools in Aurora, Colorado.

To elaborate, a school following a traditional approach to OBE would teach to and assess such traditional content outcomes as understanding the concept of democracy or the causes of the Civil

Exhibit 6.1. Sample Lifelong Learning Outcomes.

Outcome 1: A self-directed learner:

- Sets priorities and achievable goals
- Monitors and evaluates his or her progress
- Creates options for himself or herself
- Assumes responsibilities for actions
- Creates a positive vision for himself or herself

Outcome 2: A collaborative worker:

- Monitors own behavior as a group member
- Assesses and manages group functioning
- Demonstrates interactive communication
- Demonstrates consideration for individual differences

Outcome 3: A complex thinker:

- Uses a wide variety of strategies for managing complex issues
- Selects strategies appropriate to the resolution of complex issues and applies the strategies with accuracy and thoroughness
- Accesses and uses topic-relevant knowledge

Outcome 4: A quality producer:

- Creates products that achieve their purpose
- Creates products appropriate to their intended audience
- Creates products that reflect craftsmanship
- Uses appropriate resources and technology

Outcome 5: A community contributor:

- Demonstrates knowledge about his or her diverse community
- Takes action
- Reflects on role as a community contributor

Source: Redding, 1991, pp. 49–53.

War. A school following a transitional approach to OBE would also focus on traditional content outcomes. However, in addition, it would teach to and assess such nontraditional outcomes as participating in the democratic process and setting and carrying out personal goals.

Transformational OBE focuses solely on lifelong learning outcomes like those in Exhibit 6.1. Within the transformational approach, traditional content may, in fact, be covered, but only insofar as it fosters attainment of lifelong learning outcomes. Spady advocates the use of transformational OBE and sees traditional and transitional approaches as unacceptable in the long run. However, it is certainly fair to say that many educators have expressed doubts about Spady's transformational approach. In fact, few schools across the country have implemented this approach.[4] Rather, the vast majority of OBE schools and districts take a highly traditional approach and only a small number have attempted transitional approaches. (Given the conflict over the transformational approach, Spady recently has modified his view of this type of OBE, seemingly to satisfy the concerns of conservative Christian critics. See in particular *Education Newsline*, Citizens for Excellence in Education, summer 1995 issue.)

Some of the opposition to OBE is thoughtful enough to make distinctions between the various types. For example, Beverly LaHaye, president of Concerned Women for America, notes that Spady "advocates transformational OBE because it completely restructures education as we know it. Concerned Women for America opposes transformational OBE because it is a radical redefinition of education that is uncalled for and unnecessary."[5]

Others are less discriminating in their criticisms. For example, Phyllis Schlafly, founder of the Eagle Forum, levels the following charges at all OBE efforts:

> 1. OBE is packaged in a deceptive language that appears to be mischievously chosen to mislead parents. . . .

2. OBE uses students as guinea pigs in a vast social experiment. . . .
3. OBE is a dumbed-down egalitarian scheme that stifles individual potential for excellence and achievement. . . .
4. OBE sets up a computer file on each child. . . . The computer records how the child responds to behavioral modification . . . and whether he develops positive attitudes toward the mandated outcomes.[6]

Still other organizations define anything they are against as OBE. For example, in a 1994 article for the *School Administrator*, Linda Chion-Kenney reports that the Michigan Alliance of Families publishes a list of twenty-six ways to determine whether a school is using OBE. Among these are site-based management, inclusive education, team teaching, individualized education plans, professional development programs in consensus building and collaboration, cooperative learning, peer tutoring, thematic teaching, year-round schooling, portfolios, continual assessment of growth and development, multiage-level grouping, and multiyear improvement plans. Chion-Kenney also reports that the Alliance provides a long list of terms and phrases to listen for that indicate that a school is using OBE. These include *mastery learning*, *performance-based education*, *management by objectives*, *planning programming budgeting systems*, *Total Quality Management*, *Accelerated Schools*, *Effective Schools*, *Schools for the 21st Century*, *Sizer's Coalition of Essential Schools*, *Professional Development Schools*, and the *outcomes-driven development model*.[7]

A common criticism leveled at OBE is that it has no research to back up claims of its effectiveness. It is more accurate to say that transformational OBE has no research to support such claims. Traditional and transitional approaches have demonstrated their effectiveness in a number of contexts.

In 1993, the Blue Valley School District in Overland Park,

Kansas, surveyed thirty-three districts in seventeen states, all of which used either traditional or transitional approaches to OBE. Of the districts surveyed, 97 percent believed that these approaches produced positive results and 94 percent offered data to support their assertions. Table 6.1 presents some of the specific findings reported in the survey results.

In summary, no single educational reform effort can be called outcome-based education. When considering OBE reform efforts, it is necessary to determine whether they are traditional, transitional, or transformational in nature. Although transformational OBE has little research to support it as yet, traditional and transitional forms have a growing research and theoretical foundation.

The Whole Language Movement

The whole language movement is based on the principle that reading should be taught as a general process with supporting skills. (See Chapter Five.) Since its inception, whole language has taken on many forms and has caught the fancy of American educators. There are no whole language programs per se. Rather it is a basic philosophy of literacy development that focuses on the holistic, integrated aspects of reading and writing development, rather than on the discrete skills within those processes.

As with self-esteem programs, whole language is criticized for both academic and nonacademic reasons. Some politically active fundamentalists have connected whole language to the New Age. For example, the January-February 1991 issue of *Education Newsline* notes that whole language teaching is the latest of the New Age curricula. A Riverside, California, parent claimed that her children were being taught "yoga, led meditations, visualization and relaxation techniques" as part of whole language instruction.[8]

These critics also claim that whole language is another form of the "look-say" method of learning words, even though the two approaches have little in common.[9] For example, the *Phyllis Schlafly Report* warns that "all research shows that phonics is the best way

Table 6.1. Sample Results of Outcome-Based Education Survey Conducted by Blue Valley School District, Overland Park, Kansas.

Wickenburg Unified School District #9, Wickenburg, Arizona: Student performance on the Iowa Test of Basic Skills (ITBS), American College Testing Program (ACT), and Test of Academic Proficiency (TAP) was above state and national averages, which had not always been the case.

College Community School District, Cedar Rapids, Iowa: All standardized test scores increased, especially the ACT.

Metropolitan School District, Decatur Township, Indianapolis, Indiana: CTBS (Comprehensive Test of Basic Skills) scores steadily increased.

Central Montcalm High School, Stanton, Michigan: MEAP (Michigan Education Assessment Program) scores increased, as did CTBS scores.

Walker-Hackensack-Akeley #113, Walker, Minnesota: ITBS scores increased and the number of behavioral incidents decreased (K–6).

Isop, New York: The high school had an increase of AP papers submitted from 28 to 270, although school size had remained constant.

Johnson City Central School District, Johnson City, New York: Reading and math scores on the CAT (California Achievement Test) increased dramatically over an eight-year period; 55 percent of students received the highest form of diploma from the New York State Regents compared to a state average of 35 percent; and the dropout rate fell to 3 percent.

Prince George County Public Schools, Maryland: The model was adopted after data showed that black students performed twenty-five percentile points under white students on the CAT; by 1989 black third-grade students gained twenty-eight points on the test and black fifth-grade students gained twenty points.

Table 6.1. Sample Results of Outcome-Based Education Survey Conducted by Blue Valley School District, Overland Park, Kansas, cont'd.

Biloxi Public Schools, Biloxi, Mississippi: Gains on the Stanford Achievement Test were twenty-three points in reading, twenty-four points in math, and nine points in language arts during the first three years of implementation.

New York City Public School CSD #1, New York, New York: The average scores on the DRP (Degrees of Reading Power) increased from 55.5 to 68.3.

Millersport Elementary School, Walnut Township Local Schools, Millersport, Ohio: Higher scores on the MAT (Metropolitan Achievement Test) and a higher attendance rate were achieved.

Parkrose Public Schools, Portland, Oregon: Standardized test scores improved, including the DRP, state assessments, and district norm criterion-referenced assessments in math.

LaJoya Independent School District, LaJoya, Texas: The district was 75 percent Hispanic and had a high migrant population; test scores soared and attendance improved.

Yakima Public Schools, Yakima, Washington: Higher levels of achievement were achieved in reading, language, and math as opposed to a control group of students in a traditional program.

Source: Hill and Pechar, 1994, pp. 21–58.

to teach a child how to read the English language. 'Whole language' is just the trendy new name for the discredited word-guessing system known as 'whole word' or 'look-say.'"[10]

It was probably Mel and Norma Gabler of Educational Research Analysts who gave "look-say" its radical status, linking it to humanism's attempt to infiltrate much of American society. Specifically, the Gablers maintain that the drift away from a strict phonics approach to teaching reading is a way for the educational elite to retain power by keeping the masses illiterate. The educational establishment is viewed as part of the humanist plot to take over the minds of American children, and the deemphasis of a strict phonics approach is a tool to this end.[11]

It is Pat Robertson, however, who provides the most biblically authoritative reason for teaching phonics. In a section of *The New Millennium* called "The Dumbing of America," he claims that learning to read can be "a breeze . . . if reading is taught the way God made us to talk—by syllables, by what is called phonics, not by the 'look say' method forced on the schools by the behaviorist models."[12]

In addition, critics object to the whole language approach to literature because it is based on the premise that the reader creates his or her own meaning from literature. This is quite troubling to Citizens for Excellence in Education. In her book *Reinventing America's Schools*, CEE's Kathi Hudson calls this "the philosophy of relative knowledge." In addition, Hudson is disturbed by whole language advocates "heralding" the philosophy of Soviet psychologist Vgotsky, "one of the creators of Marxist psychology," as "a cornerstone" of whole language theory.[13]

In addition to their general dissatisfaction with the whole language philosophy, conservative religious activists have also targeted a specific whole language program called *Impressions*. Beginning in the mid 1980s, critics mounted an intensive nationwide attack against *Impressions*, a K-6 reading series designed to teach language arts skills using a whole language, multicultural approach to literature. *Impressions* is composed of fifteen books that contain 822 selections by such authors as C. S. Lewis, Laura Ingalls Wilder, Martin Luther King, Jr., Rudyard Kipling, and Dr. Seuss, from a variety of genres including poetry, short stories, songs, myths, folklore, and fictional and factual narratives.[14]

During the two-year period between September 1989 and August 1991, People For the American Way documented fifty-nine challenges to *Impressions* in twelve states.[15] Attacks on *Impressions* have reached the courts. For example, in 1991 in Woodland, California, parents sued the school district, seeking removal of part of the reading series from the schools. The district court's ruling in favor of the schools was upheld on appeal.[16]

Several groups have criticized *Impressions* and have been involved in challenges to its use in public schools. These groups include the American Family Association, the Christian Educators Association International, the Traditional Values Coalition, Phyllis Schlafly's Eagle Forum, and Focus on the Family, with CEE leading the attack.

Criticisms of the *Impressions* series go far beyond its whole-language orientation. According to CEE, it is a New Age reading series that promotes witchcraft, satanism, and the occult; undermines parental authority and Christian values; and is morbid, violent, and depressing. Critics claim that the stories torment even well-adjusted children with nightmares.[17] One critic said that the series promotes satanism through the use of the colors red and green, which are allegedly satanic colors.[18] According to CEE's Simonds, "the *Impressions* reading series could not only change our entire culture to an erotic witchcraft and demonized society, but it could cause psychological damage to the children reading it."[19] Although the challenges to *Impressions* have certainly curtailed its use in many schools and districts, it is still a popular approach to reading instruction.

Thinking Skills

Most of the thinking skills programs used in education are based on two learning principles: that learning involves processing information at a deep level and that knowledge once learned should be applied. (See the discussion of deep processing and application of knowledge in Chapter Five.) One thinking skills program that has received considerable attention from fundamentalists is *Tactics for Thinking*.

Published in 1986, *Tactics for Thinking* teaches twenty-two skills divided into three categories: content thinking skills, learning-to-learn skills, and reasoning skills. Learning-to-learn skills help students to remember facts and details and to develop their creative writing skills, in part through the use of imagination.[20] The *Tactics* program draws from research and theory on attention deficit disorders, goal setting, mnemonic devices, vocabulary development, advanced organizers and information organization, critical thinking, decision making, and problem solving. *Tactics* has been assailed for its alleged "experimental" use of hypnosis, mind control, New Age meditation, and imagery.

One of its most vocal opponents has been Jeanne Georges of East Gibson, Indiana, a spokesperson for an activist group called the National Citizen's Alliance. Georges argues that a *Tactics* exercise dealing with imaging is a form of mind control and could lead to the child having an out-of-body experience. Further, she states, the child could actually be in a "trance," and the teacher could then begin to influence the child's subconscious mind.[21] Georges maintains: "When a person is in a trance, the conscious mind is left behind somewhere. Scientists do not know exactly where. They don't know if it is asleep or exactly what happens. But the subconscious mind is laid bare. It is like a computer. It takes in what it is fed as the truth and processes it—good and bad. You tell it a lie, and it believes it as the truth. It cannot tell a lie from the truth. Our conscious mind is our protection from our subconscious."[22]

Through a series of convoluted arguments, Georges links the attention control and imaging exercises suggested in *Tactics* with the New Age movement's alleged goals to install a new "Messiah" and take over the world. In particular, she references a suggested *Tactics* exercise asking students to close their eyes and imagine what it might feel like to be a snowflake floating to the ground. Georges charges that attention control, relaxation, hypnosis, concentration, energy control, and meditation are all the same New Age techniques.[23]

Critics associated with the National Citizen's Alliance have also criticized another exercise claimed to induce an "altered state" in children, leaving them open to the influence of New Age thinking.[24] This exercise is a suggested activity in a section of the *Tactics* program that deals with the importance of attention control in learning. The activity is a way to introduce students to the concept and importance of focusing their attention. The teacher asks students to do some deep breathing to get relaxed and then fix their attention on a dot on the wall for sixty seconds. The teacher then asks the students to notice their reactions to deliberately focusing their attention on something. Awarenesses gained through this activity are then used by the students to develop techniques for paying attention when a class or activity is not naturally engaging.

Other vocal critics of the *Tactics* program and exercises are Mel and Norma Gabler of Educational Research Analysts and Robert Simonds, president of CEE. In a pamphlet entitled "The Drugging of Students" (commented on by Simonds in an October 1993 *President's Report*), the Gablers argue that relaxation and creativity exercises "set students up for *drug use*. . . . Such exercises teach students to value altered states of consciousness—passivity, introversion, delusion, hallucination, illusion—to which *drugs are a short cut* [emphases in original]."[25] The Gablers then charge that the "sources" of "hocus pocus" like *Tactics* are *Secrets of Shamanism*, *Buckland's Complete Book of Witchcraft*, *A Witches Bible Compleat*, and *The Satanic Bible*. Simonds states that "new-age occultic brainwashing" like this is being used in districts all across the United States.[26] Attacks on *Tactics* have had an impact on the use of the program in school districts around the country. A few districts have tabled its use; others have canceled the program. However, many districts have retained and expanded the use of *Tactics* in spite of objections.

Like *Tactics*, most thinking skills programs are designed to be used with all students. However, a significant number focus on students who have been identified as academically "gifted." In fact, in the last twenty years, interest in teaching gifted and talented students in America has grown remarkably. As Paul Torrance notes, focusing on techniques and programs specifically designed for the gifted and talented is precipitated by a desire to help individuals with exceptional talent maximize their potential.[27] The movement has spawned such innovative and popular programs as Future Problem Solving[28] and Odyssey of the Mind.[29]

In addition to their general objections to the enhancement of thinking and reasoning skills, some fundamentalists see gifted education as selectively targeted by New Agers. Johanna Michaelsen exemplifies this view in her book *Like Lambs to the Slaughter,* in which she alleges that gifted children, in particular, are New Age targets: "After all, it is the gifted and talented who will be the leaders, trendsetters, lawmakers, doctors, presidents, and teachers of the future. They are the ones who are expected to be the leaders of the New Age, and as such they *must* receive special attention and indoctrination from the social engineers [emphasis in original]."[30]

One of Michaelsen's major concerns about gifted education programs is that they attempt to enhance and activate latent abilities in students. Michaelsen warns, "The question we must deal with concerns the *source* of these abilities. If indeed these are merely neutral, latent abilities natural to mankind and potentially of great benefit, then it would certainly be backward of us to object to their development and use. If, on the other hand, they are produced by spirit beings for the purpose of drawing us into a particular belief system, as the Bible clearly indicates, then we have a real problem on our hands."[31]

Michaelsen claims that one of the ways gifted educators woo children into being open to the influence of spirits is through an emphasis on the intuitive. Referring to educators of the gifted, Michaelsen maintains, "They want the children to be 'gifted' in the 'intuitive' (i.e., psychic) abilities that they have assumed normally lie 'deep within every individual.'"[32] Later Michaelsen explains, "A euphemism for 'psychically gifted' that you may want to be aware of is 'intuitively gifted.'"[33] With the link made between intuitive knowledge and psychic knowledge, Michaelsen then explains how educational practices for the gifted are actually thinly veiled attempts to engage students in satanic rituals.

Finally, Texe Marrs, in *Dark Secrets of the New Age*, asserts that techniques that utilize intuitive knowledge are actually designed to help an individual tune "his mind in to this universal (Satanic) impulse."[34] In effect, then, gifted education is a vehicle that may directly link children to Satan.

Imagery Techniques

The use of imagery techniques is another major area of concern for critics of school reform. It is grounded in the learning principle that information should be processed at a deep level (see discussion of deep processing in Chapter Five). In her discussion of religiously based attacks on imagery, Edens explains that a vast amount of research evidence shows that mental images are a natural way to represent information and experiences in memory.[35] In effect, as Edens notes, human beings quite naturally form mental images as they think about a topic: "Individuals reported that they 'looked at' and scanned a mental image of a cat when asked questions about particular characteristics of cats."[36] From these basic principles of human information processing, instructional techniques using imagery have been developed that enhance vocabulary learning, mathematics problem solving, learning of scientific concepts, and goal acquisition.[37]

Edens notes that even if the research evidence were not so strong, an abundance of anecdotal evidence from a number of fields points to the utility of mental imagery. Anecdotal evidence is available from the fields of sports, physics, chemistry, mathematics, anthropology, genetics, astronomy, architecture, and creative writing. In addition, autobiographical reports from scientists such as Albert Einstein, Friedrich August Kekulé, Michael Faraday, James Clerk Maxwell, Nikola Tesla, and James Watson and from writers such as Samuel Taylor Coleridge, Isaac Asimov, Joan Didion, and Edgar Guest attest to the central role of imagery in their success.[38]

Some fundamentalists, however, see imagery as more than a thinking tool. In fact, they maintain, visualization activities used in the classroom are a tool to open students up to global or planetary consciousness. Further, exercises in which students relax, close their eyes, and imagine themselves in a scene may induce out-of-body experiences. As evidence of this practice in the classroom, Buehrer cites *Tactics for Thinking,*[39] in which children are asked to create mental pictures of things they wish to recall. As described by Buehrer, within the *Tactics* program, children are asked to

> picture George Washington on his horse; smell the leather of his saddle; or, before writing about snow, picture yourself as a snowflake falling through the sky.
>
> The teacher is instructed in the manual to use a warm-up exercise by having students practice creating images. The manual suggests the students imagine a blue ball hovering in space. The teacher is to make the exercise more complex by adding other objects such as colored squares.
>
> This particular exercise is alarmingly similar to rituals used to induce out of the body experiences.[40]

Buehrer maintains that developing the ability to create images is the first step before using visualization to actually leave the body. It is also a precursor to introduction to spirits in the form of spirit guides: "New Agers involved with contacting spirit guides believe that guides are essential for ushering in the new age of global consciousness."[41] Thus, what educators assert to be a natural ability that enhances the processing and recall of information is seen by some as a vehicle to contact spirits.

Self-Esteem

A number of reform efforts utilize programs and practices that are designed to enhance self-esteem. Virtually all of these are based on the learning principle that a learner must perceive himself or herself as competent and accepted by teachers and peers to perform most effectively in a learning situation. (See Chapter Five.) The sum total of these perceptions is commonly referred to as one's self-esteem. As is the case with outcome-based education, self-esteem can mean many things. Innovations designed to enhance students' perceptions of their ability to perform classroom tasks are classified as self-esteem programs, as are programs designed to help students plan and carry out goals, programs designed to help students interact better with peers, and so on.

As briefly described in Chapter Five, teachers can use many techniques to enhance the self-esteem of students. In addition, students can use some techniques independently, such as setting explicit goals and planning for their accomplishment, using affirmations, using positive self-talk, and creating and rehearsing mental images of themselves accomplishing a goal. Techniques like these are so common within psychology that they can be considered standard practices for enhancing self-esteem. Apparently their effectiveness was recognized centuries ago, as evidenced by the following account of Benjamin Franklin by psychologist Barry Zimmerman: "Benjamin Franklin wrote extensively in his 'Autobiography' about techniques he used to improve his learning, erudition and self-control. He described in detail how he set learning goals for himself, recording his daily progress in a ledger. He sought to improve his writing by studying exemplary written models and attempting to emulate the author's prose. In addition to teaching himself to write, Franklin felt this procedure improved his memory and his arrangement of thoughts, two cognitive benefits that research on observational learning has verified."[42]

Although the idea of enhancing self-esteem as an aid to learning strikes an intuitively appealing chord with most Americans, some Christians are concerned about self-esteem programs. Former CEE vice president Eric Buehrer has written extensively about his concerns about a misplaced and harmful emphasis on self-esteem in the classroom. He argues that all parents want their children to feel good about themselves. However, a healthy feeling of self-worth comes from setting standards, both academically and morally, and striving to meet those standards. Buehrer claims that the self-esteem movement often keeps teachers from applying a high standard to a student's work out of a concern that a low grade might damage the student's self-esteem. However, receiving an inappropriately high grade for poor work results in lower academic achievement. Buehrer concludes that the self-esteem movement is "concerned with justifying mediocrity, not demanding excellence. To *feel* good about oneself, rather than *be* good has become the highest pursuit [emphasis in original]."[43]

Criticisms of self-esteem programs are not limited to such academic concerns. In fact, some critics argue that the programs are anti-Christian. This position is well-chronicled in Jay Adams's book *The Biblical View of Self-Esteem, Self-Love and Self-Image*. Adams maintains that Abraham Maslow, in particular, was responsible for molding the self-esteem movement and selling it to the American public: "Abraham Maslow is the key figure involved. . . . During his days in New York City he attended Friday night seminars in Alfred Adler's home and had many talks with him. He also sought out persons like Eric Fromm and Karen Horney. . . . It was Adler's fundamental view that a person may realize fulfillment and satisfaction only when his needs for security and significance are met. Maslow took this idea, reshaped and amplified it, and then sold it under the heading of self-actualization."[44]

Adams highlights getting one's needs met as a particularly distasteful aspect of self-esteem techniques. Apparently, the major objection to this concept is that needs are closely aligned with sin:

> Now, do you begin to see what I am talking about? The supposed needs . . . are not *needs* at all.
>
> According to the Scriptures, one's *needs* are relatively few: 'If we have food and covering, with these we shall be content' (I Timothy 6:8). . . .
>
> What, then, are these so-called 'needs'? Substitute the word *desire* for *need* whenever it occurs (in these quotations) and you will have a biblical picture of what we have been talking about. . . .
>
> Under the guise of meeting needs, sin is excused [emphases in original].[45]

At a more general level, Adams objects to the self-esteem movement because it implies that humans are innately worthy of redemption. Adams corrects this notion:

> The actual teaching of the Bible (and that of the sixteenth-century reformers and all of orthodox Christianity ever since) is that it was not because of anything God saw in man that He redeemed him, but out of pure mercy and His determination to set His love on him. God's love was not the response to man's lovableness!
>
> Man was created not to become someone in his own right. . . . No, man was created to glorify God.[46]

For those ascribing to this view, programs that focus on enhancing self-esteem are a step in the wrong direction. In place of such efforts, a simple message should be sent to students. Adams explains: "One wonders how many young people will be led astray, led away from discipleship for Christ, which requires losing their 'selves,' because they were told 'Feel good about yourself' rather than being told that there is a criminal inside who needs to be put to death daily."[47]

Buehrer echoes Adams's point that the self-esteem movement

teaches students that they are innately good, which denies the biblical view of man's essentially sinful nature. Such an emphasis functions as a new kind of faith, replacing faith in God with faith in oneself.

In addition to the general concerns about enhancing self-esteem, these critics take particular exception to two specific programs, *Pumsy* and *Quest*.

Pumsy in Pursuit of Excellence

Pumsy, a program designed to build self-esteem in students, has been widely criticized by conservative Christian groups who charge the program with promoting the occult, Eastern religion, and hypnotic relaxation techniques. Created by author Jill Anderson, Pumsy is a blue storybook dragon who sometimes feels confused, unattractive, and full of self-doubt, but who learns to overcome these feelings. When Pumsy feels confused she thinks of this as "being in her mud mind," when she has positive thoughts she is using her "clear mind," and when she thinks creative thoughts she is using her "sparkle mind."

According to Anderson, these three mind-sets or attitudes were viewed by critics as "teaching children to be schizophrenic." Although Anderson dismissed these criticisms as unfounded, she made a few revisions to the curriculum to appease critics. For example, the revised curriculum explicitly states that obviously Pumsy does not have three minds.[48]

The *Pumsy* curriculum also is used to help students lead a drug-free life. Early editions of *Pumsy* recommended that students repeat Pumsy's saying, "I am me and I am enough." But critics charged that this implied that children didn't need to rely on outside authorities such as God, parents, and teachers and that the repetitious nature of the saying was akin to Eastern chanting. To appease critics, Anderson changed Pumsy's saying to "I am me and I am OK."

Critics of the *Pumsy* curriculum largely embrace the conclusions of George Twente II, a Decatur, Alabama, psychiatrist. Twente, who has written and spoken extensively about *Pumsy* and other self-esteem programs, charges that the techniques used in *Pumsy* are "extremely dangerous" and that the program "amounts to medical malpractice." Twente says that particular exercises used in *Pumsy* induce trancelike states: "Most of the *Pumsy* program is dependent on hypnotic trance induction and hypnotic suggestion in a setting psychiatry would call group therapy."[49]

Critics of *Pumsy* also argue that no scientific studies have ever shown the need for broad-based, "intervention counseling" programs such as *Pumsy*. One article criticizing *Pumsy* cites "government studies" that show that "87 percent of children *do not need* the emotional and behavioral 'help' that programs like *Pumsy* claim to provide." The article concludes, "The net effect, therefore, is potentially very harmful to a majority of elementary students."[50]

Quest

Quest is described as a "life skills" program used in some twenty thousand schools across the country. Developed primarily by Rick Little, *Quest* has three separate programs for grades kindergarten through high school: Skills for Growing, Skills for Adolescence, and Skills for Living. These programs have different units that, depending on the age of the students involved, deal differently with the topics of feelings, self-concepts, communication skills, family relationships, decision making and goal setting, financial management, and drug education.[51]

Psychologist William R. Coulson, perhaps *Quest*'s strongest critic, has made a crusade of sorts out of talking to parents across the country about the dangers of the program's "non-directive" and "affective" educational techniques. Coulson claims that nondirective techniques like those used in *Quest* leave decisions up to the student, thus promoting a subjective morality. Further, he claims, affective education inappropriately emphasizes feelings over facts.[52]

Parents are divided over *Quest*. Those who are critical of the program say that (1) it uses a "values clarification" approach to decision making that fails to take into account an ultimate moral code; (2) it uses psychotherapeutic techniques such as visualization and guided imagery that can cause emotional problems teachers are not trained to deal with; (3) it does not give a clear enough message that drugs, alcohol, and tobacco are harmful and should never be used; and (4) it undermines parental authority by encouraging children to determine their own values.[53]

However, other parents believe that *Quest* is a good program that promotes family communication and supports traditional values. One parent who attends an evangelical church stated, "We've raised our children in a Christian home with traditional values, and there is nothing I see in *Quest* that contradicts any of that."[54]

7

Literature and Curricula

Conflicts over what literature is appropriate for students have made up one of the oldest controversies surrounding the education of young people, pitting those who advocate the student's right to learn, to read, and to explore new ideas (the "right to know") against those who advocate the need to control what students are reading (the "need to protect").[1] Questions are frequently asked and complaints made about the literature available in school libraries and used in classrooms. In its 1995 *Banned Books Resource Guide*, written by Robert Doyle, the American Library Association lists 140 books challenged or banned in schools in one year alone, between March 1994 and March 1995. The books that were challenged ranged from *The American Heritage Dictionary* to *Daddy's Roommate*, a book by Michael Willhoite about a homosexual parent.[2] The *Guide* also includes a list of more than 1,100 books that have been banned or considered controversial throughout recorded history. This list includes textbooks, fiction, award-winning literature, classics, and the Bible.

Classics and young adult standards are often challenged in public schools. For example, John Steinbeck's *Of Mice and Men* ranks as one of the most frequently challenged books of the past decade. Critics have objected to the book's language and content, which has been called indecent, vulgar, profane, and offensive, and to the fact that God's name is used in vain. Other authors among the most frequently challenged are Maya Angelou, Stephen King, Alvin Schwartz, Robert Cormier, J. D. Salinger, Roald Dahl, Mark Twain, Katherine Paterson, and Shel Silverstein.

Many of the books objected to are not required reading; rather, they are available in school libraries or included on optional reading lists. People For the American Way reports that of the challenges in the 1993–94 school year, 46 percent were to books and magazines available in libraries.[3]

The majority of challenges to specific books are made by parents who share the tenets of conservative Christians or politically active fundamentalists. Some parents, however, who are unaffiliated with any organization or group simply object to books for their own reasons. One parent, in speaking before the school's review committee, challenged the use of Alvin Schwartz's *Scary Stories* books and stated, "You take it on an individual basis. We're not on a crusade. I found it very interesting, the issue of censorship versus individual rights. I had not even thought of censorship before I heard it here."[4]

Heading the list of the most frequently challenged books of the past decade are John Steinbeck's *Of Mice and Men*, J. D. Salinger's *The Catcher in the Rye*, Alvin Schwartz's *Scary Stories to Tell in the Dark*, Robert Cormier's *The Chocolate War*, Schwartz's *More Scary Stories to Tell in the Dark*, Mark Twain's *The Adventures of Huckleberry Finn*, Maya Angelou's *I Know Why the Caged Bird Sings*, *Go Ask Alice* (anonymous), Katherine Paterson's *The Bridge to Terabithia*, Roald Dahl's *The Witches*, and Shel Silverstein's *A Light in the Attic*. Criticisms leveled against these books include disapproval of offensive language, sexual scenes, negativity, violence, and an alleged promotion of the occult. See Exhibit 7.1 for more detailed reasons for these challenges.

Numerous educational and publishing organizations are ardently opposed to restricting student access to information and ideas. Groups opposing censorship include the National Council of Teachers of English (NCTE), the International Reading Association (IRA), the American Library Association, the American Booksellers Association, the Association of American Publishers, the

Exhibit 7.1. Most Frequently Challenged Books Nationwide, 1982–1995.

The Adventures of Huckleberry Finn, Mark Twain. Objections: The book is racist; it uses the word *nigger*; it damages the self-esteem of black youth.

The Bridge to Terabithia, Katherine Paterson. A Newbery Award winner. In districts reporting challenges, the book has been available primarily at the elementary level. Objections: It uses profanity and takes the Lord's name in vain.

The Catcher in the Rye, J. D. Salinger. In districts reporting challenges, the book has been used almost exclusively at the high school level. Objections: The book is obscene, negative, and blasphemous; it undermines morality; it has lurid passages about sex, uses vulgar language, and has statements that are defamatory to minorities, God, women, and people with disabilities.

The Chocolate War, Robert Cormier. In districts reporting challenges, the book has generally been available at the high school level, although some use is reported at the middle school level and (rarely) the elementary level. Objections: The book has offensive language and explicit descriptions of sexual situations; it is pornographic; it fosters disrespect in the classroom; it is "humanistic and destructive of religious and moral beliefs and of patriotism." (Doyle, 1995, p. 31)

Go Ask Alice, Anonymous. Objections: The book contains inappropriate and graphic language bordering on pornography.

I Know Why the Caged Bird Sings, Maya Angelou. In districts reporting challenges, the book has been used almost exclusively at the high school level. Objections: The book is sexually explicit (it has a rape scene); it contains profanity; it encourages premarital sex and homosexuality.

A Light in the Attic, Shel Silverstein. In districts reporting challenges, the book has been available primarily at the elementary level. Objections: It promotes disrespect, horror, and violence.

Exhibit 7.1. Most Frequently Challenged Books Nationwide, 1982–1995, cont'd.

Of Mice and Men, John Steinbeck. In districts reporting challenges, the book has been used almost exclusively at the high school level. Objections: The book uses profanity and takes God's name in vain; it is indecent, vulgar, and offensive; Steinbeck's patriotism was "questionable."

Scary Stories to Tell in the Dark and *More Scary Stories to Tell in the Dark*, Alvin Schwartz. In districts reporting challenges, these books have been available primarily at the elementary level. Objections: The books frighten young children; they show the dark side of religion through the occult, the Devil, and satanism; they talk about cannibalism.

The Witches, Roald Dahl. In districts reporting challenges, this book has been available primarily at the elementary level. Objections: The book promotes satanism and the occult; it desensitizes children to crimes related to witchcraft.

Source: Doyle, *Banned Books Resource Guide*, 1995; People For the American Way, *Attacks on the Freedom to Learn: 1993–1994 Report*, 1994; People For the American Way, *Attacks on the Freedom to Learn: 1994–1995 Report*, 1995.

National Coalition Against Censorship, The Freedom to Read Foundation, and the American Society of Journalists and Authors. These groups regularly join together to fight censorship, offering suggestions and information to concerned teachers, parents, community members, and groups. For example, a joint task force of the NCTE/IRA produced a Statement on Intellectual Freedom that set forth its common commitment to student access to diverse ideas and to bringing this principle to life in the classroom. The joint statement declared, "All students in public school classrooms have the right to materials and educational experiences that promote open inquiry, critical thinking, diversity in thought and expression, and respect for others. Denial or restriction of this right is an infringement of intellectual freedom." The task force also outlined specific recommended strategies for fighting censorship at the local, state, national, and international levels.

Each year, a number of these organizations join together to cosponsor Banned Books Week—Celebrating the Freedom to Read, in order to call attention to the problem of censorship and to take a stand for accessibility to all ideas, including those outside the mainstream. According to Judith Krug, director of the American Library Association's Office for Intellectual Freedom, which produces an annual *Banned Books Resource Guide*, "Censorship is far more dangerous to freedom than the ideas expressed in books."[5] The 1995 *Resource Guide* declares, "The essential message [of Banned Books Week] is the importance of ensuring the availability of those unorthodox or unpopular viewpoints to all who wish to read them."[6]

In the Extreme

Certainly there is a broad continuum of beliefs and viewpoints on the topic of public school educational materials and practices. Some critics of education make assertions that even most fundamentalists might consider extreme. For example, writing for the Colorado affiliate of the Eagle Forum in 1992, Samantha Smith took aim at Dr. Seuss. Warning that Seuss books "become addictive and hypnotic" when read aloud, Smith proceeded to list a number of Seuss books and their alleged objectionable content, implying that the books are dangerous. Among the Seuss books Smith criticized were *The Cat in the Hat* and *Green Eggs and Ham*. According to Smith, *The Cat in the Hat* "is a good example of how an author can compromise a child's will, all in the name of fun." After all, the Cat in the Hat bullies his way into the house while the children's mother is away, over the protestations of the fish. The Cat then lets the two "things" out, who run around tearing up the house. The children are left wondering whether they should tell their mother or not.

Smith's insinuations about *Green Eggs and Ham* are perhaps the most ridiculous and farfetched: "Reading with a *now*-critical eye [emphasis in original], illustrations become interesting in the middle of the book, where the train tunnel doesn't quite look like a train tunnel and the end of the tunnel seems to have hair on it. Could that be?"[7]

Equally extreme is an incident that occurred in 1992–93 in the small northeast Texas town of Grand Saline. Parents accused a fourth-grade teacher of devil worship and called her the Antichrist, claiming that an assigned book, *Brother to the Wind* (an African folktale), contained satanic imagery (a goat's head, for example). In addition, they insisted that a drawing of Santa Claus with a bag of books be removed from the classroom because the letters of "Santa" could be rearranged to spell "Satan."[8]

Evolution

The teaching of evolution in public schools is of primary concern to many conservative Christians, in part because of evolution's lack of reliance on a Creator. As James Dobson, president of Focus on the Family, says, "Darwin tried to tell us that the various life forms evolved on earth from a single-celled organism swimming in a primordial 'soup.' . . . From that spontaneous beginning . . . came a dazzling array of evermore complicated species, leading eventually to the arrival of human beings. This movement of life from simplicity to breath-taking complexity occurred, we are asked to believe, without the benefit of a design or a designer. . . . The assertion that God played no role in creation is highly offensive to Christians."[9] Dobson objects to evolutionary theory on other grounds as well, arguing that the theory that life evolves from disorder to order is contrary to the natural movement of all else in the observable world from order to disorder—the "downward tug on the universe and its inhabitants" described in the Bible.[10]

Other critics of evolution advance additional explanations for their opposition. For example, biblical literalists such as the Institute for Creation Research (ICR) argue that Darwin's theory of the evolution of life forms over millions—perhaps billions—of years conflicts with the biblical teaching of creation occurring over a six-day period. Further, they argue, this six-day creation occurred only six thousand years ago. Individuals subscribing to this view of creation advocate the use of such books as *What* ***Really*** *Happened to the Dinosaurs?* and *Of Pandas and People* for teaching "creationism" or "creation science" to children. (Creationism is also referred to as the "abrupt appearance theory" or the "intelligent design theory."[11]) Books like these have been introduced in schools across the country. In Louisville, Ohio, for example, a group calling itself the Origins Committee donated 100 copies of *Of Pandas and People* to the school board. Written and illustrated for the young student, *What* ***Really*** *Happened to the Dinosaurs?* features "scientists" at work at the ICR. This colorful book explains that dinosaurs lived at the same time as Adam and Eve but died in Noah's Flood because people sinned: "If Adam had not sinned, death would not have been in the world, and friendly dinosaurs would still be around."[12]

Other allegations about the teaching of evolution have a much more sinister tone. According to Henry Morris, past president of the Creation Research Society and president of the ICR, the teaching of evolution is equivalent to teaching not only humanism but satanism. In his book *Education for the Real World*, he states: "Though modern evolutionism is essentially synonymous with humanism, which deifies man, its real goal (and even this is coming more clearly into focus today, with the resurgence of astrology and other forms of occultism) is nothing less than Satanism, which exalts Satan as god."[13]

Proponents of creationism would like this view of the origin of life taught in the public schools, arguing that there is plenty of scientific evidence to back it up. Over the years a number of statutes have been proposed in individual states that would require balanced treatment of "creation science" and evolution in public school classrooms. These so-called equal-time statutes have not fared well in the courts. A brief review of Arkansas's Creation-Evolution Act 590 illustrates this.

In 1981, the Arkansas legislature passed an act requiring balanced treatment of creation science and evolution in public school teaching. The Act also prohibited any religious instruction in the treatment of either creation science or evolution science. The day the Act was passed, the American Civil Liberties Union filed suit challenging its constitutionality. ACLU lawyers argued that creation science is not a scientific model at all, but a religious doctrine, and that the claim in Act 590 that creationism is a legitimate scientific model is insupportable. A key argument given by a genetics professor at the trial was that "creation science . . . appeals to a supernatural cause, and not to a universal natural law. . . . As a consequence, it is not a testable hypothesis."[14]

Witnesses for the defense presented the argument that the general theory of evolution is not supported by scientific evidence. They also argued that, according to new evidence, the earth is not millions of years old, but only several thousand years—a view that is in harmony with the biblical account of the creation of the world. Following the trial, District Court Judge William Overton ruled that the Act was indeed an unconstitutional violation of the First Amendment. Judge Overton's ruling was based on his finding that creation science is not science; furthermore, it is based on a religious view of the world. Thus, teaching this theory of creation unconstitutionally promotes a sectarian religious belief.

The most definitive statement came from the U.S. Supreme Court in the 1987 *Edwards* v. *Aguillard* case. In *Edwards*, the Court ruled that Louisiana's equal-time statute was unconstitutional, finding it to be a clear attempt to shape the curriculum to the principles of a particular religious view.[15] In spite of this ruling, advocates of creationism want creation science taught in the classroom not as a religion, but as a science. CEE president Robert Simonds has written that it is critically important to "get the scientific evidence of creation into the classroom," declaring that "evolution is destroying our Christian kids' faith in God. . . . Evolution looks stupid and foolish when the true scientific facts of creationism are presented."[16] As evidence of this claim, Simonds quoted a 1991 *New York Times* article that reported, "A critical element of the widely accepted big-bang theory about the origin and evolution of the universe is being discarded by some of its staunchest advocates, throwing the field of cosmology into turmoil."[17]

Biblical literalists continue to look for ways to get creationism in and evolution out of the classroom. The ICR counsels parents on ways to discredit evolution, by attempting to refute its scientific basis and by linking it to immorality. In 1994, the ICR presented a "Back to Genesis" seminar in Colorado Springs, Colorado, a community where controversies over evolution and creationism in the classroom have greatly increased. Hosted by a local evangelical Presbyterian church, the seminar advised parents to openly challenge the teaching of evolution in schools and to link it to "abortion, homosexuality, racism, pornography and lawlessness."[18] Teachers are advised to simply not teach evolution. According to Citizens Project, a Colorado Springs watchdog group, at least one teacher openly teaches creationism in a life science class.[19]

The battle over creationism is not just an academic one. John Peloza, a biology teacher in the San Juan Capistrano, California, school district, was reprimanded for allegedly promoting his Christian faith in the classroom by teaching creationism. He countered with a lawsuit, insisting that he had the right to teach the theory of creationism and claiming that evolution is a religious theory. Peloza professed that he was teaching students to apply the scientific method by critically evaluating the two views of the origin of life. Claiming that he just wanted to teach "good science," Peloza argued that "theories about macro-evolution fall apart when the scientific method is applied."[20] In 1994, a federal appeals court ruled against him, finding that evolution is not a religious theory.[21]

Global Education and Multiculturalism

Political scientist Lee Anderson explains that in the past two decades a growing number of educators, governmental officials, businesspeople, and civic and religious leaders have become involved in educational innovations that attempt to "globalize" American education in a variety of ways.[22] All of these innovations have a common grounding in the learning principle that success in society requires more than academic knowledge and skills. (See Chapter Five for more on preparing for success in a diverse society.)

Global education is best described as a set of diverse movements with a variety of foci. Anderson notes that some of the movement's participants focus on expanding and improving the study of world history, world geography, world economics, world politics, or world ecology. Others seek to expand students' understanding of cultural diversity through the cross-cultural study of literature, art, music, dance, religion, and social customs. Many seek to expand and improve the study of foreign languages. Finally, some global educators devote their energies to improving instruction about often-slighted regions of the world such as Asia, Africa, the Middle East, and Latin America. In effect, notes Anderson, the term *global education* stands for a variety of efforts, all of which have the common theme of trying to expand American students' understanding of how our society interacts with other societies around the world.

In 1991, the ten authors of the annual yearbook of the Association for Supervision and Curriculum Development (ASCD), entitled *Global Education: From Thought to Action*, drafted the following definition of global education: "Global education involves learning about those problems and issues that cut across national boundaries, and about the interconnectedness of systems—ecological, cultural, economic, political, and technological. Global education involves perspective taking—seeing things through the eyes and minds of others—and it means the realization that while individuals and groups may view life differently, they also have common needs and wants."[23] This definition would seem to place global education in the mainstream of current American culture. Similar calls for an expanded understanding of the complex world in which we live came from President George Bush in his description of the new world order necessary for peaceful coexistence.

To at least one critic, global education has an agenda that reaches far beyond that described by the authors of the ASCD yearbook. In *The New Age Masquerade*, Eric Buehrer notes: "Global education has four major weaknesses. These weaknesses, however, form the very foundation for the globalists' New Age, Utopian vision. Global education crowds out the study of Western civilization; it teaches that there are no absolutes; it seeks to politically resocialize students into liberal extremism. Some global educators preach a new religion for the world based on Eastern mysticism. In fact, global education is the political side of the New Age coin."[24] Buehrer ultimately condemns the type of thinking encouraged by global education, citing James Becker, whom he characterizes as "a leader in the push for global education."[25] In his book *Schooling for a Global Age*, Becker explains that a school oriented around global education will teach the skills of comparison, analysis, and inquiry and the capacity to make rational judgments. Buehrer quotes Becker's statement that these skills include "learning modes of thinking that are relatively free from egocentric and ethnocentric perceptions,"[26] interpreting such multicultural thinking as demanding freedom from cultural and religious influences. In that event, a child should not strongly believe in anything—a dangerous educational and moral stance.[27]

For the fundamentalists, then, freedom from egocentrism and ethnocentrism is synonymous with, or closely associated with, freedom from one's beliefs and values. Further insight into fundamentalists' criticisms of global education might be gained by reviewing Douglas Groothuis's comments about the dangers of seeking a unified world order. In his book *Unmasking the New Age*, Groothuis writes that although the idea of a world government might seem appealing, the danger lies in giving absolute power to one group at the expense of the autonomy of individual nations. He explains: "Christian realism demands that no one political institution claim total power. Since all people are sinners and imperfect, political power should be counterbalanced between various institutions and nations. A centralization of power (statism) in a fallen world is even more dangerous than current national diversity."[28]

With regard to multiculturalism, fundamentalist critics maintain that they support the basic idea that children should be taught to respect and understand other cultures. However, they are concerned about the negative effects on American culture, pointing to the danger that diversity could become a divisive, rather than a uniting, force. In Volume One of *Reinventing America's Schools*, Kathi Hudson, vice president of CEE, discusses this point of view:

> America has long been made up of people from different races and cultures—that is not new. Public schools have traditionally played a great role in helping to integrate this diversity into one American culture. While it is true that most of those who initially shaped this country were Anglo-Saxon, most non-Anglos accept the essence of the ideas this country was founded upon—many have, in fact, migrated to America *because* of those ideals.
>
> *There are now some people who would like to* ***use*** *that diversity to change American culture. There is an attempt to create an America of nationalities rather than a nation of Americans* [emphases in original].[29]

Concerns about multiculturalism are also strongly voiced by individuals who are not associated with a fundamentalist perspective. For example, Diane Ravitch, former historian of education at

Columbia University and former assistant secretary for educational research and improvement at the U.S. Department of Education under President Bush, discusses two ways of integrating multiculturalism into the curriculum: the *pluralistic* approach and the *particularist* approach. Ravitch advocates the pluralistic approach, which focuses on how diverse cultures help to shape a common American culture. Multicultural studies taking the particularistic approach emphasize the unique history of specific groups. Ravitch notes that this approach, which seeks to "raise the self-esteem" of minorities, is based on lineages of "blood" and "race memory" and has the potential for fanning "ancient hatreds."[30]

Fundamentalists criticize multiculturalism on several other points. They argue that a multicultural agenda often results in a "rewriting" of American history. This takes place out of a desire to make people feel good by giving all groups of people a role in the building of America, which is not based on historical fact.[31] One well-publicized dispute occurred over the so-called rewriting of history that critics believe is reflected in the National History Standards, which were released in 1994. The three volumes, entitled *National Standards for United States History: Exploring the American Experience; National Standards for History for Grades K-4: Expanding Children's World in Time and Space;* and *National Standards for World History: Exploring Paths to the Present,* were developed by the National Council for History Standards and published by the National Center for History in the Schools as guidebooks for the teaching of history. Within weeks, a national storm of controversy erupted. At least two major publications, *U.S. News and World Report* and the *New York Times,* reported on the controversy. The heated debate surrounded new teacher guidebooks developed by the National Center for History in the Schools at the University of California, financed by the National Endowment for the Humanities and the U.S. Department of Education. (For a detailed, state-by-state report of the effort to establish content standards, see the April 1995 *Education Week* Special Report entitled "Struggling for Standards.")

Critics claim that the national standards rewrite history, severely minimizing the influence of our Founding Fathers while emphasizing instead countercultural writings and movements. By way of example, Focus on the Family maintains that the Ku Klux Klan is mentioned seventeen times in the new history standards, yet Ulysses Grant is mentioned only once; McCarthyism is referred to nineteen times, whereas Robert E. Lee, Thomas Edison, Daniel Webster, and the Wright Brothers are omitted.[32]

Leveling similar charges against the history standards is an article appearing in the April 1995 issue of Phyllis Schlafly's *Education Reporter* entitled "FOCUS: What Happened to History?" The unifying theme of the charges is that the standards are hostile to traditional American historical figures and understandings, advancing instead a host of individuals and events that had little or no impact on American history. In addition, the article maintains that the history standards exhibit "P.C. [politically correct] hostility to Western/Christian civilization" and present every event in history through the race and gender lens: "Almost every page is calculated to teach girls and minorities that they have always been oppressed classes in America. . . . It is a grievous disservice . . . to view the entire panorama of American history as one long conflict about race and gender, in which all ethnic groups except white males are portrayed as victims."[33]

Criticisms of other multicultural programs have also been made by conservative critics who are not associated with fundamentalism. Their argument is that multicultural programs often seek to have students *accept* differences in people, a step that they believe goes beyond tolerance and one that may shake the students' belief in a moral code of right and wrong. In his article "The Pitfalls of Multicultural Education," Albert Shanker, president of the American Federation of Teachers, asks:

> Do we really want them to "respect and accept" the "values, beliefs, and attitudes" of other people, no matter what they are? Do we want them to respect and

> accept the beliefs that led Chinese leaders to massacre dissenting students in Tiananmen Square? . . . Must we respect the custom of forcing young children in the Philippines or Thailand to work in conditions of virtual slavery? And must we look respectfully on Hitler's beliefs and actions?[34]

CEE asserts that multicultural programs often go beyond the learning of facts and information. Specifically, in these programs, all too often children experience the particular practices, prayers, chants, and beliefs of religions such as Islam, Hinduism, and Native American shamanism, which can include magic and witchcraft. This kind of experiential learning is even more disturbing, CEE's Simonds laments, when Christianity, America's dominant religion, cannot be discussed in the schools because educators claim that this would violate the separation of church and state.[35]

CEE is also deeply concerned that multiculturalism is being used to promote and legitimize the homosexual agenda, which is "reaching deeper into the classroom," seeking to influence children to accept homosexuality. CEE reported in 1991 that gay curricula were being developed for integration into English and social studies classes under the premise that the gay rights movement could be studied as another civil rights movement.[36]

Sex Education

Most educators would probably justify the content of sex education programs from the perspective of the learning principle that in today's complex society, more than academic knowledge is required for success or, indeed, survival. (See Chapter Five for a discussion of preparing for success in a diverse society.) Certainly a knowledge of human sexuality would be considered to be among those important life skills.

However, many religiously conservative people have strong objections to sex education. Their primary argument is that educating children and teenagers about birth control methods *increases*, rather than *decreases*, the incidence of teenage pregnancy. For example, in 1993, Focus on the Family ran full-page ads in newspapers around the country called "In Defense of a Little Virginity." Focus argued that since the 1970s, sex education programs have increasingly conveyed the idea that so-called safe sex is possible and acceptable. Citing research studies and federal government reports, the ad concluded that sex education programs like these are ineffective and dangerous, and that they have contributed to escalating incidences of sexually transmitted diseases and teenage pregnancy. The safe-sex message is a "myth." Similar arguments and federal statistics have been reported by Phyllis Schlafly's Eagle Forum.[37]

Numerous arguments have been made that sex education programs are attempts to recruit students to immorality and homosexuality and to "indoctrinate them in the new morality of indiscriminate sexual behavior."[38] In 1990–91, a coalition of conservative groups, including Dads Against Drugs (DADS) and the Michigan Decency Action Council, opposed the State of Michigan Model for Comprehensive Health Education, a curriculum that included material on human sexuality and AIDS.[39]

Fundamentalist groups also vehemently oppose the work and viewpoints of the Sex Information and Education Council of the United States (SIECUS), which strongly recommends expanded sex education programs for grades K-12. A November 1994 article in the Eagle Forum Education and Legal Defense Fund's *Education Reporter* concerned the National Sex Education Conference held in St. Louis, Missouri, the previous month by the conservative group Human Life International. Implying that a conspiracy exists in sex education between SIECUS, Planned Parenthood, and the federal government, the article reported that Planned Parenthood's use of a "'medical' perspective" was "very shrewd" in generating support for sex education, saying, "SIECUS brought the element of pornography to sex education to help desensitize subjects."[40]

The activities of SIECUS have long been opposed by fundamentalist groups. CEE opposed the SIECUS sex education guidelines released in 1991. In an October 1991 *Children's Public School*

Awareness Bulletin, CEE asserted that SIECUS was linked with Planned Parenthood and the NEA and that together these organizations have contributed to increased sexual promiscuity and abortion among adolescents, as well as teen suicide.[41] The bulletin also alleged that "students are taught to devalue human life, in the case of abortion and euthanasia, and are taught that they were not created but evolved by random chance. This teaching results in students committing suicide because they have no purpose in life and place no value upon their own life. Also, the pressures of early sexual activity, sexual diseases and teen pregnancy are too great for unmarried children."[42]

Various sex education and health education programs have been challenged around the country for being too explicit, for discussing sensitive material in coed settings, for "promoting" homosexuality, for discussing masturbation, for discussing condom use and AIDS, and for presenting abstinence as only one choice rather than as a moral absolute. One sex education practice that is especially disturbing to critics is an exercise in which the boys hold bananas while the girls practice rolling condoms onto the bananas.[43] (It is important to note that very few sex education programs utilize an activity like this and those that do get parental permission.)

Critics of sex education programs believe that the way to educate adolescents about sex and sexually transmitted diseases is to promote abstinence as the only moral and safe choice. A number of abstinence-only curricula are advocated, including Sex Respect, Teen Aid, and Facing Reality. Although supporters of these programs have been quite successful in getting them adopted in school districts across the country,[44] the programs have been challenged on the grounds that they are inaccurate, are religiously biased, and keep vital health information from young people. In Hemet, California, for example, Sex Respect has been in use since 1989, in spite of the heated controversy surrounding its use. Some parents have removed their children from the program, citing its religious bias and sexual stereotypes. Similarly, Sex Respect was challenged in 1990–91 in the East Troy, Wisconsin, school district for promoting the stereotypes that girls are "virginity protectors" and boys are "sexual aggressors."[45] The state court of Louisiana ruled in 1992 that the Sex Respect curriculum violates state law by promoting religious beliefs and disseminating medically inaccurate information. Another abstinence-only curriculum, by Teen Aid, Inc., was the subject of a suit filed against the Duval County, Florida, school district in 1992. In addition to charging inaccuracy, the suit alleged that the program promotes a sectarian religious agenda.[46]

Conflicts such as these will undoubtedly continue, pitting those who emphasize education about AIDS, birth control, and alternative sexual lifestyles against those who emphasize educating students about abstinence and the moral responsibility of sexual relations. Just such a conflict over sex education came to a head in Texas in 1994. After months of hearings before the Texas Board of Education involving advocates for and against abortion, homosexuality, and other family planning issues, the board requested a total of four hundred revisions in five textbooks being debated. The revisions included the addition of language describing the state's sodomy laws, the deletion of toll-free numbers for gay and lesbian groups, and the deletion of several clinical illustrations. The board's decision prompted publisher Holt, Rinehart and Winston, Inc., to announce that it would not sell its high school health text, *Holt Health*, in the state rather than make the revisions. Economics was a concern; however, a larger issue was ethics. A spokesperson for Holt said that the resulting product would have been one "that does not provide children with adequate instruction on life-threatening issues."[47]

An examination of the state of public education as well as school improvement initiatives, literature, and curricula under attack is only the beginning of understanding and resolving our differences. Our next task is to explore differing religious world views, religious traditions, and philosophical perspectives, and seek to understand the complexities of the First Amendment to the U.S. Constitution.

Part III

Understanding Our Differences

8

A Matter of World Views

Why do intelligent, rational, well-informed people differ so radically on issues of educational policy and practice? The fact is that people of integrity do differ from one another. When the views of one group are radically different from those of another and when public policy is at stake, debate is inevitable. How do we account for such different beliefs?

The answer seems clear once we examine patterns of thinking. Each person's thinking begins with assumptions about authoritative sources of knowledge, the self and other human beings, values, and ultimate reality. These assumptions are the building blocks of a person's world view, which, in turn, shapes his or her perceptions. What to one person may seem to be a self-evident or absolute truth may to another person seem questionable or false. These differences in judgment come about because each person starts from different assumptions and therefore arrives at a different conclusion.

Consider, as an example, the differing views in education regarding the use of imagery as an instructional technique. (See Chapter Six for further discussion about controversies over imagery.) Educators consider imagery to be a powerful tool for recall and understanding. They use imagery techniques, for example, to help students stimulate their mind while writing, process information while reading, and memorize information that has been comprehended. But where educators see imagery as a learning tool, some fundamentalist critics see a dangerous practice. One critic, Eric Buehrer, believes that visualization techniques used by educators can induce out-of-body experiences. He further maintains that the danger of imagery techniques is that "children are being prepared to become more involved in occult activity."[1]

Here two world views collide. Most educators assert that the use of the imagination in imaging techniques is a valuable method of learning. Critics, on the other hand, believe that only the Bible offers truth about subjects that might touch on values and beliefs. All other sources of gaining knowledge—the imagination, reason, experience, and scientific investigation—must be tested against the yardstick of biblical truths. The use of the imagination, therefore, must be limited by biblical admonitions to be watchful of Satan's very real and seductive influences. These very different assessments of the usefulness of imaging in the classroom result from different world views.

The Power of Paradigms

One of the most powerful findings in psychology in the last few decades is that human beings interpret information received from the senses via sets of beliefs they hold about the world at large and about their place in that world. This understanding is supported in other fields of study as well. Scientist Thomas Kuhn, in his book *The Structure of Scientific Revolutions*, made popular the concept of paradigm as a key belief or set of beliefs by which a person makes sense of the world. Kuhn argued that, no matter what the field, "at least some implicit body of intertwined theoretical and methodological belief [is present] that permits selection, evaluation, and criticism."[2]

More than a decade later, educator Frank Smith wrote that a paradigm is a "theory of the world in our heads," an interpretational structure used to organize experience. He said, "What we have in our heads is a theory of what the world is like, a theory that is the basis of all our perceptions and understanding of the world, the root of all learning, the source of all hopes and fears, motives and expectations, reasoning and creativity. . . . If we make sense of the world at all, it is by interpreting our interactions with the world in light of our theory. The theory is our shield against bewilderment."[3]

Similarly, theologian David Tracey is confident that even science does not present pure fact as truth. Rather, science itself is an interpretation of reality. He states: "With science we interpret the world. We do not simply find it out there. . . . Truth is the reality we know through our best interpretations. . . . Theologians can never claim certainty but, at best, highly tentative relative adequacy."[4]

These theories, beliefs, and assumptions through which we interpret the world, then, are called paradigms or world views. Paradigms both enable and inhibit perception. On one hand, they provide frameworks with which we organize information about people and about the world. On the other hand, they limit what we can perceive. This negative feature or downside of paradigms is that our interpretative power creates unavoidable blind spots in perception. These blind spots can be so pervasive that we become unable to see information and data that do not support our assumptions. A paradigm, then, possesses both strength and weakness, as Patton articulates: "strength in that it makes action possible, . . . weakness in that the very reason for action is hidden in the unquestioned assumptions of the paradigm."[5]

Just as the concept of paradigms has been used to explain the thinking and behavior of individuals, so too has it been used to explain the nature and function of a culture. Specifically, a culture can be defined as the shared beliefs—the shared paradigms—of a given group of people. Sathe defines a culture as a "set of important understandings (oftentimes unstated) that members of a community share in common."[6] A culture thus defined might be a community of educators, fundamentalists, mainline Christians, humanists, or secularists.

If the notion of culture as a paradigm is combined with that of the paradigm as an organizing and limiting set of assumptions, a particular culture might represent a set of parameters that circumscribe the thinking and behavior of the members of a given society. In short, culture can be viewed as a "box" within which individuals operate. This box constitutes a set of guiding principles that enable individuals to make decisions. However, it also limits individuals by creating blinders to realities that are foreign to the culture. Sociocentric thinking involves thinking within the box created by the culture in which one lives. To think outside of this box—to step outside of the paradigm of one's culture—requires objectivity about that culture. Both objectivity and intellectual self-criticism are often vehemently opposed by those who cannot conceive of a valid perspective outside of their own.

Paradigms, then, dictate what individuals perceive and do not perceive regarding the world around them. Shared paradigms form the fabric of a culture, determining what is expected and not expected, true and not true, within a society. Thus, the major reason for differences in the perceptions of fundamentalists, reform educators, secularists, liberals, and humanists—or any other group for that matter—is a difference in shared paradigms or world views.

It should be recognized that many reasons exist for differences in world views. To begin with, each of us was born into a specific culture where a common world view is dominant. We naturally adopted many, if not all, of our culture's assumptions as the basis of our thinking. We may change our world view if we are profoundly influenced by a person who holds a world view different from our own. Our thinking might also be transformed by travel, education, a traumatic experience, living in a different society, marriage, or even a religious conversion. Even so, each of us at any given time in life holds certain assumptions that influence our thinking. These assumptions are not proven facts; they are principles that we accept as a foundation for knowing and for making decisions. Thus we all approach the world and our experiences on the basis of an accepted body of assumptions, or a "faith stance."

We are therefore using the terms *paradigm* and *world view* to refer to our core assumptions and beliefs, which together shape the way each of us thinks. Four pivotal distinctions within a world view are central. They deal with (1) affirmations about authority for knowledge and truth, (2) convictions about human nature and views of the self, (3) views about values, and (4) beliefs about ultimate reality. Beliefs and assumptions, and thus world views, overlap. Each of us has our own unique bundle of experiences that helps to shape our personal view of the world. Nevertheless, some common aspects can be identified within groups of people. We will consider the differences between three broad groups—Christian fundamentalists, mainline Christians, and religious liberals—whose perspectives on these distinctions are central to the controversies surrounding education.

Authority for Knowledge and Truth

All aspects of an individual's world view are interrelated, weaving a unified fabric of perception. In fact, the world view of any person or culture, whether fundamentalist or liberal, is usually consistent. Yet no aspect of a world view is more determinative of the texture of the fabric of perception than assumptions about authority for knowledge and truth.

Christian Fundamentalists

Authority for knowledge sharply divides the world view of fundamentalist and mainline Christians. Fundamentalists assume that the Bible is their single authority for religious knowledge and truth. For these Christians, the Bible provides ultimate and unchangeable truth. From this perspective, the inerrant truth of the Bible is unquestioned as God's message for mankind. To ignore biblical truths is to make individual salvation impossible and to further the work of Satan.

It follows from this view of the absolute authority of the Bible that every aspect of books and teaching practices in the schools must be meticulously evaluated and judged. All educational materials that could possibly lead students to a view contrary to that of the Bible must be exposed and, ideally, removed. The sciences, although useful in verifying the Bible, must not conflict with the Scriptures. The social sciences must also be carefully watched, lest studies of non-Western cultures might suggest the worth of Buddhist or Hindu values and beliefs.

Mainline Christians

An important source of religious knowledge for mainline Christians is the Bible, both the Hebrew Scriptures and the New Testament. Yet the Bible is not accepted literally nor considered to be inerrant. Rather, it is an inspirational document for human spirituality, a revelation of God to the human community, and a text showing the activity of God through Jewish and Christian history. It is full of truths, insights, and inspirational literature; its ethical teachings and the moral example of biblical figures provide profound insights into spiritual matters. Moreover, the Bible contains great literature, which serves as a valuable medium in worship. Yet, for most mainline Christians, the Bible alone does not represent absolute authority for knowledge and truth.

The United Methodist Church, representing a mainline Christian world view, affirms four sources of religious knowledge: the Bible, experience, reason, and tradition.[7] Conservatives within the mainline churches put more stress on biblical authority and tradition, whereas other mainline Christians stress reason and experience. Although both mainline Christians and fundamentalist Christians assume that there are multiple sources of knowledge, including knowledge gained through the sciences, the social sciences, and the humanities, mainline Christians most often assume that sacred and secular knowledge do not conflict. Thus, for these Christians the validity of secular knowledge does not have to be checked against the Bible or other religious sources.

Religious Liberals

Religious liberals assume that the source of all knowledge is "experience and reason." To be sure, liberals, whether Christians or Jews, prize the Bible as a rich resource in the historical development of their faith and for personal spiritual growth. Yet they believe that the Bible was written not by God but by human beings who recorded their experience of God. For liberals, then, the Bible cannot be considered infallible or inerrant. Well-known Episcopal Bishop John S. Spong argues in a typically liberal way that the Bible is a prescientific book and does not document scientific data. If modern people are to be inspired by the Bible and find spiritual truths, Spong asserts, they must separate theological truth from "prescientific understandings."[8]

Religious liberals rely on a number of sources for balancing biblical insights with experience and reason. For them, knowledge begins with practical experience, whether it is subjective feeling (what the nineteenth-century theologian Friedrich Schleiermacher thought of as a feeling of dependence on God) or knowledge gained from ordinary sense experience. Another sound basis for knowledge, say liberals, is science, with its methods of investigation, hypotheses, and testing. Human reason is yet another foundation of knowledge, because human beings have the unique ability to reason and thus test the validity of ideas. Finally, religious liberals may include pragmatism in their way of knowing. In other words, an idea is true if, when it is put into practice, it works as predicted.[9]

Views About Human Nature and the Self

The second pivotal aspect of any world view concerns human nature. What is it? Are all people sinners from birth? If the self has limits, is some kind of transformation possible? If so, what causes that transformation? How do people learn and grow? Beliefs about human nature obviously influence attitudes about education and values.

Christian Fundamentalists

Those who consider themselves part of a Christian fundamentalist religious community and who take the Bible as their source of truth believe that each person inherits Adam's original sin. It is the nature of the self, a creature "fallen" from God, to live in sin. Thus, like Adam and Eve, people are continually tempted by Satan (or the Devil) to do sinful things.

Fundamentalists believe that people cannot be saved by their own efforts. Salvation is a gift from God only to those who repent of their sins and accept forgiveness. Furthermore, salvation was made possible by the crucifixion of Jesus Christ, who paid God back for the sin of all humans by His suffering on the cross. (This is the substitutionary atonement doctrine, one of the five essential doctrines of fundamentalist Christianity, discussed in Chapter Two.)

Not all fundamentalists agree on every aspect of a world view. Yet the overarching belief in original sin and the need for personal salvation is basic to fundamentalism. Although fundamentalists generally do not believe that public schools should coerce students to be "born again," they do believe that schools should not teach anything contrary to the biblical principle that all people are sinners and in need of salvation. Thus, those who hold this perspective are determined to remove from schools materials and practices they perceive to conflict with their view of human nature. For example, an emphasis on self-esteem in public schools is a sinful and worldly evil, they believe, that fails to recognize that God through Jesus Christ is the only way to a true sense of self-worth.

Mainline Christians

When mainline Christians speak of original sin, their view differs from the fundamentalist position. The prominent mainline theologian Reinhold Niebuhr, for example, believed that "to be self-conscious is to see the self as a finite object separated from essential reality."[10] The myth of the Fall, according to Niebuhr, is that evil comes into the world through the irresponsibility of people. Oftentimes people are arrogant, self-centered, or creators of evil themselves. Transformation is possible, not merely by correct beliefs or actions, but by the grace of God, who accepts all people just as they are.[11]

The language of sin and salvation, then, may be used by both mainline and fundamentalist Christians. Mainline Christians often assert, however, that original sin is a metaphor for the tendency of human beings to be self-centered. Moreover, they believe not only that all people have the capacity for growth and maturation, but that all people are part of the divinely created order. Some mainline Christians emphasize the human tendency to separate from God (sin) and thus believe that all people need salvation; others emphasize that it is not salvation from original sin that is needed, but the opportunity to grow in self-understanding, self-knowledge, and self-discipline, holding in mind a sense of the inherent dignity of all people.

Mainline Christians hold that the handicapping conditions of ignorance, lethargy, stereotypical thinking, cultural parochialism, and intense selfishness can be overcome through education and spiritual growth. It is the purpose of the schools, then, to guide children and youth in this process of growth toward more complete knowledge.

Religious Liberals

Liberals are optimistic about human nature and give no credence to the idea of original sin.[12] Their anthropocentric, or human-centered, beliefs place a high value on the potential for human ability and goodness. It might be said that liberals assume that all children can be intellectually educated and morally nurtured toward their full potentiality of wisdom, goodness, and responsibility. Human nature, according to liberals, is not entrapped in original sin, which fundamentalists believe separates everyone from God and leads to evil. Rather, liberals affirm, being human means having the potential for fulfillment.

According to the nineteenth-century Unitarian Ralph Waldo Emerson, one of the fathers of religious liberalism, life can be cruel. In spite of that, he claimed, the human soul tends toward goodness and God-ness: "Within man is the soul of the whole; the wise silence; the universal beauty, to which every part and particle is equally related; the eternal One. . . . There is no bar or wall in the soul, where man, the effect, ceases and God, the cause, begins."[13]

Values

Thoughtful religious people agree about values in some cases and differ in others. There is common agreement that values such as honesty, integrity, self-discipline, responsibility, generosity, human freedom, and courage, to name a few, need to be emphasized in families, religious institutions, and schools. But people strongly disagree about the essential nature and source of values.

The "value problem" has become acute in recent years as traditional values have eroded throughout society. Drug use and addiction have become all too prevalent among both adults and school-aged children. Violence, guns, and gangs have created uneasiness. Teenage pregnancies, spousal and child abuse, gay and lesbian issues, and the AIDS epidemic all raise value controversies. Continued violence between the races at home and abroad, along with poverty and homelessness, have led to conflicting views about what is valuable and what are correct or appropriate solutions to social problems. Nationalism and patriotism sometimes clash with concern for world justice and peace. Since World War II and the development of the United Nations, the value of world understanding has been emphasized in schools. Some parents fear, however, that school courses emphasizing an acceptance of people from foreign countries who hold diverse customs and beliefs may depreciate the love of our American way of life. This leads to value conflicts.

Christian Fundamentalists

For the Christian fundamentalist, values are objective, that is, outside human existence. Inasmuch as the Bible is believed to be inerrant as God's direct and infallible Word, the values presented in the Scriptures are absolute and objective truth. They are unchanging, written in natural law, and created by God.

The highest value for religiously conservative groups is placed on honoring and worshipping God. The value of obeying parents and maintaining conservative Christian values also ranks high in importance. Because what is right comes from God's infallible, literal Word revealed in the Bible, *religious* tolerance toward others with different values and different world views must be rejected.

Mainline Christians

Although mainline Christians generally agree with fundamentalists on the importance of values, they define values as the human judgments and actions, influenced by religion and culture, that are essential for the well-being of individuals and communities.[14] These Christians recognize that no generation begins totally fresh in deciding what to value. The Bible and other religious writings, the U.S. Constitution and its Bill of Rights, the civil laws under which everyone must live, and the example of moral heroes all provide guidelines for ethical thinking and moral action. For mainline Christians, there is no single or absolute value authority; their focus concerning values is on the welfare of people. One Christian theologian, in writing about moral values, called morality a "celebration of wholeness" in which "the integrity of the self and others is respected."[15]

For mainline Christians, then, values are not objective laws, but qualities of life that are judged to be beneficial for individual fulfillment, for community cooperation, and for a just society. Values include qualities such as beauty and other aesthetic values, recreation, and physical health, as well as all else that enhances life. Moreover, in recognizing diversity among the American population in ethnicity, race, and religious beliefs, mainline Christians emphasize the value of understanding as well as appreciating and accepting diversity.[16]

Religious Liberals

In the arena of values, religious liberals are sometimes accused of being relativists. It may be more accurate to say that they assume that everything in existence—including values—changes over time. Liberals would assert that any value decision must take into account the particulars of a situation in order to know what decision is best.[17] Values are determined by human beings as they seek to discover what is useful, beneficial, and right.

Moral values held high by liberals include self-sacrifice, generosity, justice, responsibility, and freedom. Liberals are committed to human values, including the importance of individual freedom and dignity and the opportunity to pursue happiness. They also hold to aesthetic values, such as beauty in music and the arts, as well as the values of health and recreation, all of which enhance rather than destroy life. For liberals, values are the product of human discovery and may accordingly change over time.

The Nature of Reality

A world view includes beliefs about knowledge authority, the self, and values. It also includes beliefs about reality, addressing the question, What is real—down deep and all-encompassing? For philosophers, this question is addressed in the area of metaphysics and the related fields of ontology (the study of being) and cosmology (the study of how things came to be).

Within religions, the subject of reality focuses on the topic of God. Christians, like members of other religions, believe in the *reality* of God; they differ, however, in their views about the *nature* of God. Western religions affirm that many things are real—material things, the world of nature, social institutions, and human beings. Yet all reality ultimately depends on the Creator, a creative God. What, then, are the beliefs about reality that separate those in conflict about the public schools?

Christian Fundamentalists

Christian fundamentalists affirm that ultimate reality is God—all-knowing, all-powerful, and presently alive in the world. They believe that God existed from the beginning of time and that He created the world and humankind out of nothing in six days, just as it is stated in the book of Genesis in the Bible. Such a God, who is the source of everything that exists, is believed to be perfect in knowledge, power, and love. God is a heavenly Father who exists outside the universe, as spoken of in the Lord's Prayer in the Bible: "Our Father, who art in Heaven." God, as well as Jesus Christ, who is God in human form, is the primary reality.

At the same time, fundamentalists hold to the reality of Satan, or the Devil. It was Satan, they believe, who tempted Adam and Eve, leading to original sin and man's Fall. This evil reality is active in the world today, seeking to seduce and destroy all good and loving things. Thus, people are called by God to repent of their sin, fight against the reality of Satan, and live a holy life. Fundamentalist author Dave Hunt writes, "The promise of godhood is first found at the very beginning of the Bible, in Genesis chapter 3. It is the offer that Satan, speaking through a serpent, makes to Eve. According to the Bible: this was the Lie of lies that destroyed Eve and her descendants; the human race has never escaped its seductive influence in the thousands of years since then."[18]

Mainline Christians

Most mainline Christians, like fundamentalists, are theists, believing that the doctrine of the trinity—God as Father, Son, and Holy

Spirit—best expresses the nature of God. For these Christians, God is the Creator of the world. God is also personal in that God's presence can be felt and known.

Because mainline Christians hold high the divine reality of God, which is the foundation of all that exists, it is difficult for them to take seriously the belief in a real Satan or Devil. Such a view would seem to compromise their belief in only one cosmic power—God. Mainline Christian theologians, for the most part, have struggled with identifying the source of evil in the world, without reaching any widely accepted single answer. This is the unsolved problem of theodicy, that is, how to protect the concept of God's goodness in the face of the existence of evil.

Religious Liberals

Religious liberals assume that ultimate reality, the ground of all existence, is God. But for most religious liberals, God is not a supernatural person. The metaphor of "person"—and for that matter the word *God*—is a way of speaking of ultimate reality, whose nature cannot be fully known. Religious liberals do not ignore evil. They do, however, reject belief in a literal Devil or Satan as a being who causes evil. For some liberals, evil exists in spite of God. That is, God is finite.[19] For others, sin and evil exist as the corruption of the human capacity for goodness. John Cobb writes from this latter perspective that "the possibility of pain is the price paid for consciousness and the capacity for intense feeling."[20]

Religious liberals believe that concepts of God and dominant scientific views of the world are not in conflict. Most, therefore, have difficulty conceiving of God as supernatural. Denying this supernatural quality, however, does not necessarily mean denying God. Although theologian Shubert Ogden states that "supernaturalism is . . . existentially repugnant," he insists that God can be conceived of in quite a different fashion. God can be understood as "the perfect instance of creative becoming"; that is, God can be thought of as "continually in process of self-creation, synthesizing in each new moment of his experience the whole of achieved actuality with the plenitude of possibility as yet unrealized."[21]

Some liberals are theistic and would identify with mainline Christians. Most contemporary liberals, however, emphasize the immanence, rather than the transcendence, of God in the world and in human life. A phrase such as William Wordsworth's "God is the soul of the world, an indwelling spiritual presence" is characteristically liberal. Alfred North Whitehead, a philosopher who has inspired many liberal theologians, states that God is in the world or nowhere. His words help to summarize the religious liberal's view of reality: "God is *in* the world, or nowhere, creating continually in us and around us. This creative principle is everywhere, in animate and so-called inanimate matter, in the ether, water, earth, human hearts. But this creation is a continuing process, and 'the process is itself the actuality,' since no sooner do you arrive than you start on a fresh journey. In so far as man partakes of this creative process does he partake of the divine, of God, and that participation is his immortality, reducing the question of whether his individuality survives death of the body to the estate of an irrelevancy. His true destiny as co-creator in the universe is his dignity and his grandeur."[22]

Do Educators Have a Common World View?

Most educators would probably assert that education is not based on any single paradigm or world view. Yet, researchers and theorists note that cultural paradigms are the common understandings often shared by people in a community.[23] Although certainly no written credo exists for educators, just as certainly a strong culture of education is transmitted into the community of educators through certification courses and professional journals and books. This culture of education implicitly passes on certain assumptions and operating principles that at least in part constitute the educator's world view.

One of the most influential philosophers of education in America was John Dewey (1859–1952), a longtime professor at Columbia

University. His world view has helped shape the view of educators. Dewey wrote many books detailing his philosophy of education, which emphasized the evolving *process* of learning. He believed that traditional education, relying on passive absorption and recitation of largely impractical bits of information, is out of touch with a changing society and, therefore, is a waste of a child's life. In his view, true learning takes place through living—through active, practical, self-directed engagement with the subject matter.

In *The School and Society*, Dewey wrote that "the forms and tools of learning" should be "subordinated to the substance of experience."[24] He believed that traditional education was not tapping into the natural creative instincts of the student, saying, "Our present education . . . is highly specialized, one-sided, and narrow. It is an education dominated almost entirely by the mediaeval conception of learning. It is something which appeals for the most part simply to the intellectual aspect of our natures, our desire to learn, to accumulate information, and to get control of the symbols of learning; not to our impulses and tendencies to make, to do, to create, to produce, whether in the form of utility or of art."[25]

Dewey conceived of education as child-centered. He believed that the developing interests and instincts of the student should be directed by the teacher in an ongoing and fluid process of education, one in which the curriculum would be determined on a day-to-day basis.[26] In *The Child and the Curriculum*, he urged the reader to "cease thinking of the child's experience as also something hard and fast; see it as something fluent, embryonic, vital; and we realize that the child and curriculum are simply two points which define a single process."[27] Dewey maintained that through an active, practical engagement in the process of education, the child would end up learning more information and facts than would be possible through simple memorization and recitation.[28]

Historian S. Alexander Rippa, in his work *Education in a Free Society: An American History*, notes that Dewey also saw great social benefit in this new approach to education, regarding the public schools, as did Thomas Jefferson and Horace Mann, as the best way to achieve a more democratic society.[29] In Dewey's view, traditional education's measurement of success—the accurate recitation of facts—fostered an unhealthy competition among children vying to get ahead of their fellow students. In fact, he said, this was "so thoroughly . . . the prevailing atmosphere that for one child to help another in his task has become a school crime."[30] On the other hand, the active, involved learning that characterized Dewey's philosophy of education fostered cooperation and further learning. In his essay "The School and Social Progress," Dewey stated, "Helping others, instead of being a form of charity which impoverishes the recipient, is simply an aid in setting free the powers and furthering the impulse of the one helped."[31]

Dewey believed that the result of this atmosphere was "a spirit of free communication, of interchange of ideas, suggestions, results, both successes and failures of previous experiences." The standard of measurement would not be quantity but, rather, quality—"the genuine community standard of value."[32] He concluded, "When the school introduces and trains each child of society into membership within such a little community, saturating him with the spirit of service, and providing him with the instruments of effective self-direction, we shall have the deepest and best guaranty of a larger society which is worthy, lovely, and harmonious."[33]

Dewey was an advocate of scientific inquiry and disciplined thinking. In *How We Think*, he wrote of his "conviction . . . that the native and unspoiled attitude of childhood, marked by ardent curiosity, fertile imagination, and love of experimental inquiry, is near, very near, to the attitude of the scientific mind."[34] Dewey explained that this attitude of mind is characterized by "reflective thinking," an active process in which judgment is suspended during problem solving and investigation. He emphasized his view that maintaining a "state of doubt" is essential to the systematic practice of reflective thinking.[35]

The sources of knowledge for the typical educator, then, will be many. Everything that human society has produced through its literature, its arts, and its sciences is available for the student. The method of acquiring this knowledge by each student involves active experiential learning. Contemporary educational reformers reflect this attitude by speaking of the necessity of positive attitudes toward learning and the need to develop skills in processing information.

Dewey believed that there is a difference between "religion" and "the religious." Rejecting traditional religion, he affirmed instead "religious elements in experience." In *A Common Faith*, Dewey wrote, "The sense of the dignity of human nature is as religious as is the sense of awe and reverence when it rests upon a sense of human nature as a cooperating part of a larger whole. . . . Any activity pursued in behalf of an ideal end against obstacles and in spite of threats of personal loss because of conviction of its general enduring value is religious in quality."[36]

It can certainly be said that no one had more influence over the theory and practice of public education in the United States in the twentieth century than John Dewey. This is evidenced by the fact that Dewey and his work are cited extensively in the two research volumes that underpin modern American education, *The Handbook of Research on Curriculum* and *The Handbook of Research on Teaching*.[37]

Dewey has been accused by fundamentalists of promoting an anti-Christian and even an atheistic philosophy. (See Chapter Three.) As evidence, they cite his involvement in the development and promotion of the first Humanist Manifesto, which they commonly describe as an antireligious document. The manifesto was published in 1933 by the American Humanist Association, and Dewey was one of its signers. The existence of Humanist Manifesto I and its 1973 successor, Humanist Manifesto II, and their link to education through Dewey are cited by these critics as proof of the secular humanist nature of the public schools.[38] However, most educators appear to be unaware of the existence of these documents, let alone Dewey's relationship to them. Nonetheless, critics continue to assert that education is guided by the secular humanist principles inherent in the manifestos. (For more on Humanist Manifestos I and II, see Chapter Ten.)

The lack of relevance of the manifestos to the world view of educators is perhaps best illustrated by the fact that they have not been recognized in the research and theory base upon which current educational practice is built. To illustrate, of the more than fifteen thousand scholarly citations in *The Handbook of Research on Curriculum* and *The Handbook of Research on Teaching*, not a single reference to either manifesto can be found. However, although neither manifesto is recognized in educational research or theory, John Dewey, one of thirty-four signers of the first manifesto, is cited extensively in both of these widely used research handbooks. Hitchcock contends that "the manifesto certainly represented Dewey's personal beliefs, and through it he was able to disseminate them widely and strategically."[39] Yet an open question is the degree to which the humanist principles that Dewey embraced in the manifesto have found their way into the contemporary world view of educators.

In addition, because educators belong to varied religious communities, from conservative to liberal, their world views will be shaped in part by the basic beliefs of those subcultures. Hence, generalizations about the world view of educators are imprecise at best.

9

Religious Traditions

Religion has been a major factor in American culture from the time of the earliest people. Long before the arrival of the Pilgrims at Plymouth Rock in 1620 or the founding of the Jamestown English settlement in 1607 or Coronado's expedition into the Southwest in 1540, Native Americans populated the land of North America. Their exact time of arrival is unknown, but by 1500 possibly thirty million Native Americans lived in more than five hundred different societies, following a variety of spiritual practices. In the twentieth century, more than 150 different native languages are still being spoken.[1]

Each Native American culture had its own sacred stories and rituals. At the same time, however, common elements that can rightly be called religious existed in the tribal societies. For example, Native Americans believed in a continuity and kinship between their daily lives and the sacred and mysterious aspects of the world.[2] All of history, time, and nature were considered spiritual. Sacred places such as mountains, lakes, or mesas were typically central to the Native American religions, serving as sites for special ceremonies. As one religious historian has written, "They saw power at work, awesomely and mysteriously, in every portion of nature."[3]

Probably the most widely known of the Native American tribes in the twentieth century is the Oglala Sioux, known through the popular book *Black Elk Speaks*, by John Neihardt. Information about sacred stories, ritual attention to the four directions, the sweat lodge ceremony, the sacred pipe, and many more aspects of religion have become part of general knowledge.

In the midst of popular romanticizing about Native American religion and culture on the one hand, and continuing public and private discrimination against these people on the other, stands the fact that Native Americans are part of the American religious heritage. Although Christian missionaries were successful in converting many to Christianity, the Native American religion persists in tribal beliefs and ceremonies, all types of Native American arts, and a resurgence of tribal self-identity.

Defining Religion

Our assertion that religion has been and remains a major factor in American culture from the beginning of our history to the present calls for considerable elaboration. At a very basic level, however, it raises the question: What is religion? By the term *religion* we do not mean merely an attitude or act of total devotion. If such were the case, a person's devotion to collecting guns or love of sleeping or watching television could be called religion. Saying that someone's "religion" is health food (or flying airplanes, or writing poetry) reduces the meaning of the term to something arbitrary, even trivial or idiosyncratic.

Nor is the phrase "Religion is what one does with his solitariness" (attributed to philosopher Alfred North Whitehead) useful, although one may have religious thoughts in the midst of one's aloneness. Moreover, religion is not the same as an ideology; an ideology is a body of ideas or beliefs, usually with some political or cultural emphasis, accompanied by plans for putting the ideas into operation.[4] Although any religion always involves some body of beliefs, an ordered set of ideas is not the same as a religion.

The writings of two prominent twentieth-century philosopher-theologians may be a helpful beginning. University of Chicago professor Langdon Gilkey testified in the 1981 *McLean et al.* v. *Arkansas Board of Education* creationism-versus-evolution case. In his argument that the theory of evolution is not a religious belief, Gilkey asserted that three elements are essential in any religion. First is a belief in ultimate reality (thought of as God in the Western world view), which is connected to human meaning in existence and which is expressed in myths, teachings, scriptures, doctrines, and dogmas. Thus belief in God or some ultimate reality is an essential part of religion. Gilkey emphasized that religion in Western culture is characterized as being related to God: "Religion in our culture has been shaped by the Jewish and the Christian traditions . . . of monotheism. . . . That means that all religion centers on God, and God alone."[5]

Second, Gilkey argued that religion involves a particular way of life or rules of behavior (sometimes called values) that are important for the believer. This way of life includes some way of relating oneself to ultimate reality, such as prayer or ritual. Third, religion involves a community of people with a definite structure and clear lines of authority.[6]

Professor and author Huston Smith, in his widely acclaimed book *The World's Religions*, suggests that six elements make up religion: (1) special people, such as priests, in authority in faith communities; (2) specific rituals; (3) speculation or belief systems, including a belief in moral values; (4) tradition; (5) a belief in God and confidence in God's sovereignty and grace—that is, the belief that ultimate reality is "on our side"; and (6) a sense of the infinite—a brush with mystery.[7]

The essential elements proposed by Gilkey and Smith are nearly identical, with Smith including the element of awe and mystery. Certainly other researchers might give credence to differing definitions of religion; however, in these pages we take our clue from Gilkey and Smith. Religion includes individual and group affirmations about the reality of God (sometimes thought of as ultimate reality or divine mystery), a shared tradition, commitments to specific values, and appropriate ritualistic and moral actions. This identification of religion is sufficiently specific, yet it is inclusive of many sacred traditions.[8] With this understanding of the meaning of the term *religion*, we now turn to a discussion of religion in America.

Christianity: One or Many?

Christianity first came to the territory now making up the United States with the Spanish conquistadores in the sixteenth century. Roman Catholic priests journeyed north from Mexico with Coronado, seeking to convert Indians while their leader searched for gold. A century later, waves of immigrants from Europe began to arrive, beginning with the Jamestown and Massachusetts Bay settlements. Most of those immigrants brought with them their Christian religion (although a few of the earliest settlers, such as those arriving at New Amsterdam, were Jews). In fact, a major motivation for the voyage to the new land was to overcome religious persecution and to gain religious freedom.

As the new country grew from isolated settlements to established colonies and then became the United States, Christianity flourished in its many denominational and doctrinal forms. At the present time, Christianity is the religious faith of a majority of Americans. It would be a grave mistake, however, to suppose that all Christians were or are of one accord regarding belief and practice. Despite pleas for unity and declarations from some Christians that the United States is a "Christian nation," evidence from history and contemporary life indicates that no single body of beliefs, practices, or institutional loyalties guides all people who call themselves Christians.

Huston Smith, writing about Christendom from its beginnings through the present time, states: "Nearly two thousand years of history have brought an astonishing diversity to this religion. From the majestic pontifical High Mass in St. Peter's to the quiet simplicity of a Quaker meeting; from the intellectual sophistication of Saint

Thomas Aquinas to the moving simplicity of spirituals such as 'Lord, I want to be a Christian'; from St. Paul's in London, the parish Church of Great Britain, to Mother Teresa in the slums of Calcutta—all this is Christianity."[9]

We do not wish to minimize the two thousand years of common Christian history. Over this period, men and women have been so filled with convictions about God and Jesus that many of them have suffered martyrdom, spent a lifetime in prayer, gone to war in God's name or died as peacekeepers and healers of the wounded, built huge cathedrals for divine worship, suffered privation as missionaries to convert unbelievers, copied the Bible by hand, or developed complex intellectual systems to explain their beliefs. These examples tell a story of Christian faith around the world. But history also reveals a story of schisms and divisions within the Christian communities.

Christianity is both one and many. It is one in its affirmation of one God and an emphasis on the importance of Jesus, who is believed to be Christ—son of God, anointed of God, or an incarnation of God. Christianity is also one in its common Scriptures, the Old Testament and the New Testament.

At the same time, Christianity is many in its three divisions: Roman Catholicism, Eastern Orthodoxy, and Protestantism. Each of these divisions is also split into a variety of institutional structures. Protestantism, the most divided, is separated into hundreds of different denominations. In addition to radical differences in institutional structures, Christendom also contains varied strands of thought. Whereas belief in the reality of God is commonly affirmed, little agreement can be found on the nature of God. Different beliefs about Christ abound as do different beliefs about the role of priests and clergy. Interpretations of scripture have also been controversial from the beginnings of Christendom.

One historian, commenting on the early Christian communities, wrote that "later tracings of a line of orthodox teachings through this maze of dispute cannot erase the record of contention and disunity."[10] In discussing twentieth-century Protestantism, theologian Robert M. Brown—himself a Protestant—recalled the words that Protestants sing:

> We are not divided,
> All one body we,
> One in hope, in doctrine,
> One in charity.

Then he humorously, but a bit sarcastically, suggested that a more honest version might be:

> We are all divided,
> Not one body we,
> One lacks faith, another hope,
> And all lack charity.[11]

The existence of hundreds of Protestant denominations in no way negates the deep convictions of those within a particular faith community. The devotion of people in any particular sect may be understood through several different perspectives. First, most denominations are transplanted from Europe, where the expression of belief was related to a specific tradition, language, and nationality. Immigrants thus brought their German Lutheran, Dutch Reformed, English Anglican, German Mennonite, Scottish Presbyterian, or other traditions with them.

Another reason individuals group together in their own faith communities might be attributed to what has been called "institutional families." For example, the Western liturgical family grows out of European Roman Catholicism and the Church of England. The pietist family includes traditional Moravians, Swedish evangelicals, and Methodists. Other closely related churches can be identified as the Holiness, Pentecostal, Baptist, and independent fundamentalist families.[12] Then, too, different denominations may be seen as the result of different human needs. Similarly, a denomination may have been developed by a powerful and eloquent preacher. H. Richard Niebuhr may have contributed to an understanding of varied denominations by claiming that the different organizations came about because of social and economic factors.[13]

Whatever the cause of institutional diversity, George Bedell, Leo Sandon, Jr., and Charles Wellborn, the authors of *Religion in America*, are correct in emphasizing that "the almost unbelievably broad spectrum of American religion, ranging from the most conservative to the most liberal, is a striking fact."[14] These historians also insist that far right conservatives, known as fundamentalists; mainline church members with traditional beliefs; and Christian liberals are all part of Protestant Christianity in America. Together with Roman Catholicism and Eastern Orthodoxy, they make up Christianity in America.

The history of cooperation among religious groups in the United States would suggest that the majority of church-affiliated Christians who have found a personally satisfying faith within a particular institutional structure are willing to grant the same freedom to others. A spirit of ecumenical cooperation between different Christians as well as mutual appreciation of people in all religions is not unusual. Evidence of this ecumenical spirit is seen in a 1995 document, *A Shared Vision: Religious Liberty in the 21st Century*, released by the Baptist Joint Committee, the American Jewish Committee, and the National Council of Churches. Even more striking is a document released in April 1995 under the title *Religion in the Public Schools: A Joint Statement of Current Law*. That document, endorsed by more than two dozen Christian, Jewish, Sikh, and Muslim organizations, shows a concern for the preservation of the religious liberties of a wide spectrum of Americans of diverse beliefs and faith communities.[15]

Nevertheless, divisions exist within American Christendom. With the emergence of politically active fundamentalists, whose organizations and publications are discussed in this book, interdenominational and interfaith cooperation all too often has given way to disputes. Doctrinal and value conflicts have erupted within the Southern Baptist Convention and in other major denominations. Mainline religious leaders, for example, organized the Interfaith Alliance to counter the influence of conservative groups such as the Christian Coalition.

There is dissention even among evangelicals. In June 1995, a coalition of more than eighty prominent moderate and liberal evangelicals, mainline Protestants, and Orthodox and Roman Catholic Christians released a statement titled "The Cry for Renewal," in which it declared that Christian faith has come to be associated with Religious Right politics.[16] Jim Wallis, editor of the evangelical magazine *Sojourners* and a principal author of the statement, declared that the "public perception of a right-wing evangelical juggernaut is a false impression that we would like to correct."[17] The statement was released shortly after the Christian Coalition unveiled its Contract with the American Family.

Judaism: The Broad Perspective

Being a Jew in the United States is as American as being a Protestant or Catholic. Sociologist Will Herberg, publishing his volume *Protestant, Catholic and Jew* in 1955, argued that the brand name for people in the United States is their religion: Protestant, Catholic, or Jew. Each identification, he argued, is equally acceptable and equally American.[18]

Like Christianity, Judaism is a religion that is both unified and divided—it is one and many at the same time. A tie links Jews together into one people, in spite of national, political, or theological differences. A sense of peoplehood transcends every difference. Three fundamental attitudes make up this sense of being one people. First, Jews, both secular and religious, understand themselves as having a common history. Abraham, Isaac, and Jacob are key figures in this history. The exodus from Egypt is recalled by the words "Remember how God led us out of slavery in Egypt," which are found over and over in the Hebrew Bible. Second, Jews have a shared history of persecution and suffering. The Holocaust has solidified this attitude of peoplehood. Third, especially among observant Jews, oneness is tied to the sense of a covenant with God from the time of Abraham to the present.[19]

If Judaism expresses unity, it also has plurality; it is divided into Orthodox, Conservative, and Reform groups, with further divisions within these three main categories. Orthodox Judaism strictly maintains the authority of the Torah and all Jewish dietary and ritualistic laws. Reform Judaism, on the other hand, emphasizes the importance of adapting Judaism to the modern world. The Conservative movement, organized in 1913, stands between the Orthodox and Reform categories in adherence to the Torah and in belief and practice.

Alan J. Yutter, writing in the *Jewish Spectator*, states that the Torah does not permit any Jew to hate another Jew.[20] Nevertheless, people in the Orthodox community often look down on less strictly observant Jews. At the same time, the Reform group often considers Orthodox Jews as hopelessly parochial. Peoplehood, yes, but divisions, too.

The Jewish population in the United States is thought to be between six and seven million, or about 3 percent of the American population. Nevertheless, the influence of Jews on the fields of medicine, the arts, business, and education and on the overall American culture is believed to far outweigh their small representation in the American populace.

Buddhism and Islam

East Asian people transplanted to the United States in the nineteenth century brought their religions with them. Enclaves of Chinese or Japanese in major cities had small Buddhist temples or houses of worship, which were often visited by curious tourists who hardly considered these temples a part of mainstream religion. Yet

Buddhism, along with Hinduism from South Asia, began to receive attention in the United States in connection with the 1898 Parliament of World Religions in Chicago. Since then, the broad picture of religions in America has expanded to include traditions from Asia.

Recognition of the legitimacy of Asian traditions in America was encouraged with the growing study of comparative religions in colleges and universities. One influential historian of religion, Max Muller, is often quoted as saying that "he who knows [only] one religion knows none." Thus, from the early days of the twentieth century, academic institutions contributed to the general recognition that many religions exist side by side in America.[21]

The number of courses about various religions of the world has steadily grown in most institutions of higher education along with growth in the number of Buddhist adherents in the United States. In a 1976 volume called *Buddhism in America*, Emma M. Layman indicated that Buddhism, especially Zen Buddhism, had grown rapidly in the United States throughout the twentieth century. Some new followers of Buddhism were students within the counterculture movement. Others were professional men and women, businesspeople, and housewives who practiced meditation and a Buddhist way of life. Still others were newly arrived Asians such as Vietnamese. Many types of Buddhism continue to flourish, to the extent that "Buddhism in America is characterized by great diversity."[22] Layman cited the 1973 *Britannica Book of the Year*, which estimated that 300,000 people were practicing some form of Buddhism at that time in North America.[23]

The presence of Muslims in this country, made evident by the presence of mosques in every major city, adds to the pluralistic religious landscape. Yvonne Y. Haddad and Jane I. Smith, editors of a 1994 book called *Muslim Communities in North America*, assert that among the wide variety of religious groupings is the community of Muslims. Haddad and Smith report that by 1992 North America had over twenty-three hundred Islamic institutions.[24] Although it is difficult to know the exact numbers of Muslims in this country, a 1995 estimate by an official of the Arab-American Anti-Defamation League was that over two million Arab Muslims live in the United States.[25] This number does not include non-Arab Muslims from such countries as Pakistan, India, and Bangladesh, or Black Muslims among African Americans. Whatever their numbers, Muslims in the United States make up a larger group than some Protestant Christian denominations, including the Protestant Episcopal Church, the United Church of Christ, and the Disciples of Christ.

New Religions and the New Age Religion

Each century gives birth to religions that do not fit any previous category and are hence thought of as "new" religions. These religions may emphasize various aspects of a religious tradition, blend elements of several religions, or create something new out of their distinctive culture. In so doing, they often initially suffer harsh criticism from established religious groups. Nineteenth-century America was filled with an outbreak of such religions. Joseph Smith, for example, believed that he had a direct revelation communicated by a heavenly messenger. Inspired by this vision, the Church of Jesus Christ of Latter-Day Saints—now commonly called the Mormon church—was born. Once severely criticized, the Mormon church is now considered an established American religious community.

The nineteenth century is acknowledged as a period of tremendous religious enthusiasm, generating numerous religious communities. In particular, religious historian Whitney R. Cross describes the emotionally charged groups that spread across upstate New York during this period. The fervor of these groups fed the flames of a great religious revival, perhaps accounting for Cross's characterization of this area as the "burned over district."[26] These religious groups claimed to be part of authentic Christian history, even though their communal living, beliefs, and practices differed significantly from mainline groups of their day. Each of these utopian and communitarian groups, such as Brook Farm, the Millerites, the Oneida Community, and the Shakers, emphasized a special theological and ethical belief system as well as a distinctive community arrangement. For example, among these groups property was usually held in common. Differences did exist, however. For example, among the Shakers, sexual activity was forbidden, yet among residents of the Oneida Community, heterosexual activity was given considerable freedom in what were called "complex marriages" or nonexclusive relationships. Other groups—most notably the Millerites—emphasized the apocalyptic expectation that the world was coming to an end. Syracuse University professor Michael Barkun sees a clear connection between the nineteenth-century utopian communities and the new religious movements of the 1960s and later.[27]

One "new" religion of the twentieth century that has been the focus of attacks by critics of education is the New Age religion. (See Chapter Three). The New Age movement, although often considered a spiritual movement, has many characteristics of a religion. It has leaders. It includes belief systems, specific rituals, affirmation of the reality of God, codes of ethics, a growing tradition, and a powerful sense of mystery. It does not have, as yet, a definite organization or clear lines of authority.

New Age thinking ranges from the writings of Roman Catholic priest Thomas Keating and Episcopal priest Matthew Fox to the books of Hollywood actress and writer Shirley MacLaine. Practitioners include business executives attending retreats and young intellectuals attending seminars, as well as street-corner groups enthralled by a gesticulating speaker. New Age practices, including prayer, sacred dance, and ritual chanting, at times are similar to practices found in mainline or evangelical churches.

Mixing innovative ritual activities with traditional prayer and meditation, the New Age movement presents a contemporary example of an age-old pattern of people on a spiritual journey. That journey involves a search for one's own authentic being and a quest for divine mystery, which is intuitively felt to enrich life. From the perspective of this search, New Age thinking may be found even in the Bible. Throughout the New Testament are images about new life, a new creature, new man, or a new heaven and earth. Clearly, the Christian Scriptures are concerned with a creative God who transforms humans to become something new. Christian mystics in medieval Europe may have been historical prototypes of individuals who embrace New Age thinking. Through the discipline of meditation and prayer, mystics believed that they found unity with God. Some even believed that they discovered God within themselves.[28]

New Age religion as we know it today began to take shape in the 1960s. Many people sought personal authenticity and spiritual fulfillment in different ways from those they learned in the religions of their childhood. Yoga and the popularity of Eastern teachers, Zen Buddhism, and Western mysticism received attention. The movement also incorporated Native American religious practices with special concern for the sacredness of nature.

New Age thinking favors seeking relationship with God, who is perceived as being within the world of nature and within human beings. New Age spirituality also includes a concern for the unity of all humanity, an interest in psychic powers, a belief in reincarnation, a search for one's potential, and the hope for a better society.[29]

New Age religion cannot be precisely defined, yet some elements may be identified as follows:

- Practices aimed at making the earth a healthier, happier, and more peaceful place to live
- Practices of meditation, eating only natural foods, and activism regarding peace and protection of the natural environment
- Disciplines that are believed to lead toward transformation of consciousness
- An emphasis on the indwelling presence of the divine spirit

GOVERNORS STATE UNIVERSITY
UNIVERSITY PARK
IL 60466

- Study and practices of mysticism as understood from all major religious traditions
- A belief in holistic healing
- An interest in the world's mythologies as revealing truths[30]

That there is a New Age religion (or, more accurately, New Age religions, because the New Age movement has no single orthodoxy or institutional orthodoxy) seems evident. Bookstores are filled with volumes on various spiritual paths. Psychologically oriented self-help spiritual seminars and workshops are advertised in every city newspaper. Community centers schedule regular yoga sessions. Even some mainline Christians and Jews have been known to show interest in crystals, tarot cards, or even a belief in reincarnation.

Any observant and thoughtful person can reflect on New Age patterns of belief and practice and try to guess the future of the New Age. Each person's conclusions will probably be different. Some will conclude that certain New Age themes will gradually be absorbed into mainline religious traditions. Others may conjecture that the novelty of the New Age religion, if it is shallow, will die out; if it is profound, it will persist as part of the dominant culture. Still others will insist that New Age religion is not new at all. Rather it is a combination of various aspects of many traditional religions. In whatever way New Age spirituality may be evaluated, the extreme fear it arouses in critics of education is scarcely warranted.

What Religion Is and Does

The previous sections have shown that religion is found in many forms within groups with varying national origins and ethnicities. It is clear that no one has a monopoly on religion in this country. We exist within a plurality of religions, with additional diversity within each religious grouping. This diversity is so great that these pages could not possibly include references to every religious community or begin to touch on the multitude of existing belief systems.

Joseph Campbell's words give a positive hint of the importance of religion in culture. Campbell describes the stories and myths that encompass the religious experience as "the secret opening through which the inexhaustible energies of the cosmos pour into human and cultural manifestation."[31] If the religions provide a channel for cosmic energy to come to individual and corporate life, they seem to function in several common ways. Each religion provides a tradition and a community within which people find their psychological and social identity and, hence, their sense of stability. A religion also offers a belief system that links each self to the cosmos; this belief system supplies meaningful answers to questions about pain, suffering, and death. In addition, a religion conveys a cluster of values that are transmitted to each succeeding generation by the community. Religion thus creates and legitimizes the social values that are believed to be essential to that faith community, and even to the larger society. The sense of mystery that leads people to ponder eternity and, in the West, to affirm the reality of a God who cannot be fully known is conveyed in religion.

Reports from empirical studies also contribute to an understanding of what religion does in people's lives. One study concluded that students who belonged to a Christian group at the University of Western Ontario were healthier and happier and handled stress better than a comparison group with no such affiliation. More specifically, the nonaffiliated students were more oriented to personal success and materialism. Those who were affiliated with the religious group held high values such as getting along with others, friendship, parents, family, and God; they also had significantly better health and used health services less frequently than others. The last conclusion was that religiously affiliated students were more satisfied with their lives than were nonaffiliated students.[32] Another empirical study sought to discover the psychological function that the devout practice of religion serves in human lives. Researchers concluded that devout personal religion serves as a buffer against the sense of helplessness related to feelings of isolation, loneliness, and rejection.[33]

The examination of religion in America undertaken in this chapter has been essential precisely because of the cultural and spiritual crisis of our time. This crisis can be understood through an awareness of conflicting views about the proper role of religion in public life. One view is that the United States is a Christian nation, a nation intended by its founders to be Christian without genuine separation of church and state. Those ascribing to this view would have us believe, moreover, that there is but one true religion—a particular brand of Christianity. An opposing view, a completely secular one, would deny this country its powerful religious roots. Such a view holds that religion should have little or no role in public life.

Both views, we maintain, are damaging to the traditional and protected role of religion and religious faith in a democratic society. Rather, we affirm the vital moral and spiritual role that religion plays in both our public and private lives, but we would equally stress the dangers of efforts supporting the establishment of any one religion or of denying the freedom of individuals to espouse a purely secular ideology.

10

Philosophical Perspectives

Fundamentalist critics of the public schools have often focused on what they believe to be the evils of humanism and secularism. These critics fear that secular humanism is an "official" religion advanced by schools in place of traditional Christianity. Reflection on these criticisms points to the need for a careful examination of the key terms *humanism*, *secular*, *secularism*, and *secular humanism*. This chapter will point out the varied meanings of these terms.

Humanism

The word *humanism* is ambiguous; a variety of intellectual systems and ethical philosophies have carried that label. Historians, in writing about humanism, often refer to the early Greek philosopher Protagoras, who is quoted as saying, "Man is the measure of all things, of things that are, and of things that are not." The writings of other Greek philosophers such as Socrates and Plato contained the seeds of what was later to become Renaissance humanism. In the fifteenth-century Italian Renaissance, the study of the humanities was born, from which both the words *humanist* and *humanism* are derived. One meaning of the term *humanist*, then, is one who is interested in the intellectual and academic disciplines known as the humanities—so called because these disciplines dealt with human nature in its fullness, the beyond-rational as well as the rational side of humanity. This type of humanism refers to those who taught and studied the humane or liberal arts and whose basic quest was for human good. Their intellectual interests were primarily literary, historical, and ethical; they wrote poems, orations, letters, plays, histories, and other scholarly works.[1]

During the Renaissance, *humanism* referred to the state of mind of those who sought to achieve genuine humanity through cultural studies such as literature and philosophy. An unquenchable appetite for learning, a commitment to political and social freedom, and a dedication to the worth and dignity of every human being were all characteristic of this kind of humanism. The authors of *Western Heritage of Faith and Reason* declare, "It is probably not too much to say that the principles of democracy have their root in Humanist ideals."[2]

Another kind of humanism has been called Christian humanism. Within this perspective, human values are at the heart of religious faith; human beings are believed to have inherent value, and what they do can be both noble and inspiring. The biblical lines from the Eighth Psalm express this kind of humanism: "What is man that thou art mindful of him? . . . Yet thou has made him little less than God." Possibly the most famous Christian humanist was Erasmus (1466–1536), who criticized what he believed to be the weaknesses of the institution of the church of his time. At the same time, Erasmus espoused a simple Christian morality, a universal system of ethics built upon belief in God and what he called a "Philosophy of Christ."[3] In this view, all Christians may be called humanists if they believe that everyone is created by God and if they support the moral teachings of Jesus.

These three types of humanism—ancient Greek, Renaissance, and Christian—are part of the fabric of Western religions and cultures. The values inherent in Christian humanism could be said to have grown out of the biblical and theological foundations of Christianity.

In response to critics who superficially charge that all humanists seek to destroy traditional values, it is imperative to note the values espoused by a typical humanist, writer James Huxley. In discussing virtues, Huxley wrote that hope, purpose, and skill are virtues to be developed in children. Adults, he believed, should practice love, care, and wisdom.[4] Humanist James Hemming identified other values prized by humanists including "reverence for individual personality, respect for truth, honesty in dealings and relationships, responsibility for one's own actions, love of justice, care for the weak and needy, open-mindedness to new ideas, and responsible involvement in the betterment of mankind."[5]

A recent study by psychologist Nelson Gould suggests that many people who belong to humanist organizations are themselves believers in traditional religion. His study focused on the religious beliefs of counselors and psychologists who belong to the Association of Humanistic Education and Development (AHEAD). Gould noted that, in a random sample of 388 members responding to his questionnaire, "the respondents were representative of the total AHEAD membership in proportion to sex, geography and lengths of membership."[6] Gould found that a clear majority of respondents believe in a Judeo-Christian God and 83 percent stated that humanistic and religious values are highly compatible. He concluded, "The supposed humanist aversion to religion is not supported by these findings."[7]

However, a radically different kind of humanism maintains its emphasis on human values but rejects any traditional religious foundation for its ideology. It is this type of humanism—secular humanism—that elicits harsh criticism from conservative Christians.

The Secular and Secularism

The terms *secular* and *secularism* are key concepts in clarifying the meaning of secular humanism. According to the 1988 *Random House College Dictionary*, *secular* means "of or pertaining to worldly things or to things not regarded as religious, spiritual, or sacred."[8]

Leo Pfeffer appears to be using a similar definition of secular when, in writing about the First Amendment to the U.S. Constitution, he states that the amendment requires the government to be secular, or "religion-blind."[9] Thus, tax-supported institutions should neither advocate a specific religious faith nor do anything to hinder religious faith. In this sense, then, *secular* is neutral to religion. If these definitions are utilized in respect to education, the schools must grant religious freedom to students, but they must also teach about religion objectively. They must be cautious to avoid the establishment of any particular religion in school policies or curricula.

The primary definition of *secularism*, conversely, is "a system of political or social philosophy that rejects all forms of religious faith." A second definition is "the view that public education . . . should be conducted without the introduction of a religious element."[10] In the first sense, secularism can be construed to carry an antireligious tone. When put into practice, it is an ideology in contradiction to religious neutrality. Thus, the advocacy of secularism, which denies any place for religion, could not be legitimate public policy. This ideology of secularism excludes God, highlighting instead the belief that autonomous people must rely entirely on their own resources.

For advocates of secularism, whether in the antireligious sense or in the nonreligious sense, the empirical sciences provide the foundation of all knowledge, and human reason is an adjunct to the process of gaining knowledge. Secularists do not look to the Bible or revelation as sources of knowledge, authority, or truth.

Historian Richard Tarnas, writing about the foundations of modern secularism, states, "Between the fifteenth and seventeenth centuries, the West saw the emergence of a newly self-conscious and autonomous human being—curious about the world, confident in his own judgments, skeptical of orthodoxies, rebellious against authority, . . . assured of his intellectual capacity to comprehend and control nature, and altogether less dependent on an omnipotent God."[11] The eighteenth-century emphasis on reason gave secularism an additional cultural boost.

The capitalist, industrial economy sparked by modern technology has also pushed secularism along. The desire of every businessperson to make money, along with the rising economic level of the majority of people in the West, may have minimized the traditional role of religion as a giver of meaning. Technological advances in transportation make it easy for people to spend weekends on the ski slopes or at the beach, rather than in church. Population mobility works against maintaining a close-knit, continuous religious community. Ironically, the "Protestant work ethic," a concept attributed to the sixteenth-century Christian leader John Calvin, may contribute to the desire for increased financial rewards—not a primary goal of most traditional religions.

The perspective of secularism assumes that the universe is impersonal, is governed by natural laws, and can be understood only through measurable means. In other words, the ancient philosophy of materialism is characteristic of secularism. This philosophy is based on the doctrine that existence is determined by matter and motion and by the laws that govern materiality; God is not the foundation of existence. Writing about the development of modern secularism by the nineteenth century, Tarnas describes its psychological makeup: "The direction and quality of that character reflected a gradual but finally radical shift of psychological allegiance from God to man, from dependence to independence, from otherworldliness to this world, from the transcendent to the empirical, from myth and belief to reason and fact."[12]

Those who wish to preserve the beliefs and values of the past are harsh critics of secularism. To be critical of secularism, they believe, is to stand firm against the rapid, sweeping, and extensive changes occurring in society. Because traditional values are believed to be given and shaped by religion, it is feared that without religious foundations society will fall into immoral chaos. Fundamentalists are not alone in being concerned about the impact of secularism. Yale University Law School professor Stephen Carter, in his book *The Culture of Disbelief*, argues that a secular culture may well erode not only traditional values but democracy itself. Democracy cannot survive, Carter maintains, without a foundation of moral character and strong independent institutions that mediate between individuals and government—two important roles that religions fulfill.[13]

A study of history does not provide clear clues as to whether religion or secularism is winning in modern society, especially when measured by church membership. In 1787, the year of the Constitutional Convention, fewer than 10 percent of the population belonged to a church or synagogue.[14] In contrast, reports of religious participation in the 1990s indicate that over 60 percent of the population in the United States are listed as members of a religious community and 96 percent say that they believe in God.[15]

Nevertheless, if secularism is growing, as politically active conservative Christians claim is happening at the present time, then it is imperative for all religious people to be vigilant in finding appropriate roles for religion and traditional values within a pluralistic society and within the framework of the Constitution. If secularism were to eliminate most religion and religiously based values from society (an unlikely prospect), then a fundamentalist countereffort to develop a theocratic government might become a possibility.

Secular Humanism

When secularism is joined with humanism, then we can speak of secular humanism. This type of humanism can be more adequately characterized as an ideology than as a religion. Secular humanism is a radically different kind of humanism than Renaissance or Christian humanism. It is a philosophy that emphasizes the potentiality of human beings and rejects any supernatural power. As characterized by philosopher Corliss Lamont, it is an ideology that declares that God does not exist. Lamont asserts that secular humanists believe that "all forms of the supernatural [are] myth" (by which he means false). This philosophy views nature "as the totality of being and as a constantly changing system of matter and energy which exists independently of any mind or consciousness."[16]

Secular humanists maintain that a belief in God is a destructive illusion. Further, they promote a way of life that systematically excludes God. Instead, they adhere to a belief in the inherent potential of human beings, affirming that autonomous human beings must rely entirely on their own resources for self-fulfillment. Historian James Hitchcock notes, "Obviously Christians, Jews, Moslems, and adherents of most other religions of the world cannot possibly be humanists in this sense."[17]

Secular humanists deny any religious foundation for their values and find no need for religious legitimation for those values. Whereas fundamentalist Christians believe that values are given by God as revealed through the sacred Scriptures, secular humanists insist that values are the qualities of life discovered by individuals using the tools of reason as they reflect on human possibilities. Furthermore, society will be made better, they believe, through this human struggle for values. Affirming this positive view of humankind, Lamont quotes poet Carl Sandburg's lines:

> And man the stumbler and finder, goes on,
> Man the dreamer of deep dreams,
> Man the shaper and maker,
> Man the answerer. . . .
>
> Man is a long time coming.
> Man will yet win.[18]

Studies in twentieth-century humanism in America commonly mention two important documents. These are Humanist Manifestos I and II.[19] The first manifesto originated in 1933 when the American Humanist Association published the creed for their movement and entitled it "The Humanist Manifesto." (See also Chapter Eight.)

This document expresses an ideology that is secular, even though it uses the term *religion* to refer to a passion for creative living and the desire to enhance all humanity. Specifically, the manifesto asserts that (1) the universe is self-existing and not created, (2) the ultimate purpose of life is self-realization, and (3) science illustrates the folly of any supernatural or cosmic guarantees of human values. In using the term *religion*, the authors of this first manifesto were striving to create a broader definition of the word, declaring, "There is great danger of a final, and we believe fatal, identification of the word *religion* with doctrines and methods which have lost their significance and which are powerless to solve the problems of human living in the Twentieth Century. Religions have always been means for realizing the highest values of life."[20] Although the manifesto claims that traditional doctrines and methods of religion have lost their power to solve the problems of human living, it also calls for a religion appropriate for the twentieth century.

Yet what the authors call religion is more like an ethical ideology than a religious faith. The word *God* is not used. Rather, the document asserts, "the nature of the universe depicted by modern science makes unacceptable any supernatural or cosmic guarantees of human values."[21] Even more specifically, it denies any validity in either theism or deism. Old attitudes of worship and prayer are to be replaced by attitudes of cooperation and social well-being. In addition, the statement denies any distinction between sacred and secular values. It leaves no place for the "brush with mystery" so characteristic of Western religion. (See Chapter Nine.)

In 1973, forty years after the publication of the first manifesto, Humanist Manifesto II was published. Although this second manifesto followed the basic tenets of the first, it was more explicit in its antireligious, anti-God tone. The document elevates human needs and experience above traditional religions, expressing optimism about human potentialities and encouraging independence rather than dependence on others or on a God. For these humanists of the 1970s, moral values grew out of human experience and did not need any religious sanctions. Finally, the 1973 document endorsed confidence in an open and democratic society, civil rights for all people, the separation of church and state, and the hope for a world community of peace without divisive nationalistic loyalties.

The humanism expressed in the second manifesto has moved away from any religious identification. The document can be seen as secular in the neutral sense of the term or it can be interpreted as a statement reflective of secularism. In the first, neutral sense, Humanist Manifesto II declares that "the state should encourage maximum freedom for different moral, political, religious and social values in society. It should not favor any particular religious bodies through the use of public monies, nor espouse a single ideology and function thereby as an instrument of propaganda or oppression."[22] In this neutral sense, the manifesto could be interpreted not as antireligious, but as nonreligious.

However, secularism, with its antireligious tone, pervades the document. The authors of this second manifesto articulate a philosophy that is clearly antagonistic toward traditional religion, declaring, "Traditional dogmatic or authoritarian religions that place revelation, God, ritual, or creed above human needs and experience do a disservice to the human species." Such a belief in traditional theism or salvation is characterized as "harmful."[23] In addition, the dogmas and myths of traditional religion do not pass the test of scientific evidence: "We find insufficient evidence for belief in the existence of a supernatural."[24] All of this suggests a position clearly characteristic of secularism.

The secularism of the second manifesto has been rejected by those with a conservative religious orientation, especially Christian fundamentalists. Religious people adhering to mainline or liberal points of view who support human values in theory and in practice may also regret the secularism expressed in the manifesto. They, too, often fear that values that are unsupported by some religious faith may, in time, disappear. Our observation, however, reveals that acts of violence against others and acts of gross immorality have been done by the deeply religious as well as the nonreligious. Similarly, attitudes and actions of bravery, kindness, self-sacrifice, responsibility, and other moral values have been exhibited by both religious and nonreligious people. Therefore, individuals of all persuasions need to cooperate in identifying motivations for living high moral values and techniques for transmitting those values to each succeeding generation.

In conclusion, the question of whether secular humanism is a religion has been the center of analysis and debate. Conservative school critics contend that secular humanism is a religion. As Steven Lee explains in arguing the same point, at least for First Amendment purposes, secular humanism is "a comprehensive belief system that addresses ultimate concerns."[25] Lee reasons that secular humanism addresses an ultimate source of morality—in this case, human experience—which is a fundamental aspect of religion.[26]

Humanist Irving Babbitt declares that humanism is not a religion. He adds, however, that humanism can "work in harmony with traditional religion."[27] Theologian Julian Hartt, in a published debate with secular humanist J.A.C. Auer, claims that "humanism . . . is not understood even by the humanists as being a 'substantive' or systematic and organic religion. . . . [it] is left as an ethic, as a conviction about human values and what we should do about them."[28] Hartt goes on to write that since ethics is part of religion, at most humanism is a fragment of religion.

Those who argue the religiousness of secular humanism, however, trivialize religion. Lee's assertion that all systems of thought that compete with conventional religions should be treated as religions has the effect of calling virtually any firmly held set of beliefs a religion.[29] As argued in Chapter Nine, to claim that any belief held firmly is a religion is to minimize the significance of authentic religion.

But more importantly, perhaps those who declare secular humanism's religious status do so needlessly. For an endorsement of secular humanism, whether as a religion or an ideology, by public school educators would be unconstitutional. Secular humanism denies a belief in God—the central component of traditional Western religions—and the First Amendment to the Constitution clearly mandates neutrality in matters of religious faith, requiring all public officials, public school educators included, to neither advance nor inhibit religion. It is to the First Amendment and its religion clauses that we now turn.

11

Church and State

Any discussion of public education, values, and religious beliefs necessarily calls into question the appropriate relationship between government and religion. Participants on all sides of the debate raise the rights embodied in the First Amendment to the U.S. Constitution as a banner. However, interpretations of these rights and their application in public life differ. What is more, disagreement seems to be widespread about the First Amendment, particularly the so-called wall of separation between church and state. In this chapter we review these related issues. We also review landmark court cases that apply principles of constitutional religious liberty.

A Wall of Separation?

Thomas Jefferson, so often cited by both sides in the public school debate, called religious liberty "the most inalienable and sacred of all human rights."[1] This most-important freedom is protected by the First Amendment, embodied in its first two clauses, known as the religious liberty clauses: the establishment clause, "Congress shall make no law respecting the establishment of religion," and the free exercise clause, "or prohibiting the free exercise thereof."[2] Taken together, these clauses protect freedom of conscience in everything that gives meaning to life. No doubt religious persecution by the

English government was an impetus for the framers of the Constitution to grant religion special protection. In fact, although it may seem today that the clauses were meant to protect the state from the church, they were originally designed to protect the church from the state.

When asked about the relationship between church and state, most Americans would undoubtedly reply that a wall of separation is mandated by the Constitution and the courts. Yet considerable disagreement exists concerning what this means. "Wall of separation" is a metaphor, created by Thomas Jefferson to describe his view of the purpose of the First Amendment. Jefferson's own religious beliefs are unknown. Nevertheless, historians agree that he introduced the "wall" metaphor in an 1802 letter to the Danbury Baptist Association, written eleven years after the ratification of the Bill of Rights, which included the First Amendment. In it he said, "I contemplate with sovereign reverence that act of the whole American people which declared that their legislature should 'make no law respecting an establishment of religion, or prohibiting the free exercise thereof,' thus building a wall of separation between church and state."[3]

The 1879 *Reynolds* v. *United States* decision was the first case before the U.S. Supreme Court dealing with religion in the First Amendment context and the first case to rely on Jefferson's separation metaphor. In the opinion, Chief Justice Morrison Waite called Jefferson's description of the wall of separation an "authoritative declaration of the scope and effect" of the First Amendment.[4] Sixty-eight years later, Jefferson's metaphor gained infamy, as well as an enduring relationship with the First Amendment, in the *Everson* v. *Board of Education* case. In the 1947 *Everson* decision, the Supreme Court affirmed the *Reynolds* reasoning, deciding one of the most important and influential cases dealing with the relationship between church and state. Writing for the majority of the Court, Justice Hugo Black wrote, "The First Amendment has erected a wall between church and state. That wall must be kept high and impregnable."[5]

At issue in *Everson* was the constitutionality of reimbursing parents for the cost of transporting their children to parochial schools. Justice Black wrote that the establishment clause prevented the establishment of a national church and required governmental neutrality in religious matters, precluding government from passing laws that "aid one religion, aid all religions, or prefer one religion over another."[6]

The justices unanimously agreed on the rhetoric of strict separation, but they were sharply divided over the application of this rhetoric to the facts in the case. In a 5–4 decision, the majority concluded that the reimbursement was indeed constitutional. The four justices who strongly disagreed with the conclusion found the majority's rhetorical commitment to strict separation "utterly discordant" with its decision.[7] Thus began a controversy over the interpretation of the religious liberty clauses that continues to the present day.

For nearly twenty-five years after the *Everson* decision, the Supreme Court followed separation doctrine in a number of cases involving public education. In 1948, one year after the *Everson* decision, the Court outlawed sectarian religious teaching in the public schools in *McCollum* v. *Board of Education*. In 1962, in *Engel* v. *Vitale*, the Court banned state-sponsored prayer in public schools. And in 1963, in *Abington School District* v. *Schempp*, the Court outlawed required Bible reading in public schools, declaring that government could neither advance nor inhibit religion. Finally, in 1968, the Court struck down a state antievolution statute in *Epperson* v. *Arkansas*, resulting in a complete reversal of its reasoning in the *Scopes* decision some forty years earlier.

The Supreme Court's view of separation evolved after 1947 from one of strict separation to a more flexible approach. In 1971, in *Lemon* v. *Kurtzman*, Chief Justice Warren Burger noted that the language of the religion clauses "is at best opaque" and that the "lines of demarcation" between government and religion are hard to perceive.[8] In the *Lemon* decision, the Court outlined its three-pronged test for determining whether a state action violates the religion clauses, a test that is especially relevant to the controversy over public school educational materials. In a 1985 decision, the Court noted that it has "particularly relied on *Lemon* in every case involving the sensitive relationship between government and religion and the education of our children."[9]

The *Lemon* test mandates that in order for a state action to pass constitutional muster under the religion clauses (1) the action must have a secular purpose, (2) its primary effect must neither advance nor inhibit religion, and (3) the action must not foster "an excessive government entanglement with religion."[10] This test represented a shift in the Court with regard to the notion of the separation of church and state. Writing for the Court, Justice Burger declared that "total separation is not possible," declaring that the line of separation is not a "wall" but a "blurred, indistinct, and variable barrier depending on all the circumstances of a particular relationship."[11] Nevertheless, the Court ruled in *Lemon* that Pennsylvania and Rhode Island statutes providing reimbursement to church-related schools in specific circumstances were unconstitutional because they had the effect of excessively entangling government and religion. However, the Court approvingly summarized its previous rulings that found that the state could constitutionally provide services such as bus transportation, school lunches, and public health services to church-related schools.

Scholars and writers, as well as Supreme Court justices, have criticized the so-called *Lemon* test, noting the seemingly discordant rulings in which the test was applied. Focus on the Family's Dobson and others point to the ridiculousness of the *Lemon* test's results—one action is okay, but another action that is seemingly the same is not. These varying rulings in which the *Lemon* test was applied have been reached in cases dealing with aid or support to religious schools. For example, the Supreme Court ruled that a state may lend geography textbooks containing maps of the United States to religious schools, but in another case the Court ruled that it may not lend maps of the United States for use in geography classes. Similarly, the state may lend textbooks on American colonial history, but not a film on George Washington or a projector to show the film in a history class.[12]

Chief Justice William Rehnquist, an outspoken critic of the "wall of separation" doctrine, attacks the *Lemon* test: "The *Lemon* test has no more grounding in the history of the First Amendment than does the wall theory upon which it rests. The three-part test represents a determined effort to craft a workable rule from a historically faulty doctrine; but the rule can only be as sound as the doctrine it attempts to service."[13]

The Free Exercise Clause

Although the religion clauses sometimes work together to protect religious freedom, there is an inherent tension between them. This tension has long been recognized by the courts and by legal scholars. For example, governmental accommodation of an individual's right to the free exercise of religion could be viewed by some as open support, that is, establishment, of religion.[14]

When the First Amendment was written, Christianity was the predominant religion. Some writers argue that the founders were motivated to protect one sect from gaining power over another and to prevent a national religion from being established. Since then, the American population has diversified tremendously, mostly as a result of mass immigration in the nineteenth and early twentieth centuries. Similarly, over time the Court's definition of religion for free exercise purposes has broadened from a theistic one to one that reflects the diversity so evident in the American populace today.

In the 1890 *Davis* v. *Beason* case, the Supreme Court allowed for a broad, individual interpretation of religion, but one that was limited to theistic beliefs. The Court wrote, "The term 'religion' has reference to one's view of his relations to his Creator, and to the obligations they impose of reverence for his being and character, and of obedience to his will."[15]

Over the first half of the twentieth century, however, the landscape of the American population changed dramatically, and the Court's definition of religion for First Amendment purposes broadened. By the 1940s, the Court had begun to move away from an exclusively theistic definition of religion. In 1961, in *Torcaso* v. *Watkins*, Justice Black wrote that the protection granted by the religion clauses—at least for free exercise purposes—was broad and not limited to theistic beliefs. In what has become a well-known and often-quoted footnote, Black identified several nontheistic "religions" falling under this protection: "Among religions in this country which do not teach what would generally be considered a belief in the existence of God are Buddhism, Taoism, Ethical Culture, Secular Humanism, and others."[16]

In 1965, the Court again dealt with the definition of religion in *United States* v. *Seeger*. The *Seeger* case dealt with a 1951 congressional statute exempting religious objectors from combat training and service. In a unanimous decision, the Court held that the test of a belief that would exempt an objector from combat was whether a "sincere and meaningful belief" held a place parallel to a belief in God.[17] This decision sparked considerable opposition by members of Congress who viewed it as granting conscientious objector status to virtually anyone who disagreed with the war. Consequently, in 1967, Congress passed a revised version of the 1951 statute that attempted to narrow the Court's expansive definition of religion in *Seeger* to theistic beliefs.[18] However, two years later, several U.S. district courts ruled that the new law was an unconstitutional violation of the establishment clause because it discriminated in favor of objectors with more orthodox religious views.

When a particular case implicates the free exercise clause, courts generally use another three-pronged test, first outlined in the

Supreme Court's 1963 decision in *Sherbert* v. *Verner*. This test applies a "strict scrutiny" standard in requiring that (1) the state action not impose a burden on the free exercise of religion unless (2) there is a compelling state interest for the action and (3) the state interest is accomplished through the means least restrictive to the religious practice.[19]

The free exercise clause protects the individual's right to religious belief. In applying the free exercise test, the courts must first determine whether the state has required an objecting party to make some affirmation or to take action that conflicts with deeply held religious beliefs. Mere exposure to offensive views does not constitute a violation of the free exercise clause. This has been an important distinction in court cases dealing with public school controversies (see Appendix A).

School Prayer

The landmark, highly controversial, and widely misunderstood *Engel* v. *Vitale* case originated in New York State and concerned a prayer adopted in the 1950s by the New York State Regents, who control the state's educational system. Ten parents brought suit against the New Hyde Park, New York, public school district, challenging the daily, although voluntary, recitation of a prayer that read, "Almighty God, we acknowledge our dependence upon Thee, and we beg Thy blessings upon us, our parents, our teachers and our country." The case eventually reached the U.S. Supreme Court. In 1962, the Court struck down the prayer, noting the wall of separation mandated by the Constitution. Writing for the Court, Justice Black reasoned that it was not the business of school officials to compose official prayers for recitation by students, even if the participation was voluntary. Since the 1962 *Engel* decision, school prayers composed or read by school officials or teachers have been unconstitutional.

A common misconception is that the *Engel* decision meant that public schools had no place for religion. The Supreme Court, in fact, warned that its decision should not be read as hostility to religion. More to the point, the justices endorsing the majority decision wrote that they were protecting religion from governmental interference, since "a union of government and religion tends to destroy government and degrade religion."[20]

The following year, the Court ruled in the *Abington School District* v. *Schempp* case that public school Bible reading and recitation of the Lord's Prayer were also unconstitutional. This case concerned required Bible reading in Pennsylvania public schools and recitation of the Lord's Prayer in Maryland public schools. The Court found that these school exercises had the effect of sponsoring a religion and declared that the First Amendment "requires the state to be neutral in its relations with groups of religious believers and nonbelievers."[21] The Court also rejected the argument that recitation of the prayer and Bible reading were constitutional because they were the wishes of the majority, maintaining that the First Amendment's free exercise clause "never meant that a majority can use the machinery of the State to practice their belief."[22]

In the decades since these watershed decisions, misunderstanding and misapplication of the Supreme Court's principles have been widespread. Students have the right to pray alone or in groups, to speak about their religious perspectives in classroom discussions, and to share their faith with others as long as it is not disruptive and does not infringe upon the rights of others. Prayers led or organized by teachers, however, are a different story, because teachers hold positions of authority over impressionable students.

The 1992 *Lee* v. *Weisman* Supreme Court ruling was a landmark decision that clarified the prohibition against official school prayer as extending to prayers or invocations composed or read by local religious leaders at the request of school officials. The case originated in Providence, Rhode Island, where it had been the policy of the school district to invite members of the clergy to give invocations and benedictions at middle school and high school graduations. A graduating middle school student and her father objected to any prayers at the graduation ceremony. After unsuccessfully objecting to the principal about the prayers, the parent filed a motion for a temporary restraining order to keep school officials from including prayers in the ceremony. The motion was denied and the ceremony, including the prayers, took place. The parent filed suit, seeking a permanent injunction barring school offices from inviting clergy to deliver prayers at any future middle school or high school graduations.

In spite of the school board's argument that graduation prayers were deeply meaningful to many students and parents, the district court ruled that school officials could not invite religious leaders to recite or organize any form of prayer at graduation ceremonies. Such a practice, the court wrote, had the effect of endorsing religion and subtly coercing students to take part in a religious exercise; thus it was a violation of the establishment clause. The case was appealed to the Supreme Court, which affirmed the decision in 1992.

The Court highlighted the school board's argument that students who objected could simply choose not to attend the graduation ceremony, noting that graduating is "one of life's most significant occasions. . . . A student is not free to absent herself from the graduation exercise in any real sense of the term 'voluntary.'" The Court also wrote that public graduation prayers had the effect of coercing students, concluding that "the Constitution forbids the State to exact religious conformity from a student as the price of attending her own high school graduation."[23]

In spite of the *Lee* decision, prayers at graduation ceremonies are constitutional under certain circumstances. One of the requirements is that prayers must be voluntary, student-initiated, and nonsectarian. However, after the *Lee* decision, two lower courts interpreted the *Lee* ruling differently, reaching conflicting conclusions.

In 1992, the Fifth Circuit Court of Appeals ruled in *Jones* v. *Clear Creek Independent School District* that school prayer is constitutional if it is student-initiated, nonsectarian, and nonproselytizing.

The *Jones* decision was appealed to the Supreme Court, which declined to review the case. Two years after the Fifth Circuit decision, the Ninth Circuit Court of Appeals ruled in *Harris* v. *Joint School District No. 241*, a case involving an Idaho school district. The court ruled that the delegation to students of decision making regarding whether there would be prayers at graduation violated the establishment clause. Citing the U.S. Supreme Court's 1992 *Lee* decision, the court reasoned that school officials still controlled graduation. This ruling was in opposition to the Fifth Circuit's *Jones* decision. However, in June 1995 the Supreme Court set aside the Ninth Circuit's *Harris* ruling, ordering the lower court to dismiss the case. This action resolved the apparent conflict between the rulings of the Fifth Circuit and the Ninth Circuit, at least for the time being.

Since the 1962 *Engel* decision, numerous efforts have been made at the federal and state levels to return some kind of prayer to the public school setting. The most successful efforts have been those proposing a "moment of silence." Students are free to pray, meditate, or think about whatever they choose during this time. As long as such "moment of silence" laws or practices do not force prayer on students, they are likely to be held to be constitutional. "Moment of silence" laws are currently in place in several states.

Colorado Springs, Colorado, psychiatrist Deane Berson developed an eighteen-page proposal for what he calls a "values-affirming moment of silence." Berson sent the proposal to Colorado state representatives and to Colorado Senator Ben Nighthorse Campbell. Noting America's social problems, Berson maintained that his proposed moment of silence, reflecting the principles of the Golden Rule, "would help American students develop a moral core to guide their conduct and help avoid these problems."[24] Berson proposed the following statement, which would be read by the teacher:

> This moment of peace is for us to silently think about what inspires us to be the best person we can be, practicing compassion and justice, courage and accountabil-

> ity, honor and community, and showing the respect for students and teachers throughout the day that we wish to receive from them.[25]

Berson advocates this moment of silence because it encourages a sense of community and provides a moral affirmation, yet avoids the unconstitutional entanglement of church and state. Students would be free to reflect on God, someone they admire, an inspiring poem, or some other source of inspiration. Focus on the Family's president, James Dobson, is not too keen on "moment of silence" legislation, calling it a "meager measure . . . a foot in the door—but not much more than that."[26]

Like evolution and appropriate literature for children, school prayer has been a hotly debated topic over the years. The level of the controversy rises and ebbs for a variety of reasons. Since the November 1994 congressional elections and conservative sweep, the national debate about religious liberties and school prayer has been recharged. Citing numerous examples of increasing hostility toward religious expression, particularly in public schools, many conservative Christians, including Speaker of the House Newt Gingrich, advocated amending the Bill of Rights to emphasize the importance of religious belief in America. Gingrich initially promised a vote on a constitutional religious liberty amendment by July 4, 1995. After a storm of controversy, however, the vote was put off until later in 1995.

Calling the battle for religious freedom "one of the seminal fights of the decade,"[27] Gingrich proposed public hearings in all fifty states to open the debate "on spiritual life and reestablishing our Creator at the center of American policy."[28] Gingrich advocated a constitutional amendment specifically addressing the issue of school prayer and proposed the following wording as a starting point in the debate: "Nothing in this Constitution shall be construed to prohibit individual or group prayer in public schools or other public institutions. No person shall be required by the United States or by any state to participate in prayer. Neither the United States nor any state shall compose the words of any prayer to be said in public schools."[29]

Conservatives have voiced numerous reasons for their support of some form of school prayer. Some link prayer to patriotism. A letter to the Colorado Springs *Gazette Telegraph* expressed this view, stating that a simple school prayer "should offend no one who is proud to be a citizen of the United States."[30] A more widely used argument is that since 1962, when the Supreme Court declared official school prayer unconstitutional in the *Engel* v. *Vitale* decision, America has been suffering a precipitous moral decline. Dobson sums up this view, writing, "Many people, myself included, believe that the deterioration of public education in recent years can be linked directly to our inability to teach values and show respect for God in the classroom."[31]

A coalition of conservative Christian groups has joined to endorse the Religious Equality Amendment. Focus on the Family and James Dobson assert that it is necessary to pass a constitutional amendment that would explicitly protect public religious expression. Dobson asserts, "We believe in the concept of pluralism, which acknowledges the widely differing values and beliefs among our citizens. We believe that the right to hold and express those diverse convictions can only be assured by passage of a broad-based amendment to the Constitution."[32] Organizations supporting this effort include Concerned Women for America, the National Association of Evangelicals, the Christian Coalition, and the American Center for Law and Justice. The proposed Religious Equality Amendment would, they assert, lend much-needed legal support to student prayer and other forms of religious expression in public schools. In advocating such an amendment, these organizations point to polls that show a wide majority of Americans favoring an amendment allowing student-led prayer in public schools.[33]

Although these groups are firmly committed to broadening the role of religion in public life, they do not advocate officially mandated or organized teacher-led prayer in public schools for a number of reasons. A primary reason is the acknowledgment that the landscape of American religious belief is quite diverse. If some kind of official school prayer were to be permitted in public schools again, it could lead to a watered-down prayer acknowledging some kind of "lowest common denominator deity" or to a kind of "affirmative-action" plan in which prayers would be offered to all kinds of deities and goddesses.[34]

A constitutional amendment regarding public school prayer is opposed by leading religious liberties expert Charles Haynes. Such an amendment, he believes, reflects widespread frustration and concern about the prevailing cultural attitude toward religious expression in public life. Haynes calls the drive for public school prayer "the wrong solution to a real and urgent problem: confusion about the proper rôle of religion in public education."[35] Haynes maintains that the push for constitutional amendments concerning school prayer will disappear when freedom of conscience is truly protected in American public life and when education about religion is returned to the curriculum. (For more on educating about religion, see Chapter Twelve.)

The complex and varied interpretations of the First Amendment, court cases addressing the relationship between government and religion in the public school context, and differing religious convictions will in all probability not be resolved in the immediate future. However, these continuing problems call for vigilance in understanding both the content and the intention of differing perspectives in order to preserve both religious plurality and free discussion.

Part IV

What Educators Can Do

12

Religion and Values in Public Education

A widespread misconception about the relationship between public schools and religion is that schools cannot discuss religion. This is not true. In fact, the U.S. Supreme Court has *encouraged* objective teaching about religion. In recent years more and more professional educational organizations have recognized this and developed guidelines for teaching about religion.

Influence of the Courts and Professional Organizations

Supreme Court decisions during the twentieth century, although consistently ruling against sectarian teachings and devotional exercises, have left the way clear for more, not less, religion, especially through teaching about religion. During this time, the Court has strived to distinguish between the unconstitutional practice of teaching particular religious philosophies and the constitutional practice of teaching *about* religion. Government's relationship with religion was articulated, in part, by the Supreme Court in the 1947 *Everson* v. *Board of Education* case. Writing for the Court, Justice Hugo Black stated that courts must be careful, in seeking neutrality, not to promote hostility toward religion: "State power is no more to be used so as to handicap religions than it is to favor them." He stated that the First Amendment's purpose is to be neutral toward religion, not its "adversary."[1]

Perhaps the most definitive endorsement by the Supreme Court for teaching about religion in the public schools came in the 1963 *Abington School District* v. *Schempp* case. In writing for the Court, Justice Tom Clark made a clear distinction between school-sponsored Bible reading, which the Court found unconstitutional, and studies about religion, which it encouraged: "In addition, it might well be said that one's education is not complete without a study of comparative religions or the history of religion and its relationship to the advancement of civilization. It certainly may be said that the Bible is worthy of study for its literary and historical qualities. Nothing we have said here indicates that such study of the Bible or of religion, when presented objectively as part of a secular program of education, may not be effected consistent with the First Amendment."[2]

By the time of this decision, some professional educational organizations had already developed guidelines for including teaching about religion in curricula. For example, in 1953 the American Association of Colleges for Teacher Education, with a grant from the Danforth Foundation, conducted a research project concerning the development of curricular materials about religion. Of importance was the conclusion that "teaching about religion" is the phrase that most accurately refers to the legitimate place of religious studies in tax-supported institutions.[3] That language has remained in use to the present day.

During the same period and in the next two decades, colleges and universities were rapidly expanding. Along with enrollment growth came the rapid development of religious studies departments, even in tax-supported institutions. By 1973 the National Council on Religion and Public Education (NCRPE) began publishing its quarterly journal, *Religion and Public Education*. Professional groups such as NCRPE have encouraged educators to include information about religion whenever it is a natural part of any subject—for example, in literature, world history, American government, the arts, and especially American history.

In spite of Supreme Court approval—even encouragement—of teaching about religion, and in spite of a plethora of available resources, study materials have been far too silent on the subject of religion. In the early 1980s, then U.S. Secretary of Education Terrel H. Bell coined the phrase "dumbing down" to describe the deterioration of textbooks. (Bell appointed the National Commission on Excellence in Education, which produced the well-publicized report *A Nation at Risk.*) Perhaps to avoid controversy, textbooks were found to have removed references to religion or watered down controversial subjects such as evolution. For example, a 1985 study of social studies textbooks, funded by a grant from the National Institute of Education, found textbooks that did not mention that Martin Luther King, Jr., was a clergyman or discuss the religious background of the Pilgrims. Instead, Pilgrims were referred to as "people who go on long journeys."[4]

In recent years, however, increased attention has been paid to the study of religion, due in part, no doubt, to studies such as the one funded by the National Institute of Education, and *A Nation at Risk.* One person who has taken a leadership role in developing materials for study about religion and many other issues dealing with religion and public education is Charles C. Haynes, visiting scholar at the Freedom Forum First Amendment Center at Vanderbilt University in Nashville, Tennessee. Haynes and the Center are widely acknowledged as leaders in helping educators understand and implement the First Amendment's religious liberty principles in public school classrooms, teaching them how to teach about religion and honor diverse expressions of religion.

Excellent curricular materials continue to be developed. One particularly noteworthy volume is Haynes's *Religion in American History: What to Teach and How,* published in 1990 by the Association for Supervision and Curriculum Development. The book includes a comprehensive listing of important religious influences in American history (including recommended readings), original source documents concerning religion (which Haynes explains how to naturally incorporate into already existing curricula), and consensus statements and guidelines concerning teaching about religion in public schools. Among the consensus statements is one adopted over a decade ago by the National Council for the Social Studies. This statement insisted that "religions have influenced the behavior of both individuals and nations, and have inspired some of the world's most beautiful art, architecture, literature, and music. History, our own nation's religious pluralism, and contemporary world events are testimony that religion has been and continues to be an important cultural value. . . . The study about religions, then, has a 'rightful place in the public school curriculum because of the pervasive nature of religious beliefs, practices, institutions, and sensitivities.'"[5]

Fourteen specific guidelines for teaching about religion that were developed by the National Council for the Social Studies are also included in Haynes's text. They are given here in full:

1. Study about religions should strive for awareness and understanding of the diversity of religions, religious experiences, religious expressions, and the reasons for particular expressions of religious beliefs within a society or culture.
2. Study about religions should stress the influence of religions on history, culture, the arts, and contemporary issues.
3. Study about religions should permit and encourage a comprehensive and balanced examination of the entire spectrum of ideas and attitudes pertaining to religion as a component of human culture.
4. Study about religions should investigate a broad range, both geographic and chronological, of religious beliefs, practices, and values.
5. Study about religions should examine the religious dimension of human existence in its broader cultural context, including its relation to economic, political, and social institutions as well as its relation to the arts, language, and literature.

6. Study about religions should deal with the world's religions from the same perspective (that is, beginnings, historical development, sacred writings, beliefs, practices, values, and impact on history, culture, contemporary issues, and the arts).
7. Study about religions should be objective.
8. Study about religions should be academic in nature, stressing student awareness and understanding, not acceptance and/or conformity.
9. Study about religions should emphasize the necessity and importance of tolerance, respect, and mutual understanding in a nation and world of diversity.
10. Study about religions should be descriptive, nonconfessional, and conducted in an environment free of advocacy.
11. Study about religions should seek to develop and utilize the various skills, attitudes, and abilities that are essential to history and the social sciences (that is, locating, classifying, interpreting data; keen observation; critical reading, listening, and thinking; questioning; and effective communication).
12. Study about religions should be academically responsible and pedagogically sound, utilizing accepted methods and materials of the social sciences, history, and literature.
13. Study about religions should involve a range of materials that provide a balanced and fair treatment of the subject and distinguish between confessional and historical fact.
14. Study about religions should be conducted by qualified and certified teachers selected for their academic knowledge, their sensitivity and empathy for differing religious points of view, and their understanding of the Supreme Court's decisions pertaining to religious practices and study about religions in the public schools.[6]

Equally instructive regarding the relationship between religion and public schools is a document included in *Religion in American*

History called "Religion in the Public School Curriculum: Questions and Answers." Another product of Haynes's efforts to find common ground, the agreement represents broad consensus from religious and educational groups and provides specific answers to questions educators often ask about teaching religion and values in the public school context. The document outlines reasons for asserting that teaching about religion in public schools is constitutional and necessary and distinguishes between objective teaching and indoctrination, echoing many of the social studies guidelines included above. The groups that jointly sponsored "Questions and Answers" are as important to note as is the content of their statement:

American Academy of Religion

American Association of School Administrators

American Federation of Teachers

American Jewish Congress

Americans United Research Foundation

Association for Supervision and Curriculum Development

Baptist Joint Committee on Public Affairs

Christian Legal Society

Church of Jesus Christ of Latter-Day Saints

Islamic Society of North America

National Association of Evangelicals

National Conference of Christians and Jews

National Council for the Social Studies

National Council of Churches of Christ in the U.S.A.

National Council on Religion and Public Education

National Education Association

National School Boards Association[7]

Consensus Efforts

In recent years, great strides have been made toward a wider consensus among groups with differing beliefs on a number of issues concerning religion in public schools and on the broader issue of religion in public life. One of the most noteworthy examples is the 1988 Williamsburg Charter, developed in connection with the bicentennial of the U.S. Constitution. The document declares a rededicated commitment to the First Amendment's religious liberty principles and the need for vital, responsible, public debate as a citizenry through which to mediate our differences. The two hundred signers of the Charter, representing a broad spectrum of beliefs, made the following affirmation: "The Charter sets forth a renewed national compact, in the sense of a solemn mutual agreement between parties, on how we view the place of religion in American life and how we should contend with each other's deepest differences in the public sphere. It is a call to a vision of public life that will allow conflict to lead to consensus, religious commitment to reinforce political civility. In this way, diversity is not a point of weakness but a source of strength."[8]

The signers of this compact called for civil public dialogue and debate among all people—those who hold differing religious faiths or those who hold none. Noting the increasing pluralism of America, the Charter declares that "religious liberty, or freedom of conscience, is a precious, fundamental and inalienable right . . . for citizens of all faiths or none."[9]

The two hundred people who signed the Williamsburg Charter included former presidents Jimmy Carter and Gerald Ford, Chief Justice William Rehnquist and the late Chief Justice Warren Burger, and leading members of Congress of both parties. Signers also included religious leaders from Catholic, Jewish, Protestant, Muslim, Buddhist, and Christian Science communities; business leaders from Fortune 500 companies; educators; and labor union leaders. It is worth noting that individuals from differing perspectives involved in public school debates also endorsed the document, including James Dobson, president of Focus on the Family; Charles Colson, chairman of Prison Fellowship Ministries; Phyllis Schlafly, founder of the Eagle Forum, who served here as a member of the Bicentennial Commission; Norman Lear, founding chairman of People For the American Way; and Robert Maddox, executive director of Americans United for Separation of Church and State.

In reflecting on the work accomplished by the collaborative efforts of these organizations, Haynes wrote, "For the first time in the history of public education, a broad spectrum of religious and educational groups agreed on at least some of the issues that have divided us for so long. . . . These statements acknowledge the importance of study about religion in public education, and warn against both religious indoctrination *and* hostility to religion in policies and curriculum [emphasis in original]."[10] After the publication of the Williamsburg Charter, Haynes acted as a catalyst for the development of a new social studies curriculum, *Living with Our Deepest Differences: Religious Liberty in a Pluralistic Society*, inspired by the driving principles of the Charter. These materials for upper elementary, middle school, and high school students and teachers are designed to help students understand the democratic principles, freedoms, and inherent civic responsibilities of the Bill of Rights, in particular the First Amendment's rights of religious liberty and freedom of conscience. (To find out more about this curriculum, contact the Freedom Forum First Amendment Center. See Appendix B at the back of this book.)

In 1995, another ground-breaking consensus document was signed. Charles Haynes and the Freedom Forum First Amendment Center, along with a host of educational and religious organizations, offered *Religious Liberty, Public Education, and the Future of American Democracy: A Statement of Principles*. This statement, which specifically addresses the role of religion and values in public schools, was signed by, among others, the American Association of School Administrators, the American Center for Law and Justice, the Association for Supervision and Curriculum Development, the Christian Coalition, Citizens for Excellence in Education, the National Association of Evangelicals, the National Education Association, and People For the American Way. (For more information, contact the Freedom Forum First Amendment Center, listed in Appendix B.) The statement's six guiding principles are:

1. Religious liberty is an inalienable right of every person.
2. Citizenship in a diverse society means living with our deepest differences and committing ourselves to work for public policies that are in the best interest of all individuals, families, communities and our nation.
3. Public schools must model the democratic process and constitutional principles in the development of policies and curricula.
4. Public schools may not inculcate nor inhibit religion. They must be places where religion and religious conviction are treated with fairness and respect.
5. Parents are recognized as having the primary responsibility for the upbringing of their children, including education.
6. Civil debate, the cornerstone of a true democracy, is vital to the success of any effort to improve and reform America's public schools.[11]

Efforts are being made at the state and local levels to implement the principles and responsibilities underscored in these documents. In order to build consensus within school districts and communities, agreement must first be reached on what Haynes calls the "civic ground rules, rooted in the 'three Rs' of religious liberty: Rights,

Responsibilities, and Respect."[12] Haynes, along with the Freedom Forum First Amendment Center, worked with community leaders and the California County Superintendents Educational Service Association to develop the California Three Rs Project: Educating for Citizenship in a Diverse Society. The Three Rs Project sponsors, for example, seminars that teach ways to gain consensus on issues of religious and ethnic diversity in schools. Curriculum workshops provide guidance for teaching about religion and for the in-depth study of specific religious traditions. This project may serve as a model for other communities that have a desire to take seriously issues of religious liberty in the public school setting.

A useful manual for any district interested in developing a curriculum in religion studies is *Finding Common Ground: A First Amendment Guide to Religion and Public Education*, edited by Charles Haynes, which is available from the Freedom Forum First Amendment Center. The manual offers guidelines and suggestions for school administrators, principals, and teachers on creating a proper role for religion and religious expression in public education.

There are, to be sure, risks for the schools when study about religion is included in a subject such as literature or in a specific course such as comparative religions. Some critics at the far right of the religious spectrum may attack the schools, insisting that teaching about religion leads to tolerance of religions other than Christianity, destroys the values of traditional Christianity, and falsely conveys the belief that all religions are legitimate. These critics may proclaim that religion, especially Christianity, is a matter of faith and commitment, and that intellectual inquiry may weaken or even destroy that faith. By the same token, atheists may accuse the schools of promoting religion, arguing that schools should be free of all religion. Yet discussion does not equate with either inhibiting or fostering religion. Objective teaching about religion fulfills both constitutional intent and the recommendations of national professional educational societies. The school's task is to foster the intellect. The nurturing of faith—quite a different matter—is the function of the home and church.

Another risk is that a teacher who is a devout member of a particular religious sect may be so enthusiastic about some aspect of religion that she or he may seek to persuade students of its exclusive truth. Conversely, a teacher's bias against the significance of a given religious belief or practice may be so strong as to be persuasive. In either case, if guidelines concerning teaching about religion are followed, such problems can be minimized.

In addition to the materials mentioned above, a wealth of materials is available to school systems seeking to provide a complete education that takes seriously and appreciates the place of religion in society. Course outlines for different grade levels, filmstrips, videotapes, teacher's guides, and many more resources are readily available. A number of nonsectarian, nonpartisan professional educational groups can provide information about available resources. (See Appendix B.)

Public Schools and Values

Considerable agreement has been reached regarding teaching about religion in the public schools. Similarly, programs focusing on core values are spreading throughout our schools, even in the midst of conflicting views about values. Agreement about values exists on a number of points. First, participants on all sides of the debate, as well as courts and legal scholars, agree that a "valueless" education is not possible.[13] In fact, the very nature of the public school environment makes it impossible *not* to convey values, whether consciously or unconsciously. Purpel and Ryan, authors of several books on the subject of moral education, note that the sheer number of hours a child spends in the classroom is a significant argument: "It is inconceivable for the schools to take [a] child for six or seven hours a day, for 180 days a year, from the time he is six to the time he is eighteen, and not affect the way he thinks about moral issues."[14]

Further, teachers serve as role models for students, as even the U.S. Supreme Court has acknowledged, "exerting a subtle but important influence over their perceptions and values."[15] In addition, as one legal scholar notes, "all curricula convey certain assumptions about the nature of the world and of humankind."[16] One might argue that fact-based instruction avoids values. However, even the most fact-based instruction conveys a set of moral or value-laden assumptions. For example, history books may speak of American settlers' battles against savage, heathen Indians as "fact." That so-called "fact" for one person is another person's value judgment or slanderous comment.

A value-free education is not only impossible; it is not desirable. Certainly it is the responsibility of a civilization to pass values on to the next generation. In his book *Educating for Character,* Thomas Lickona writes: "A society needs values education both to survive and to thrive—to keep itself intact, and to keep itself growing toward conditions that support the full human development of all its members. Historically, three social institutions have shared the work of moral education: the home, the church, and the school. In taking up values education, schools are returning to their time-honored role, abandoned briefly in the middle part of this century."[17]

The U.S. Supreme Court has concluded that values education is necessary in order to maintain a democratic society. Public schools are to inculcate the values that students must learn in order to participate fully as citizens.[18] Yet they must fulfill this responsibility within the limits of the First Amendment and avoid imposing orthodoxy in opinion or belief in the classroom.[19] This is especially delicate given the impressionability of schoolchildren and the fact that students are indeed a "captive audience" in an environment in which the pressure to conform is high.[20]

Value questions are not easily solved. Some community leaders and educators will argue that the values to be taught have their source in the civilized, democratic society at large. Others will declare that the God of the Jewish and Christian Bible is the source of all true values. Anthony Podesta of People For the American Way advocates promoting "shared civic values" such as justice, pluralism, and participation.[21] Rabbi David Gordis of New York City advocates "core values" such as "patriotism, the dignity of the individual, respect for knowledge, appreciation both of continuity and of change, sensitivity to the moral weight of decisions that we all make, and respect for law coupled with the appropriateness of challenging unjust laws."[22] Still others would include the teaching of the values that are common to the great religious traditions.[23]

Some scholars and educators have advocated promoting "secular" or "democratic" or "neutral" values. But what are these, and how are they defined? "Neutral" values are an illusion. Furthermore, as Yerby so aptly states, "The neutrality of any such claim to truth rests solely upon perspective. A relativistic approach may seem neutral to the relativist, but it will not seem neutral to the absolutist."[24] Similarly, a problem exists with the Supreme Court's admonition that schools must promote the values needed for citizenship in a democratic society. Justices, even Supreme Court justices, seem to disagree about what these necessary values are. A reading of legal decisions written by former Supreme Court Justice William Brennan and Court of Appeals Justice Lively reveals an emphasis on the values of tolerance and respect for diversity.[25] Decisions authored by Supreme Court Justice Rehnquist, on the other hand, emphasize the transmittal of absolute values of right and wrong that serve as a standard for attitudes and actions.[26]

In facing value conflicts, we often forget how much consensus there is among diverse religious people and even secularists about many values. For example, more than 250 people attended a conference in 1987 entitled "Values, Pluralism, and Public Education," sponsored by People For the American Way. Held in Washington,

D.C., the conference was attended by parents, teachers, administrators, scholars, and publishers from some twenty states. Fourteen speakers, both conservative and liberal, agreed on one thing: we must teach values in our public schools.

Recent values education efforts have focused on "character education." One coalition formed in 1992, the Character Education Partnership (CEP), offers guidance and resources to schools across the country that are committed to fostering good character in students. In spite of political and religious differences, CEP affirms, core ethical values are widely shared among community members, including "caring, honesty, fairness, responsibility, and respect for self and others."[27] These core values must be promoted in all phases of school life from discipline policies, curriculum, and parent and community relationships to management of the overall school environment. A critical ingredient in any successful character education program is a full, working partnership with parents, who are the primary moral educators of their children.

Effective character education programs are being implemented across the country. For example, after years of discussion, the Baltimore County, Maryland, Task Force on Values Education and Ethical Behavior has developed a handbook for school administrators. It suggests procedures for setting up a values education program that will involve the community in partnership with the school. Other resources on character education suggested by the CEP include "How to Institute a Values Education Program" in *Teaching Values and Ethics: Problems and Solutions*, a report by Kristen J. Amundson.[28] In addition, the Association for Supervision and Curriculum Development and the Network for Educational Development in St. Louis, Missouri, have material available on teaching values in the schools.

There appears to be widespread public support for values education, as reported by a Phi Delta Kappa/Gallup Poll. This 1993 poll found that 69 percent of the public believe that their communities could agree on basic values that public schools should teach. More than 90 percent support public schools teaching honesty (97 percent), democracy (93 percent), acceptance of people of different races and ethnic backgrounds (93 percent), patriotism (91 percent), and moral courage (91 percent).[29]

Like programs that teach about religion, successful character education programs are rooted in community consensus on the three Rs: rights, responsibilities, and respect. Within any community, reasonable people of integrity will differ on how core values should be applied. Sincerely held, diverse beliefs among the American people will always exist; they are, in fact, one of the strengths of our democratic society. The task is to provide a civic framework in which these differences can be respectfully discussed and debated.

13

Responding to Parental and Community Concerns

The roots of any successful response to criticisms of educational materials and programs can be found in the school's ongoing efforts toward developing a strong sense of community among parents, teachers, administrators, community members, and students. A vital community with an established network of working relationships has laid groundwork to successfully deal with controversies should they arise.

Creating this sense of partnership among everyone in the school community is an ongoing process that should be grounded in an appreciation for a shared commitment to creating the best possible educational environment for students. For educators, this means being responsive to questions and concerns, seeking parental input concerning all aspects of the school, and educating parents about the school's curriculum, its goals, and its underlying philosophy. A key component is getting to know and appreciate the values and ideals prized by the school's unique community. For parents, this means supporting the school, volunteering to help out in the classroom, working on any one of a multitude of committees available in most schools, and interacting with educators and administrators with the respect due any professional, especially one who is so intimately involved in the child's education. Obviously, the time to work on developing a strong, healthy school community is now—before controversies arise.

Selection and Reconsideration Policies

An essential element of a successful school community is the development of democratic policies, both for the selection of educational materials used in the classroom and for reconsideration of materials should their use be challenged. The development of a sound, written policy that guides the selection of instructional materials should be a priority for every district. Such a policy articulates the overall educational philosophy, clarifies specific goals for various subject areas, and spells out the step-by-step details, including naming the people involved and explaining the variety of criteria used in the selection process.

A well-designed selection policy serves a variety of purposes. First and foremost, it fosters educational excellence by ensuring that the best resources are available to students. It also helps to educate parents and community members, providing a common basis of understanding about the district's educational goals and objectives. These ends are served when the policy clearly sets out:

1. A statement of the philosophy that guides the school district, which should recognize that academic freedom carries with it academic responsibility, and which should also speak to the importance of a shared partnership with the school community
2. A statement that educational materials selected include not only textbooks but library works and supplementary materials such as newspapers, charts, films, and computer programs
3. The overall educational goals and objectives of the district, including the need to teach specific facts and knowledge as well as to develop analytic and thinking skills
4. A clear description of each step in the selection process from initial consideration to final approval and identification of the people involved in each step

5. The specifics of the regular review process for revising and updating curricula
6. The criteria used by qualified professionals to select specific, age-appropriate educational materials

Developing written reconsideration policies is another vital step in creating an open and democratic school community, one that can withstand controversies. Reconsideration policies should be well thought out and should clearly lay out the steps to follow if materials or teaching techniques are challenged—whether by a parent, a community member, a teacher, a librarian, or an administrator. Broadly speaking, these policies should include:

1. A statement encouraging complainants to read the *entire work*, rather than isolated passages, and to consider the work in light of the program's overall educational goals
2. A clear, detailed description of the steps in the review process, which should include the steps to follow if the complainant wishes to appeal the review committee's decision
3. Clear guidelines on filling out written, detailed complaints that cite specific examples
4. A requirement that review committees be as broad-based as possible and include teachers, parents, administrators, and librarians, as well as students, when appropriate
5. A statement that encourages ongoing communication between parents and teachers and recommends that every effort be made to resolve concerns and complaints at the classroom level on an individual basis

It should be emphasized that professional organizations recommend taking an "innocent until proven guilty" stance. In other words, challenged materials should remain in the library or in the curriculum during the reconsideration process. This sends a message of respect not only for educational materials in general but for the original selection process.

It is vitally important to publicize selection and reconsideration policies. Every opportunity should be sought to help familiarize the school community with the educational philosophy, the goals, and the specifics of policies. Parent-Teacher Association meetings and other school events, as well as faculty meetings and workshops, are natural opportunities for explaining policies and answering questions. Mailings, special meetings, and even the media might also be used to "get the word out" to the entire school community.

The importance of these written policies cannot be stressed enough. If your district does not have such policies, get busy developing them. If policies are available, make sure that people are familiar with them. When sound, articulate, and democratic policies are in place, controversies are minimized and those that do arise are more easily and fairly resolved. (For an excellent model selection policy implemented by the Appleton, Wisconsin, School District, see *Protecting the Freedom to Learn: A Citizen's Guide* by Donna Hulsizer, available from People For the American Way. Another resource offering guidelines for developing reconsideration policies is *The Students' Right to Read*, published by the National Council of Teachers of English. See Appendix B.)

Rationales and Educational Plans

Key aspects of any sound educational plan are reflecting on goals, conducting research concerning potential materials and resources, and engaging in thoughtful planning. It is important to develop in advance a written educational plan as well as written rationales for the books, materials, and teaching methods used in the classroom.

A rationale serves as an educationally based defense for using a specific piece of literature or specific materials in the classroom. Rationales can be especially helpful concerning works of fiction, which, as a broad category, have had more than their share of challenges. Developing a rationale is a process of reflecting on both the value and the potential downside to a work in meeting students' educational needs and interests. The process includes collecting professional reviews and analyses of materials and considering the materials' contribution to an overall educational program.

Many written rationales already exist. Check with other educators or contact your professional organization. The National Council of Teachers of English's Support for the Learning and Teaching of English (SLATE), for example, keeps an ever-expanding file of written rationales. One vital SLATE resource is an April 1994 Starter Sheet, written by educators Jean Brown and Elaine Stephens and entitled *Rationales for Teaching Challenged Books*.[1] This Starter Sheet contains excellent guidelines for developing rationales. It also includes a list of 227 titles for which rationales were available at that time. The list of available rationales continues to expand as educators share their rationales with fellow educators and with their professional organizations.

According to Brown and Stephens, at a minimum a rationale should contain:

- A bibliographic citation and the intended audience
- A brief summary of the work and its educational significance
- The purposes of using the work and how it will be used
- Potential problems with the work and how these can be handled
- Alternative works an individual student might read or view[2]

Realistically, creating a fully developed rationale for every book used in the classroom would take a tremendous amount of time—

far more than most busy professionals have available. Thus, educators should expend their energies in focusing on key works or works that have been controversial in other communities and, for other works, writing a brief statement of the reasons for choosing them. In writing rationales, teachers should ask themselves how the literature or curricular material being considered fits into the overall educational plan. Is it the best material for students given their age and level of maturity? Is it the best material for achieving the goals developed for the students?

Becoming involved with a professional organization is an excellent opportunity to exchange information and support with other professionals and to develop an awareness of what is happening in the field across the nation. Developing close relationships with other professionals helps educators become more sensitive to the issues surrounding the teaching of books or works that have been controversial. It also helps in gaining a perspective of how the needs and standards of individual communities differ across the country.

One-on-One with Parents

Experience has shown that the best way to work out problems is at the personal, local level—the classroom. It is vitally important to work with parents and concerned citizens on an individual basis. Teachers often ask, What should I do if a parent approaches me and questions a book or curricular materials? Here are some commonsense suggestions, compiled, in part, from publications written by the NCTE and People For the American Way, among others:

1. Talk with the parent and listen. Find out what his or her concerns are about the material. Review your reasons for choosing the material and explain how it fits into and meets the needs of the educational plan you have developed for the class. What are the educational merits of the material? It helps if you have already put these criteria and your reasoning in writing.

2. Find out if the parent has read the book or curricular material. If not, encourage the parent to read it in its entirety. Sometimes challengers have not personally read the material and rely on what they have heard about it from another individual or an organization. At times a challenger may be taking a particular section of a book out of context. Viewing it as a whole often gives the parent a different perspective.

3. If, after reading the material in its entirety, the parent still objects to his or her child reading it, offer an alternative reading assignment for that child.

4. If the challenger wishes to have the material removed entirely from the curriculum, refer him or her to your school's written reconsideration policies, which should already be in effect in your district (if not, this is a policy that your school should develop immediately).

5. Remember that challengers, whether they are part of a larger group or not, are individuals. The media will report the most sensational and extremist remarks made by individuals on any issue, and certainly people with extreme views do exist. However, many challengers are rational people who care just as much as you do about exposing students to alternative viewpoints and helping them to become critical thinkers.

As we have seen in this book, many who object to educational materials do so on religious or moral grounds. They are concerned about what they see as a degeneration of the moral fiber of this country. In short, they believe that many societal problems have resulted from the increasing secularization of society and public institutions. In addition, they are concerned that a belief system, tantamount to a religion, is being promoted in the public schools. Whether you agree with this assessment or not, remember that their view of the world is just as clear and right to them as yours is to you. Respect these differences rather than resisting them. Find out more about why they see things the way they do. Encourage dialogue. Such respectful debate will help strengthen our schools.

Finally, it is vitally important to be informed. In short, this means becoming familiar with the ideas and activities of groups battling "censorship," as well as of groups concerned about books, educational techniques, and elements of educational reform. (See Appendix B at the end of this book for a list of recommended organizations to contact for information.)

14

The Community at Work

School Wars has been written with the assumption that all points of view in the ideological conflict should be part of the public debate. Yet "school wars" may be an unfortunate metaphor, albeit one that is all too accurate. In a war, one side wins; the other loses. Rhetoric of this sort has been quite common among zealous participants of all political persuasions involved in public school controversies. Hopefully, such an "us-versus-them" mentality is losing its grip on the debate and more and more citizens are replacing it with respect and careful listening.

As we saw in the previous chapter, wide community involvement early in the textbook and materials selection process is vitally important in helping to prevent these divisive battles. A democratic process that involves all members of the community will not prevent heated disagreements, but it may prevent larger community schisms. One example that resulted in widespread community strife is the well-publicized controversy over New York City's *Children of the Rainbow* elementary curriculum guide, produced by the New York City Board of Education and under consideration as a supplement to its multicultural curriculum.[1] Purportedly designed to help students understand cultural, ethnic, family, and religious diversity, the guide included a bibliography listing books on gay parenting and recommended that teachers positively acknowledge different family structures, including gay and lesbian parents.

Controversy erupted in the 1991–92 school year when members of the Queens school board and other objectors charged that the program promoted homosexuality and did not reflect the heterosexual family standards of the community. In spite of several revisions, the school board refused to adopt the curriculum. In response, Joseph Fernandez, New York City's chancellor of schools, suspended the school board. Shortly thereafter, the board of education overturned the suspension and, in February 1993, voted to fire Fernandez.[2]

Given their vastly different perspectives on the issues described in this book, one might conclude that educators and conservative Christians, particularly those sharing a fundamentalist world view, have little possibility of reconciliation. Indeed, a logical case can be built for such a conclusion, but if it is accurate, few appealing courses of action remain. An all-out war can ensue that will yield an ultimate "winner" relative to control of the content and values taught and reinforced in American schools. Certainly the casualties will be high in such a battle. Another option is to dismantle public education in favor of a privatized system. Although no country we currently seek to emulate has such a system, some of those in the fundamentalist and politically conservative ranks advocate taking this path.

A more favorable alternative is to embrace the controversy and honestly seek to reconcile differences. American educators might have to reach out and create more opportunities for interested parents, particularly those sharing a fundamentalist world view, to take part in selecting educational programs and materials.

At the same time, fundamentalists might have to desist in their blanket assault on all educational innovations and their assertion that educators are knowingly or unknowingly part of a conspiracy to woo the minds of American youth away from Christian beliefs. Additionally, they will surely have to tolerate the existence of world views other than their own, with the caveat that their own world view will be appreciated and included. Ultimately, such concessions might enlighten members of both sides and render public education a true "marketplace of ideas," where no group has a monopoly on what is learned and how it is taught.

What would it be like if the tremendous energies that are currently focused on disrupting public education, on one side, and defending it, on the other, were refocused on the goal of collaboration? For illustrative purposes, we ask that you reread the scenario at the beginning of Chapter One of this book. That hypothetical scenario represents the dynamics that currently exist when educators and fundamentalists disagree. Then read the scenario below, which represents the dynamics that might occur if true collaboration were the working principle underlying these interactions.

The lead article in the local newspaper read, "Local School Accused of Fostering a New Religion." It went on to explain that a war was raging in the local school district—not a war of bullets, but a war of ideas. On one side was a highly vocal and aggressive group of community members who were convinced that the changes the school district was trying to make were actually a thinly veiled attempt to promote a new satanically based religion. This group became a formal organization calling themselves Concerned Citizens for Educational Change, or CCEC. On the other side were teachers, administrators, and community members who had planned to systematically make significant changes in the district over the next few years. They saw the attempts of the community group as the first step toward undoing two years' worth of work in upgrading their educational system.

For the first few months after CCEC members made their feelings and intentions known, the district was in utter chaos. Members of CCEC made demands for information and insisted that they participate in meetings and decisions. These demands began to severely tax the resources of the district. Nothing the district could do was sufficient to satisfy them. District teachers and administrators began labeling the members of CCEC as "crazies" and characterized their efforts as a "witch-hunt" to the media. The local chapter of the

National Education Association mobilized and even began discussing a teachers' strike if CCEC was successful in its efforts to stop the proposed innovations in the district. A full-scale war was about to erupt.

Fortunately, at some point in those first few months, the superintendent and some of his key administrators came to the same conclusion as some of the leaders of CCEC: if the controversy was allowed to continue, nobody was going to win. A phone call from CCEC's leader to the superintendent set up the first private meeting. They agreed that they had to at least try to divert the impending disaster. Luckily, a member of the community was skilled at negotiation and arbitration. In addition, she had taken part in a number of community-based initiatives across the country that had sought to reconcile differences concerning religious belief and public education. She was called in to facilitate the initial meetings between CCEC and the district administrators.

Within a few meetings, several key issues were identified. The district administrators wanted CCEC to call off their media campaign against the innovations proposed by the district and to stop draining district financial and temporal resources. In return, the district promised to seriously consider all CCEC requests regarding the curriculum and instructional practices. With the help of the facilitator, CCEC's four key concerns and requests were identified:

1. The infusion of a creationist perspective into the science curriculum as an alternative to the strict evolutionary theory currently presented
2. Dropping the district's whole language approach to literacy instruction
3. Teaching that abstinence was the preferred mode of premarital sexual behavior
4. Dropping the district's plans to implement an outcome-based approach to school

It was decided that these issues should be addressed by a small group of individuals who represented the CCEC and the school district's team that had planned the proposed innovations. This group was called the reconciliation team. The target date for a resolution was the beginning of school the following year. Until then, all changes proposed by the district were put on temporary hold.

Many meetings of the reconciliation team ensued, during which both sides earnestly presented their perspectives. At first, differences in opinions were so vast that it looked as though no resolution was possible on any of the issues. However, as time went on, members of the group began to form the opinion that those from the other side were not as intent on harming their opponents as they were on protecting and preserving ideas that were important to them. Each side eventually began to comprehend the logic behind the opposing group's position.

Gradually, and sometimes painfully, agreements were reached around each of the four issues that had been identified. Science teachers agreed to present evolution as a theory rather than as established fact and note that other rival theories existed. The district agreed that creationism could be discussed in religious studies classes, although not in science classes, inasmuch as the courts had determined that creationism promotes a religious view, not a scientific one. Members of CCEC conceded that their concerns about the district's whole language approach to literacy were fueled by a fear that children would not receive proper training in phonics. The district's administrators agreed to make sure that phonics instruction would be available for all children who needed it, yet phonics would be taught in the context of a whole language philosophy.

The district also agreed to encourage abstinence as a preferred mode of premarital sexual behavior. Members of CCEC agreed that the information about contraception currently in the sex education program would also be taught with the consent of parents. They also agreed that a traditional outcome-based approach that focused solely on academic outcomes in mathematics, science, history, geography, reading, and writing was compatible with their emphasis on a "basic" education; the district agreed to remove the proposed implementation of the nonacademic "transformation" outcomes that dealt with such skills and abilities as goal setting and cooperation. However, both sides agreed that such skills were important for students to develop. Probably the most important action of the reconciliation team was their resolution that their public school system would not shrink from future controversial issues but, when appropriate, would present all sides of those issues as a regular part of schooling in the district.

When the school year began the next fall, the decisions of the reconciliation team were implemented. Not surprisingly, support for these decisions was not unanimous. Many individuals and a few special interest groups accused both sides of "selling out." However, the vast majority of the community members applauded the spirit of cooperation and compromise exhibited by both sides. The editor of the local paper even agreed to support the efforts of the reconciliation team by making a concerted effort to print articles that were not inflammatory. A weekly column written by members of the team was established to keep the community informed about proposed changes in the district.

In all, it had been quite a year since CCEC had first challenged the district's proposed innovations. Strong emotions and beliefs had come to the surface, but, in the end, most agreed that it had been well worth the initial turmoil. A community that had been deeply divided now was beginning to create new areas for cooperation. The school system was no longer perceived as a bureaucracy run by a small group of elite educators, but a true extension of the beliefs, values, and concerns of the community. Remarkably, the future looked bright.

Is a scenario such as this possible? To use a worn but relevant cliché, only time will tell. However, the indications are that individuals and groups are making overtures for reconciliation. For example, during the winter of 1994, a meeting of organizations representing educators and fundamentalist groups was convened by the American Association of School Administrators. Among the more than thirty people attending were Ronald Brandt of the Association for Supervision and Curriculum Development; the Reverend Barry Lynn of Americans United for the Separation of Church and State; attorney Elliot Mincberg of People For the American Way; Marjorie Ledell, an educational consultant from Littleton, Colorado; Stinson Stroup, executive director of the Pennsylvania Association of School Administrators; Robert Simonds, of Citizens for Excellence in Education; Janet Parshall, of Concerned Women for America; and attorneys from Christian as well as Jewish organizations.[3] The purpose of the meeting was to explore ways to productively resolve conflicts between public educators and fundamentalist groups.

At a more individual level, William Spady, chief architect and proponent of transformational outcome-based education (one of the primary targets of school critics), and Robert Simonds, founder and president of Citizens for Excellence in Education and one of the more outspoken and vehement critics of transformational OBE, have engaged in a series of discussions about their differences and possible resolutions to those differences. As described by Spady, some progress has been made in those discussions. Specifically, Spady identified the following positive outcomes from the meetings:

1. A much deeper appreciation of each other as human beings with a common goal
2. A much stronger common understanding of what OBE and related reforms are about and how schools can approach them from a "legitimate alternatives/win-win approach"
3. A sincere commitment to establish a program/vehicle/center on educational reconciliation and reform in which to work with districts experiencing major conflict to provide a basis for productive dialogue and successful reconciliation of what are now highly polarizing issues and tactics

4. An invitation to appear together on the 1995 national conference programs of the American Association of School Administrators and the Association for Supervision and Curriculum Development[4]

These initial meetings have led to further productive exchanges of ideas. At the May 1995 convention of the American Association of School Administrators, Simonds presented the Enhanced Basics-Based Education (EBBE) model as an "option" to transformational OBE programs. According to Simonds, the essential principles of the EBBE model include a focus on academics and content knowledge as a "prerequisite to higher-order thinking skills and creative expression," factual and objective academic testing, and the establishment of in-school partnerships between parents and students to maximize achievement.[5] (Information on this model may be obtained from CEE.)

This new level of conversation is a refreshing contrast to past clashes. In a speech delivered at the March 1995 conference of the Association for Supervision and Curriculum Development in San Francisco, Simonds expressed regret at some of the harsh rhetoric he has used in the past.[6] Such efforts are highly encouraging and perhaps are portents of a new era in the relationship between fundamentalist and educational organizations. However, a great deal of confusion and misinformation still exists. It is our hope that this book will help remedy that condition by identifying and clarifying the central issues and principal players so that more productive interactions may prevail in the future.

New Areas of Conflict

New areas of conflict will surely erupt beyond those presented in this book. For example, author Michael Barkun wonders how we will deal as a society with flagrant and violent racism. Barkun points out that up to fifty thousand people throughout the United States openly espouse racism and anti-Semitism.[7] A public that has mastered the art of civilized debate will be better able to cope with fascist forces than a public pulled apart by religious divisions, where little attempt has been made to accommodate honest differences.

Issues of race will no doubt continue to raise concerns in education—both concerns about insensitivity and concerns that too much "sensitivity" leads to preferential treatment. Each year, charges are made that public school materials are racist in some way. For example, during the 1993–94 school year, a number of library staples were charged with anti-Semitism or with racism against African Americans or Native Americans, including *Peter Pan*, the *Little House on the Prairie* series, *The Adventures of Huckleberry Finn*, and *The Complete Fairy Tales of the Brothers Grimm*.[8] Concerns about racial sensitivity are not limited to works of fiction. In an article entitled "The Hijacking of American History," John Leo maintains, "Anyone trying to write an honest history of America has a problem: how to write about the national commitment to liberty and equality while facing up to the two great stains on the national character—the destruction of the Indians and the enslavement of Blacks."[9]

Such fact-based areas of study are already under scrutiny, as we have seen in the controversies over history standards. No doubt controversy will continue regarding what should be emphasized in the study of history, inasmuch as the selection of material is itself an interpretation of what happened and what is important for students to learn.

Future battles will inevitably come as schools increasingly tie into the Internet, the electronic thoroughfare. A 1994 *New York Times* article by Stephen Bates noted, "Schools can keep a porno book off the library shelf but they can't keep it from entering the building through cyberspace."[10] Bates pointed out that many students will be able to access programs that include everything from nude photographs to recipes for making marijuana brownies. He asks if school boards will limit computer use that includes e-mail.

Those who want all religious issues kept out of schools may object to modem connections to on-line religion forums. One computer analyst claims that by 1994, 160,000 people had renewed or discovered a connection to faith through electronic bulletin boards. Prayer partners may be established via computers, and students may participate in discussions of creationism versus evolution in the Religious Forum on Compuserve.[11] These and other conflicts promise future controversy. Thus, it is imperative that we find effective and empowering ways of resolving our most basic differences.

Let All Voices Be Heard

World views among people ranging from conservative to liberal may not only differ but also frequently collide. Conflict and confrontation can create mistrust, suspicion, and fear. Conflict can, however, serve a useful role in a democratic society if it leads to dialogue. Worthwhile dialogue necessitates careful listening and intellectual integrity on the part of all participants. In dialogue, participants can avoid dismissing those who hold firmly to a belief simply because it is a religious one. (Author Stephen Carter warns that this is all too often the state of affairs in American society.[12]) Without dialogue, differences that disrupt a community will only be hidden beneath the political victories of whatever segment of the public gains predominant power.

Diversity is a fundamental part of our American heritage. This diversity unites us, yet it also threatens to divide us, particularly when it comes to religious ideals. Our nation, like our world, is no stranger to clashes over religious beliefs. Issues such as those raised in controversies over textbooks have divided people for centuries. Around the globe are countless reminders of religious intolerance, persecution, and centuries-old wars motivated by religious fervor. Aroused by zeal and passion, people feel compelled to cling tenaciously to a set of meanings, often at any expense. Thus far the controversy over American educational materials has not become that extreme, although the same intense passions have been ignited.

If we shared José Ortega y Gasset's views, these historical conflicts would not surprise us. In his book *The Revolt of the Masses*, Ortega stated, "[Liberty] is the supreme form of generosity. . . . It is a discipline too difficult and too complex to take firm root on earth."[13] Ortega might have argued that human beings have a natural inclination to be intolerant as well as ego- and ethnocentric. Indeed our own history reveals this propensity for creating spheres of intellectual security and isolation. As McClosky and Brill point out, colonial America contained "many small 'closed enclaves' making it possible for an individual to search out and 'settle in with his co-believers in safety and comfort,' from which vantage point 'he could help [to impose] group beliefs on all within reach.'"[14]

Our founders recognized the importance of reaching out beyond these "closed enclaves" of thought and opinion. Only then is there any chance that "truth" will be discovered. However, reaching out beyond our own sphere is a taxing proposition. As McClosky and Brill assert, "The impulse to strike down a threatening enemy seems to require little learning or knowledge."[15] Educators, communities, parents, and citizens must continue to strive for resolution in these controversial areas. The alternative is a continued state of controversy and potential lawsuits, resulting in further divisiveness in our communities and schools.

Imagine for a moment some possible insights by participants in a dialogue between fundamentalist, mainline, liberal, and secularist parents and educators. Mainline Christians may find it difficult to understand the sharp distinction fundamentalists make between absolute truth and falsehood, right and wrong. Yet certainly they would affirm the stable foundation that standards of right and wrong provide, both for society and for the individual life. Fundamentalists may have a hard time grasping the willingness, or even the desire, of those with a different world view to accept a measure of ambiguity in matters of truth and values. These conservatives, however, would understand the importance of individual freedom and individual responsibility in decision making.

Teachers may discover that most fundamentalists are not interested in having public schools exclusively teach the tenets of their particular religion. Rather, they may learn that these religious conservatives are trying to overcome a widespread secular view of the world. Fundamentalists may come to realize that educators are not atheists merely because they see fossil forms as evidence that the world is millions of years old. Instead, these educators are following their accepted source of empirical data that indicate that this is an old world still in the making. Fundamentalists, as well as liberals, may agree that interpreting the world through the scientific lens is valid; yet they both may point out that this lens does not fully convey the rich meaning and purposiveness of the world. For example, the religious affirmation of God as Creator expresses a certain conviction about the order, the beauty and worth, the mystery and majesty, of the natural world.

In dialogue, mainline Christians may discover that fundamentalists are deeply committed to concrete facts—the hard data sometimes thought to be the private possession of secular scientists. Fundamentalists may discover that the educator's concern for creativity in music and the arts, as well as for the cultivation of the imagination in literary studies, is close to the deep religious currents of inspiration in the Bible.

Dialogue may demonstrate that world views overlap. For example, both fundamentalists and mainline Christians believe in sin. Although the word *sin* has different meanings, there may be room for discussion about the limitations as well as the possibilities inherent in being human. Similarly, a shared understanding about the use of language might be discovered. It is not always clear whether people who speak of God are using literal or metaphorical language. If God, at least in part, is mystery and beyond human knowing, these groups may agree that poetic and metaphorical language is necessary in religious discourse. If believers from fundamentalists to liberals express clearly their assumptions about sin, God, and evil they may discover common elements expressed in different language symbols.

Fundamentalists speak about the fallen angel, Satan. This devil seeks to glorify himself and seduce people into a false sense of the self. Through Satan's influence, people come to think they can be gods. Most mainline and many liberal Christians also recognize evil in the world, yet they tend to place responsibility for arrogance, false pride, and evil behavior not on Satan but on individuals themselves. Moreover, some liberal participants in dialogue, upon careful listening, may discover that their own psychological perspective is similar to that of fundamentalist and mainline Christians. Some people distinguish the lower self from the higher self—self-will from God's will. They may even consider the ego as the self-centered aspect of a person, the pull toward narcissism. This tendency, they recognize, can become all-consuming, characterized by conceit, selfishness, and greed.[16] All participants, then, may discover a common thread about evil, whether expressed in language about Satan or through other words.

Dialogue might even reveal that secular scientists have much in common with fundamentalists in their concern for precision in thinking and for objective truth. Mainline Christians and secular scientists might also converse on the possible division between fact and value, to the end that religious reflection on science can focus on meaning and value in interpreting scientific theories.

Dialogue will certainly also reveal fundamental differences in values and beliefs that cannot be reconciled. These deeply held convictions should not be sacrificed in the name of dialogue; yet important understandings and collaboration can be reached nonetheless. Differing beliefs are inevitable. In fact, where liberty and human growth are prized, such divergent views should be sought out.

The First Amendment to the Constitution, perhaps our most prized democratic principle, was greatly influenced by a philosopher who held high the value of such a marketplace of ideas in dialogue. John Milton argued that truth could best be discovered in an environment of open debate. Milton left his indelible mark on our democratic philosophy, one that is all too often forgotten in the present controversy. Consider the following passage from Milton's *The Areopagitica,* written in 1644: "And though all the winds of doctrine were let loose to play upon the earth, so Truth be in the field, we do injuriously by licensing and prohibiting to misdoubt her strength. Let her and Falsehood grapple; who ever knew Truth put to the worse in a free and open encounter?"[17]

The motto "Let all voices be heard" offers rich possibilities for the future.

Appendix A

Key Public School Cases

Most challenges to public school instructional and library materials are resolved in one way or another within the school system at the local, community level. However, dissatisfied parents, community members, and religious groups across the country continue to file suits to press for changes in public education.

Early Textbook Battles

Two of the earliest controversies over public school textbooks took place in 1974 in Kanawha County, West Virginia, and in 1977 in Warsaw, Indiana. These cases are presented here as examples of the extreme emotions that can become inflamed in public school controversies. They also seemed to set the stage for continuing challenges to public school materials. As discussed in Chapter Two, attempts to restrict or terminate student access to certain educational materials increased dramatically in the years following these two incidents.

Kanawha County, West Virginia, 1974: The Battle of the Books

The Kanawha County "battle of the books," as it is often called, began when a group of five public school teachers submitted a list of language arts textbooks to the school board for approval. The books were recommended, in part, to meet the requirements of a multicultural and multiethnic mandate outlined in a 1970 West Virginia state law.[1] The textbook selection committee screened the books using a list approved by the state, then recommended that the books be adopted, and at an April 1974 school board meeting, the books were approved for use. However, Alice Moore, a school board member and the wife of a local conservative Protestant minister, made a motion to delay purchase of the texts until they could be studied more thoroughly. The school board unanimously passed this motion.

Moore contacted Mel and Norma Gabler of Educational Research Analysts for their advice on the books. Subsequently, she objected to a number of the selected books. She maintained that most of the books on the language arts list contained material that was disrespectful of authority and religion, destructive of social and cultural values, obscene, pornographic, unpatriotic, or in violation of individual and family rights of privacy. The controversy escalated during a series of school board meetings held in May and June of 1974. Moore attended the initial meeting. Ten local ministers attended the next meeting. At a meeting two days later, twenty-seven ministers described the books as indecent and immoral. And at the next meeting, attended by nearly one thousand people, the school board voted to drop eight of the most controversial textbooks from the list.

However, Moore and other fundamentalists were not satisfied. They protested the books by keeping eight thousand of the district's forty-six thousand students out of school; in addition, more than four thousand coal miners stayed away from work and pickets closed bus stations, grocery stores, and construction sites. The windows in the board of education building in Charleston were blown out by gunfire. The school board announced that all of the adopted textbooks would be submitted to a citizen's committee for review, and that some of them would be removed from classrooms during the review process. The next day high school students staged a walkout protesting the removal of the controversial textbooks. Shortly thereafter, the Reverend Charles Quigley declared, "I am asking Christian people to pray that God will kill the giants that have mocked and made fun of dumb fundamentalists."[2]

Violence continued over the next two months. School buses were the targets of gunfire. A car belonging to parents who sent their children to school during the protest was firebombed, and a state police car escorting a school bus carrying children to school was hit by sniper fire. After one person was shot and another wounded in a protest, the schools were temporarily closed.

In early November, the school board voted to return all of the controversial books to the schools with the exception of two series, which were placed in school libraries and restricted to use subject to parental approval. At the end of November, the board adopted new textbook selection guidelines. This represented a resolution of the controversy, although it was an unsatisfactory one for many people. The National Education Association established an inquiry panel to review the Kanawha County textbook controversy. It concluded that the new procedures would make the adoption of instructional materials "a nearly impossible task—and a nightmare." It also declared that by the time texts worked their way through the system, the materials left to choose from "may have been so narrowed as to make a mockery of the selection process."[3]

Warsaw, Indiana, 1977

Three years later, in 1977, a similar controversy took place in Warsaw, Indiana. The problems began with the school board's decision to review the Individually Guided Education (IGE) program at Washington Elementary School following numerous complaints from parents, who said that their children were not learning basic skills such as reading, writing, and arithmetic. During the summer of 1977, the school board met in a special session and voted to drop the IGE program and to establish "strict parameters" in all elementary schools in the county.

At another school board meeting that summer, the board voted to drop the Values Clarification class from the English department at the high school and to remove the textbooks and destroy them as soon as possible. Board members were concerned that exercises in the book asking students to share their views on personal subjects such as premarital sex and masturbation could encourage students to reject family and religious values.[4]

At later board meetings, English teachers at the high school protested the board's action. In August 1977, the school board voted to discontinue several English courses, including Gothic Literature; Black Literature; Whatever Happened to Mankind?; Good Guys, Folklore, and Legends; Detective and Mystery Fiction; and Science Fiction. In the fall of 1977, a group of senior citizens (no doubt representing only a small portion of the community at large) burned forty copies of the textbook used in the Values Clarification class, *Values Clarification: A Handbook of Practical Strategies for Students and Teachers*, by Sidney B. Simon, Leland W. Howe, and Howard Kirschenbaum. (The book had become part of the high school English curriculum after the district's former superintendent invited the Indiana Department of Public Instruction to conduct an in-service training program on the principles advanced in the book.)

Around this time, the coordinator for the high school English department, who had been a teacher for thirty years, resigned her position. She stated that she felt that the board did not have enough trust in her and said that board members should have consulted her about the English curriculum before changing it. Another teacher, who taught a course entitled Women in Literature, was told by the principal that the reading list for the course included books that might offend the community. She was ordered not to use several of these books in her class. She protested and, near the end of the school year, was dismissed. Ten other teachers were asked to resign.

Before the beginning of the following school year, the school board approved a policy that stated that any "multi-page teacher-made" instructional material needed the approval of the principal and superintendent before it could be formally used in a classroom. In the fall, the principal sent out a memo to teachers telling them to bring any material that "might be objectionable" to his office. Later that school year, the board adopted a resolution that school officials should "teach students to avoid the use of profanity and obscenities, also books and materials that could be construed as objectionable in this community shall not be used."[5]

In January 1978, the president of the Warsaw Community Education Association filed a complaint with the state education employment relations board alleging unfair labor practices. After a hearing, the examiner recommended that the school board be ordered to reverse all its policies. The board appealed the decision. Meanwhile, board members and teachers reached a compromise.

However, several lawsuits were subsequently filed against the school board. The Indiana State Teachers Association filed suit on behalf of two teachers who had been dismissed. The Indiana Civil Liberties Union filed suit on behalf of high school students, alleging that the school board's actions had violated the students' "right to know" and "the right to read." The district court judge stated that school boards have the right to determine curriculum and library materials as part of their role in developing citizenship in students. He further stated that board members have to rely on their own personal moral and political beliefs in making such decisions.[6]

The decision was appealed. The appellate court judge agreed with the district court's conclusion that students' constitutional rights had not been violated, stating that high school students do not have the same academic freedom as college students. However, he considered the allegations to be serious, noting that the burning of the Values Clarification books was a "hateful ceremony." He instructed the plaintiffs to amend their complaint if they could provide evidence of actual constitutional violations.[7]

The Warsaw and Kanawha County cases had much in common. Both were characterized by a clash of deeply held beliefs and a struggle for control over public education. And in both cases, although a resolution was reached, they were uneasy and failed to resolve the underlying conflict of ideas and values about the education of American students.

Notable Court Cases

Four notable cases involving conflicts over public school materials reached the higher courts in the 1980s. Later in this appendix we review each of these cases. These rulings relied heavily on three earlier U.S. Supreme Court decisions concerning the nexus of freedom of conscience and the authority and duty of public school officials. Here we highlight these earlier decisions that articulated important constitutional principles regarding officially prescribed orthodoxy, the state's relationship with religious belief, and the First Amendment liberties of students in the public school setting.

Avoiding Orthodoxy

West Virginia State Board of Education v. *Barnette*, decided in 1943, set an important precedent concerning the issue of officially prescribed orthodoxy in the public schools. The suit was originally brought by citizens in West Virginia who sought an injunction to restrain the state board of education from enforcing its flag-salute statute against Jehovah's Witnesses.

Three years earlier, in the 1940 *Minersville School District* v. *Gobitis* case, the U.S. Supreme Court concluded that "national unity is the basis of national security" and that state authorities have "the right to select appropriate means for its attainment.[8] After that decision, the West Virginia legislature amended its statutes to require all schools to teach courses in history, civics, and the Constitution "for the purpose of teaching, fostering and perpetuating the ideals, principles and spirit of Americanism, and increasing the knowledge of the organization and machinery of the government of the United States and of the state of West Virginia."[9]

In response, the West Virginia State Board of Education adopted a resolution ordering schools to make the salute to the flag and its companion pledge a regular part of the school day. Their resolution stated that refusal to salute would be considered "insubordination" and would be "dealt with accordingly."[10] By state statute, any child refusing to obey "the lawful requirements of the school" was to be expelled, or suspended and denied readmittance until he or she complied.[11]

Objections were made to the required "stiff-arm salute" by several groups, including the Jehovah's Witnesses. The Witnesses objected on religious grounds, viewing it as violating the Bible's mandate not to "bow down" to or serve "any graven image."[12] In lieu of the required flag salute, the Witnesses offered to "periodically and publicly" make another pledge acknowledging their allegiance to God, their respect for the United States flag, and their obedience to all U.S. laws "consistent with God's laws."[13] Representatives for the Witnesses filed suit in district court seeking an injunction against the salute; the injunction was granted. The board of education appealed to the U.S. Supreme Court, not because it wanted to enforce the salute, but because it sought a broader ruling overturning the *Gobitis* decision and the state law, declaring that they were an unconstitutional denial of the First Amendment rights to religious liberty and free speech.

The Supreme Court overruled its decision in *Gobitis*. The Court wrote that in spite of the West Virginia legislature's desire to promote the worthy goal of national unity, the compulsory flag salute and pledge were an unconstitutional compulsion to "declare a belief."[14] Although the Court acknowledged the important functions of school boards, it stated that these functions can be performed within the parameters of the Bill of Rights. In fact, school officials must vigilantly guard these freedoms in order to teach students, by example, important democratic principles. The Court wrote: "That they are educating the young for citizenship is reason for scrupulous protection of Constitutional freedoms of the individual, if we are not to strangle the free mind at its source and teach youth to discount important principles of our government as mere platitudes."[15]

Concluding its opinion, the Court declared that the Bill of Rights was designed precisely to protect freedom of conscience from officials or majorities of any kind:

> Freedom to differ is not limited to things that do not matter much. That would be a mere shadow of freedom. The test of its substance is the right to differ as to things that touch the heart of the existing order.
>
> If there is any fixed star in our constitutional constellation, it is that no official, high or petty, can prescribe what shall be orthodox in politics, nationalism, religion, or other matters of opinion or force citizens to confess by word or act their faith therein.[16]

Thus, with the *Barnette* decision, the Supreme Court brought to life a fundamental constitutional principle concerning the relationship between individual freedoms and authority. Since then, this principle has been cited by the courts in numerous decisions.[17]

Affirming Neutrality

The Supreme Court's 1968 *Epperson* v. *Arkansas* ruling is particularly relevant to controversies concerning religious belief and public schools. With this decision, the Court found Arkansas's antievolution statute to be unconstitutional, thus firmly applying the principle of governmental neutrality articulated in the 1947 *Everson* v. *Board of Education* decision to the public school selection of teaching materials. The *Epperson* decision established a precedent that led to the overturning of antievolution statutes in other states that had been established in the wake of the 1927 *Scopes* v. *Tennessee* decision.

One year after the *Scopes* decision, the Arkansas legislature passed its own antievolution statute. Anyone who taught evolution or used a textbook dealing with evolution would be guilty of a misdemeanor, subjecting the violator to dismissal. Subsequently, for more than thirty-five years, the public schools used textbooks that did not discuss evolution.

In the 1965–66 school year, however, the Little Rock, Arkansas, school district adopted a textbook that contained a chapter on evolution. Susan Epperson, a high school biology teacher, wanted to use the textbook but knew that to do so was a criminal offense. She filed suit in the state's chancery court, challenging the constitutionality of the statute. The chancery court ruled that the statute was unconstitutional because it "tend[ed] to hinder the quest for knowledge, restrict the freedom to learn, and restrain the freedom to teach."[18] On appeal, the Arkansas Supreme Court reversed. In a two-sentence opinion, it declared that the statute was "a valid exercise of the state's power to specify the curriculum in its public schools."[19] The case was appealed to the U.S. Supreme Court.

The Court wrote that because American public education is generally in the hands of state and local authorities, any kind of judicial intervention should be approached with restraint. However, such intervention is warranted, the Court noted, when basic constitutional freedoms are at issue. Quoting its precedents, the Court declared, "The vigilant protection of constitutional freedoms is nowhere more vital than in the community of American schools. . . . The First Amendment does not tolerate laws that cast a pall of orthodoxy over the classroom."[20] The Arkansas statute had been passed specifically because of "fundamentalist sectarian conviction"; therefore, the justices ruled, it must be found unconstitutional. Citing a series of "separation" cases beginning with *Everson* v. *Board of Education* and *McCollum* v. *Board of Education* (forbidding school prayer and Bible reading, respectively), the Court concluded: "There is and can be no doubt that the First Amendment does not permit the State to require that teaching and learning must be tailored to the principles or prohibitions of any religious sect or dogma."[21]

Students' Rights

Although *Tinker* v. *Des Moines Independent Community School District*, decided in 1968, did not involve a controversy over library books or textbooks, it was a landmark case with regard to students' rights in the public schools. The *Tinker* case established another key constitutional principle applicable to public school controversies.

Plaintiffs were two high school students and one junior high student who wore black armbands to school to protest the Vietnam War. They were asked to remove the armbands but refused to do so. Two days earlier, school principals in the city of Des Moines had instituted a ban on armbands in anticipation of such a protest of the war. Consequently, the students were sent home and suspended from school until they agreed to return to school without the armbands. The students sought a federal injunction restraining school officials from suspending them. However, the lower federal courts upheld the constitutionality of the school officials' actions, concluding that they were reasonable in order to prevent a disturbance that might result at school from the wearing of the armbands. The case was appealed to the U.S. Supreme Court.

The Court cited *Barnette*'s pronouncement that school boards have a special duty to perform their functions within the parameters of the Bill of Rights, since school authorities are "educating the young for citizenship," but acknowledged the broad authority local school officials have to regulate and control school conduct. The Court stated, as it did in *Barnette*, that the problem it faced dealt with the conflict between the rights of students and the authority of school officials.[22]

Declaring its opposition to orthodoxy, the Court stated that students have First Amendment rights to free speech and that these rights were not outweighed by school officials' right to protect the orderly operation of the schools, since the students' wearing of the armbands caused no disruption. The Court echoed *Barnette*'s condemnation of officially prescribed orthodoxy of opinion and speech, declaring: "State-operated schools may not be enclaves of totalitarianism. School officials do not possess absolute authority over their students. Students in school as well as out of school are . . . possessed of fundamental rights which the State must respect. . . . In our system, students may not be regarded as closed-circuit recipients of only that which the State chooses to communicate. They may not be confined to the expression of those sentiments that are officially approved."[23]

The Court set forth the heart of its decision in a statement that seemed to be its guiding principle: "It can hardly be argued that either students or teachers shed their constitutional rights to freedom of speech or expression at the schoolhouse gate." Although the Court's language had the effect of expanding the First Amendment rights of students, the Court did state that these rights had to be applied within the unique framework of the school environment.[24]

Although the *Barnette*, *Epperson*, and *Tinker* decisions dealt with different sets of facts, the Court faced the same fundamental dilemma: where to draw the line in the sensitive area where the authority of the state and the protected freedoms of the individual conflict. As we have seen here, a majority of the Court in each case gave more weight to First Amendment liberties, concluding that these rights grant the student the freedom to differ with officially or commonly held beliefs—especially those that lie in the realm of accepted "truth," such as American patriotism and religious doctrine.

These Supreme Court decisions established principles that later courts could look to when resolving public school controversies: the mandate against officially prescribed orthodoxy, parameters for tailoring local school curricula, and the recognition that students have First Amendment rights. As such, these cases had the effect of limiting local school boards' authority. Taken together, these decisions established the principle that state actions in the public school context should be strictly scrutinized when they implicate the essential liberties protected by the First Amendment. This principle was again followed in the highly divisive 1982 Supreme Court *Board of*

Education, Island Trees Union Free School District No. 26 v. *Pico* decision and in three "secular humanism" cases before the high court in the ensuing years.

The Cases of the Eighties

Litigation concerning religious freedoms multiplied in the 1980s. More lawsuits were filed in the 1980s than in the entire history of the United States.[25] During this time, four challenges concerning textbooks or library materials made their way to the higher courts: *Board of Education, Island Trees Union Free School District No. 26* v. *Pico*, decided by the Supreme Court in 1982; *Grove* v. *Mead School District No. 354*, decided by the Ninth Circuit Court of Appeals in 1985; *Mozert* v. *Hawkins County Board of Education*, decided by the Sixth Circuit Court of Appeals in 1987; and *Smith* v. *Board of School Commissioners of Mobile County*, decided by the Eleventh Circuit Court of Appeals in 1987.

In the 1982 *Pico* case, plaintiffs were students who were protesting, on First Amendment grounds, the school board's removal of books. In contrast, plaintiffs in *Grove*, *Mozert*, and *Smith* were fundamentalist Christians who brought suit seeking to have materials removed from schools. These cases illustrate how the courts must balance the First Amendment rights of students with the responsibility of school boards to select textbooks and materials. They also illustrate the sincerely held beliefs of those who stress the need to protect students, those who stress students' right to know, and the reasoning the courts followed in resolving these conflicting views.

Board of Education, Island Trees Union Free School District v. Pico

Board of Education, Island Trees Union Free School District v. *Pico*, decided by the Supreme Court in 1982, resulted in seven separate opinions, revealing a severely split Court. This case came before the courts after seventeen-year-old high school student Steven Pico and other students filed suit against school officials in Island Trees, New York, for banning eleven books from the public school libraries.

In September 1975, the board of education president, its vice president, and a board member attended a conference sponsored by Parents of New York United, a politically conservative organization concerned about educational legislation in the state of New York. At the conference, the board president obtained a list of books that he described as "objectionable."

After returning to Island Trees, board members went to the high school library one night, reviewed the card catalog, and found that nine of the listed books were in the high school library. (The nine books in the library were *Slaughterhouse Five*, by Kurt Vonnegut, Jr.; *The Naked Ape*, by Desmond Morris; *Down These Mean Streets*, by Piri Thomas; *Best Short Stories of Negro Writers*, edited by Langston Hughes; *Go Ask Alice*, by an anonymous author; *Laughing Boy*, by Oliver LaFarge; *Black Boy*, by Richard Wright; *A Hero Ain't Nothin' but a Sandwich*, by Alice Childress; and *Soul on Ice*, by Eldridge Cleaver.) Board members subsequently determined that one of the listed books, *A Reader for Writers*, edited by Jerome Archer, was in the junior high school library and that another, *The Fixer*, by Bernard Malamud, was being used in the curriculum of a twelfth-grade literature course. In February 1976, the board ordered the principals of the junior high and high schools and the district superintendent to search the schools for copies of the "objectionable" books and to send them to the board office so that board members could read them. The superintendent of schools objected to this directive in a memo to the board, stating that a policy already existed that called for appointing a committee to review challenged books.

After the board's actions became public, it issued a press release in which it stated that some books in schools across the country were "anti-American, anti-Christian, anti-Semitic, and just plain filthy. . . . It is our duty, our moral obligation, to protect the children in our schools from this moral danger as surely as from physical and medical dangers."[26] When they were asked to give an example of how the books were anti-American, board members referred to

A Hero Ain't Nothin' but a Sandwich, which at one point notes that George Washington was a slaveholder; this "negative" portrayal of Washington, they argued, made the book anti-American. The book was also objectionable because the title contains the word "ain't." *The Fixer*, which describes the persecution of Jews in the Soviet Union, was described by board members as "anti-Semitic" because it used derogatory terms to describe Jews. The board claimed that *Go Ask Alice*, the diary of a teenage drug addict, encouraged students to use drugs and glorified sex.

After the controversy became public, the board appointed a committee of parents and school staff to review the books and make recommendations. The committee recommended that five of the books be retained in the school library, that two be removed, and that one be made available to students only with parental approval; the committee could not agree on two of the remaining books and took no position on one. The board rejected the committee's recommendations and banned ten of the eleven books anyway. The superintendent left the school district the following year.

Steven Pico and other students sued the board, alleging that the board's removal of the books denied them their First Amendment rights. The U.S. District Court for the Eastern District of New York granted summary judgment in favor of the school board. After years of appeals, the case found its way to the U.S. Supreme Court. The Court's *Pico* decision, which includes seven separate opinions, is an excellent record of the conflicting world views that are at the heart of the controversy over public school instructional materials. A comparison of these opinions reveals the diverse meanings assigned by the individual Court justices to First Amendment freedoms in the educational context—meanings that inevitably guided the individual justices toward their respective conclusions.

Their differences revolved, in part, around the question of the role of the state as the educator of youth in American society. Both the majority and dissenting justices based their respective opinions on the well-established idea that public schools must prepare students for participation as citizens. The justices differed significantly, however, in their interpretation of this vital public school responsibility.

Writing the plurality opinion for the Court, Justice William Brennan, Jr., cited the *Epperson* and *Tinker* decisions in acknowledging the broad discretion school boards have in managing school affairs. Federal courts should not intervene, he wrote, unless First Amendment rights are at stake. In this case, the school board's removal of books from the school library might be a violation of students' constitutional right to *receive* ideas if the board's motivation was to suppress ideas with which it disagreed, and thus to promote orthodoxy.

The plurality opinion declared that a school board's discretion to determine library holdings "may not be exercised in a narrowly partisan or political manner." Brennan noted that removing books because they were pervasively vulgar or because they did not meet an "educational suitability" standard would be an acceptable motivation.[27] However, if, by removing books, the board's primary intention was to deny students access to ideas with which the board disagreed, then the board's actions were unconstitutional. The Court proclaimed, "Our Constitution does not permit the official suppression of ideas."[28] Brennan emphasized that the Court's decision only related to the removal of books from school libraries, not to the addition of books, and that school boards may have wide discretion in establishing curricula.

The plurality opinion noted that school libraries are particularly important in promoting the First Amendment principles of tolerance, respect for diversity, and access to diverse, unpopular, or unorthodox ideas. Brennan distinguished the regular curriculum from the school library. Using language from a case dealing with public colleges and universities, he asserted that the public school library is "the principal locus" of the freedom "to inquire, to study and to evaluate, to gain new maturity and understanding."[29] The Court also emphatically pointed to established court doctrine, notably *Barnette* and *Epperson,* which decried orthodoxy in the public schools. Brennan declared that the removal of books from school libraries for the purpose of suppressing ideas and prescribing orthodoxy "stand[s] inescapably condemned by our precedents."[30]

Brennan's interpretation of the role of public education emphasized inculcation of the democratic principles of free speech, tolerance, and access to ideas rather than of moral values and beliefs. He highlighted the responsibility of the schools to prepare students for citizenship in a democracy in which the First Amendment right of free speech is of paramount importance. Brennan cited the *Tinker* case's admonition that students are not "closed-circuit recipients of only that which the State chooses to communicate" in declaring that students must necessarily be exposed to a variety of ideas and viewpoints. Brennan wrote: "In sum, just as access to ideas makes it possible for citizens generally to exercise their rights of free speech and press in a meaningful manner, such access prepares students for active and effective participation in the pluralistic, often contentious society in which they will soon be adult members."[31] Writing for the Court, Brennan quoted *Barnette*'s 1943 statement that school boards have a special duty to educate students for citizenship by way of example. Thus, school boards must vigilantly perform their functions within the parameters of the First Amendment.

The dissenting opinion in the *Pico* case was written by Chief Justice Warren Burger, who was joined by justices Lewis Powell, Jr., William Rehnquist, and Sandra Day O'Connor, all of whom filed dissenting opinions. Their opinions stand in marked contrast to Brennan's plurality opinion. These justices maintained that the school board's actions were a valid exercise of its discretion, not an unconstitutional suppression of ideas. Like Brennan, they stressed the inculcative character of the public school institution, asserting that "by its very nature . . . [it] is a place for the selective conveyance of ideas."[32] However, Burger argued that in order for schools to fulfill their obligation to inculcate "fundamental values," school officials must necessarily express their views and make content-based decisions on material taught in the classroom.

The dissenters argued that the majority was recognizing a "previously unheard of" right of access to ideas, a right that the dissenters clearly did not view as emanating from the First Amendment, especially the First Amendment rights of public elementary and secondary school students. They highlighted the differences between public school students and other American citizens, stressing the fact that children are impressionable and teachers have great influence over them. Burger argued that a school board should not be obligated to act as a "courier" of ideas, especially since students are free to check out any book they desire at the local public library. In short, they wrote, the right to receive ideas is inconsistent with the role of public education.[33]

The dissenters asserted that the Court's reasoning in examining the motivations of the school board was vague and illogical, and that Brennan's "educational suitability" test for constitutionality was "standardless."[34] Burger argued that such a conclusion would no doubt be reached in most instances in which school officials retained or removed a book because they considered it to be unacceptable for students. Further, Burger argued, the majority opinion would have the effect of making school board decisions concerning library holdings subject to review by the federal courts. In Burger's dissent, he facetiously questioned whether local schools should be administered by elected school boards or by "federal judges and teenage pupils."[35] In short, when balancing student rights against the authority and responsibility of school officials, the dissenters gave more weight to school officials.

After the *Pico* decision, the character of book-banning cases evolved from questions concerning general objections to materials to questions concerning the alleged advancement of the so-called religion of secular humanism. Between 1985 and 1987, three secular humanism cases were decided by the appellate courts, after an initial determination at the district court level. The facts and issues before the appellate courts in *Grove, Mozert,* and *Smith* were strikingly similar, as were the philosophies that guided the respective courts in the review process. In each of these cases, plaintiffs were parents of public school children who claimed that the schools were exposing their children to ideas they found offensive to their fundamentalist Christian beliefs. The plaintiffs concluded that the schools were inhibiting their religion in violation of the First Amendment's religion clauses.

Grove v. Mead School District No. 354

In 1985, the Ninth Circuit Court of Appeals ruled on *Grove* v. *Mead School District No. 354*. Sophomore high school student Cassie Grove was assigned *The Learning Tree* by Gordon Parks as part of her English literature class at Mead High School in Washington state. She read part of the book, which deals with racism from the viewpoint of a black teenage boy from a working-class family, and found it offensive to her fundamentalist Christian beliefs. She showed it to her mother, who read the entire book and agreed with her. The Groves complained to the teacher, who assigned another book for Cassie to read and gave her permission to leave the classroom during discussion of *The Learning Tree*. However, she chose to remain. Her mother filed a formal complaint with the school district anyway, seeking the book's removal from the curriculum. A committee evaluated the book and concluded that *The Learning Tree* was an appropriate part of the sophomore English curriculum. Grove appealed to the school district's board of directors, who, after a hearing, denied her request to remove the book from the curriculum.

Grove brought suit against the school district, alleging that the board's use of *The Learning Tree* violated both the free exercise clause and the establishment clause of the First Amendment in inhibiting the Groves's fundamentalist religious beliefs and in advancing the "religion of secular humanism."[36] Grove stated that she believed *secular*, *humanism*, and *secular humanism* were synonymous. She defined secular humanism as "a religion dedicated to affirmatively opposing or showing hostility toward Christianity. It has declared its pulpit to be the public school classroom and its 'bible' is adolescent literature like *The Learning Tree*."[37] Grove claimed that "the book . . . clearly teaches anti-Christian concepts, values, and beliefs." She asserted that "eternal religious consequences" would result from exposure to or even discussion of *The Learning Tree*.[38]

The U.S. District Court for the Eastern District of Washington granted summary judgment to the school district, finding that there had been no constitutional violation. The Groves appealed to the Ninth Circuit U.S. Court of Appeals. Writing for the court, Chief Judge Robert J. McNichols concurred with *Epperson*'s statement that local school boards generally have broad discretion in managing schools and that courts should only interfere when constitutional values are implicated, which he obviously thought was so in this case. The court then quickly evaluated Grove's contention that her free exercise right to control the religious upbringing of her child had been violated. McNichols applied a strict scrutiny test similar to the test articulated in the 1963 *Sherbert* v. *Verner* case (see Chapter Eleven), concluding that the burden on Grove's free exercise of religion was "minimal" because the school had given her daughter an alternate reading assignment as well as permission to leave the classroom during discussion of the book.

The court concluded that accommodation of the Groves' request to remove the book from the curriculum would excessively burden the state's compelling interest in providing well-rounded public education. Further, the state's interest in education would be "critically impeded" if it banned a book every time someone objected to it. The court used language directly from the 1948 *McCollum* decision (which found official classroom Bible reading to be unconstitutional) in declaring that tailoring the public schools to meet every possible objection would ruin the school system: "If we are to eliminate everything that is objectionable to any of [the religious bodies existing in the United States] or inconsistent with any of their doctrines, we will leave public education in shreds."[39]

With regard to the alleged establishment clause violation, the court used the *Lemon* test in ruling that although secular humanism may be a religion, the primary effect of the book in question was secular and its use did not constitute establishment of religion or nonreligion. The court stated that *The Learning Tree* "was included in a group of religiously neutral books in a review of English literature, as a comment on an American subculture."[40]

A concurring opinion by Circuit Judge Canby provides insight into the court's reasoning and interpretation of the First Amendment's protection of religious freedom. Canby thoroughly analyzed the plaintiff's allegations, particularly Grove's assertion that secular humanism is a religion. The opinion asserted that Grove had "erect[ed] an insurmountable barrier to meaningful application" of the establishment clause because she viewed all "value-laden thought" as either religious or antireligious, and interpreted all secular views as antireligious. Canby argued that, in the language of *Lemon*, "secular" necessarily means "nonreligious," and not "antireligious," as the plaintiff claimed. In addition, he argued, even if *The Learning Tree* is representative of secular humanism, it is far removed from a "comprehensive belief system" supported by a formal organization with tenets. He concluded that the plaintiffs had provided no facts to support their claim that secular humanism had been established in the public schools as a religion.[41]

Canby also stated that Grove might have a free exercise claim if her daughter had been forced to read *The Learning Tree*, to be present while the book was discussed in class, or to declare a particular belief. However, noting that Grove sought to have the book removed from the curriculum, Justice Canby wrote that the free exercise clause does not protect individuals from being "religiously offended" by governmental actions that expose them to divergent attitudes and beliefs. He concluded that removing *The Learning Tree* because of the plaintiff's "hostility to ideas" would be a threat to First Amendment values. He noted *Pico*'s declaration that "our Constitution does not permit the official suppression of ideas."[42]

Both McNichols's and Canby's views of public education are

similar to those advanced by Brennan in the *Pico* decision. Their language endorses the view that public schools should expose students to diverse, competing views. For example, Canby noted that *The Learning Tree* was included in the curriculum for the "commendable purpose of exposing students to different cultural attitudes and outlooks."[43] These opinions reveal the appellate court's view that public school education does and should educate students about diverse lifestyles and beliefs and expose them to diverse ideas and viewpoints, including religious ones, as long as such "education and exposure do not become advocacy or endorsement."[44]

Mozert v. Hawkins County Board of Education

Two years later, a similar decision was reached by the Sixth Circuit Court of Appeals in another secular humanism suit. *Mozert* v. *Hawkins County Board of Education* was concluded four years after the plaintiffs challenged a Tennessee public school reading series on grounds that repeated exposure to the reading series offended their religious beliefs.

In the spring of 1983, the Hawkins County, Tennessee, Board of Education adopted the Holt, Rinehart and Winston Basic Reading Series for use in the public elementary and junior high schools. The series was used as part of a "critical reading" approach in grades 1–8 designed to develop higher-order cognitive skills that would enable students to compare ideas and to evaluate and understand complex material and characters. In grades 5–8, reading was taught as a separate subject at a specific time each day. However, ideas appearing in the reading program were discussed in other courses as part of the school's commitment to an integrated curriculum. In grades 1–4, reading was not taught as a separate subject. Instead, teachers used the reading texts in other subjects throughout the day.

At the beginning of the 1983–84 school year, Vicki Frost, the mother of three students in the Hawkins County, Tennessee, public schools, read a story in her daughter's sixth-grade reading text that dealt with mental telepathy. As a self-described "born-again

Christian," Frost objected to any teaching of mental telepathy; she also objected to other themes in the book. She discussed her concerns with other parents, who joined with her in forming an organization called Citizens Organized for Better Schools (COBS).

Members of COBS made their objections to the Holt series known at school board meetings in the fall of 1983. On several occasions, Frost and other parents discussed their concerns with the middle school principal. Initially, the principal agreed to provide an alternative reading program for students whose parents objected to the Holt reading series. During the reading classes, these students left the regular classroom and worked on reading assignments from an older textbook series. Students in two elementary schools were also provided with alternative reading material.

However, in November 1983, the school board voted to eliminate all alternative reading programs and to require attendance at regular classes for all students. In response, students who had objected to the Holt series refused to read the texts or to attend classes where the series was used. Several students were subsequently suspended for brief periods. A number of them eventually withdrew from the public schools and enrolled in private Christian schools. Two students made special arrangements with the teacher in spite of the board's order: one was excused from reading the Holt series; the other read the series, but the teacher made notes on the student's worksheets indicating that the student did not have to believe the stories.

In December 1983, seven families filed suit against the Hawkins County Board of Education, alleging that compelled and repeated exposure to the Holt reading series burdened their rights under the free exercise clause of the First Amendment. Plaintiffs were supported by Beverly LaHaye's Concerned Women for America; People For the American Way created the People For Legal Defense Fund to secure legal counsel and pay fees associated with defense of the Hawkins County School District.

Eventually, a trial was held in the U.S. District Court for the

Eastern District of Tennessee. During the trial, Frost provided extensive testimony concerning her beliefs and her position about the Holt series. She testified that the word of God as found in the Christian Bible "is the totality of my beliefs."[45] The court noted that other members of their churches and even their pastors did not agree with the plaintiffs' position in the case.[46]

Frost testified that after spending more than two hundred hours reviewing the Holt series, she discovered numerous passages that offended her Christian beliefs. These passages fell into seventeen categories, including evolution, secular humanism, pacifism, "futuristic supernaturalism," magic, the occult, the improper use of imagination, false views of death, and teaching that "Man is God." As an example of this last category, she referred to a passage that described Leonardo da Vinci as the man with the creative mind that "came closest to the divine touch." Frost used a story called "A Visit to Mars" as an example of the "futuristic supernaturalism" category, stating that the story portrays thought transfer and telepathy in such a way that "it could be considered a scientific concept."[47]

Although the plaintiffs did not dispute the value of developing critical reading skills in students, Frost objected to many elements of the critical reading program used by the school. For example, she testified that the poem "Look at Anything" presented the idea that by using imagination, a child can become part of anything and thus understand it better. She stated that she felt it was an "occult practice" for children to use their imagination beyond the authority of the Bible, declaring that "our children's imagination has to be bounded."[48] She also testified that she did not want her children making decisions and judgments in areas where the Bible provided answers. She also strongly objected to language in the teacher's manuals for these reading texts. She stated that she felt the manuals encouraged teachers to present the ideas in the texts as "truth" rather than as ideas.

Another plaintiff witness was Bob Mozert, father of two students in the Hawkins County system. He echoed many of Frost's objections. In addition, he testified that he had found objectionable passages in the reading series that dealt with role reversal or role elimination, especially biographical material about women who had been recognized for achievements outside their home. He also objected to passages that he felt emphasized a one-world or planetary society.[49]

Both Frost and Mozert testified that they did not want their children exposed to other forms of religion or to the feelings, attitudes, and values of other students that contradicted their religious views without a statement that the other views were incorrect and that their views were correct. Frost stated that she objected to stories that developed "a religious tolerance that all religions are merely different roads to God. . . . We cannot be tolerant in that we accept other religious views on an equal basis with ours."[50] She also stated that she opposed books like *The Wizard of Oz* because they convey the idea that qualities such as courage, love, and wisdom can be learned and are not just God-given. Frost and Mozert both testified that after reading the entire Holt series, a child might adopt the views of a feminist, a humanist, a pacifist, an anti-Christian, a vegetarian, or an advocate of a "one-world government."[51]

In response, the school board contended that shaping the school curriculum to meet the desires of the plaintiffs would be an excessive state entanglement with religion that would violate the establishment clause. The board also argued that unless the religious beliefs that plaintiffs claimed had been burdened were central to their faith, the plaintiffs were not entitled to protection under the free exercise clause. The board also argued that exposure to the Holt series did not amount to teaching or indoctrination and that the schools were not inculcating religious doctrines. In addition, the board argued, the critical reading approach used in the schools furthered the role of the public schools in bringing together diverse ideas and people on common ground. It was vital, therefore, to have a uniform reading series in the schools.

The district court applied a free exercise test similar to the *Sherbert* v. *Verner* test in concluding that plaintiffs could opt out of the required reading series because their free exercise rights had been violated. The court granted an injunction against the reading requirement and awarded damages of more than fifty thousand dollars as reimbursement for legal costs and the cost of sending the plaintiffs' children to alternate schools. The school board appealed.

The U.S. Court of Appeals for the Sixth Circuit reversed the district court's decision, finding that the district court had erred in its application of the free exercise test to the facts in this case. In order to violate plaintiffs' free exercise liberties, the court wrote, the plaintiffs must be compelled to take some action that offends their religious beliefs. Simply being exposed to the diverse ideas found in the reading series did not amount to compulsion.

Frost, Mozert, and other witnesses had argued that *Barnette*'s prohibition against coercion applied in this case, but the appellate court distinguished the present situation from *Barnette*. The court reasoned that mere exposure to diverse or offensive ideas did not amount to the compulsion to "declare a belief" that *Barnette* forbade. The court also maintained that the purpose of the free exercise clause is to grant individuals protection from governmental coercion, not to grant individuals the power to dictate governmental policy. The court further noted *McCollum*'s declaration that accommodation of every objection to public education would ruin the schools.

In his majority opinion for the appellate court, Chief Judge Lively affirmed earlier Supreme Court decisions articulating the purpose of public schools as an educator of the values that are necessary to a democratic society. Foremost among these values is tolerance of diverse political and religious views, a tolerance the critical reading approach attempted to foster. The court described tolerance of divergent religious beliefs as "a civil tolerance, not a religious one. It does not require a person to accept any other religion as the equal of the one to which that person adheres. It merely requires a recognition that in a pluralistic society we must 'live and let live.'"[52]

The court went one step further and advocated more than mere tolerance, declaring that schools bring together "diverse and conflicting elements," a goal that the critical reading approach advanced. A concurring opinion by Judge Cornelia G. Kennedy wholeheartedly endorsed the critical reading program because it exposed students to a variety of ideas and encouraged them to form their own opinions concerning complex moral and ethical issues. Thus, the court viewed the contemplation and analysis of diverse ideas as an important part of the educational process. It concluded that the reading requirement did not create an unconstitutional burden under the free exercise clause. Contrary to the district court's opinion, the appellate court did not look favorably on allowing plaintiffs to opt out of the required reading series. Kennedy's concurring opinion maintained that this would violate the "compelling interest" that the school district had in avoiding religious divisiveness.

Smith v. Board of School Commissioners of Mobile County

While the Sixth Circuit Court of Appeals was deciding the *Mozert* case, the Eleventh Circuit was addressing a similar situation in *Smith* v. *Board of School Commissioners of Mobile County*. However, whereas the plaintiffs in *Mozert* challenged a required public school reading series on free exercise grounds, the plaintiffs in *Smith* challenged public school textbooks on establishment grounds.

The *Smith* case arose out of a series of school prayer cases in which plaintiffs had intervened. In 1982, the Alabama senate adopted legislation allowing prayer services in the public schools. Ishmael Jaffree, a parent of three children attending the Mobile County schools, filed suit against the school board, its superintendent, and various principals and teachers, seeking an injunction that would keep the defendants from holding prayer services or other religious observances in the public schools in keeping with the new Alabama legislation.

Douglas Smith, a teacher in the public schools, along with others, filed a motion to intervene in the case as defendants, claiming that their right to free exercise of religion would be violated if

Jaffree's injunction was granted. The motion to intervene was granted. Subsequently, more than six hundred additional names were added as intervenors along with Smith. The intervenors requested that, if Jaffree's injunction was granted, the injunction be expanded to preclude "the religions of secularism, humanism, evolution, materialism, agnosticism, atheism, and others," which they claimed had been established in the public schools.[53]

The District Court for the Southern District of Alabama upheld the constitutionality of the prayer statutes. However, the Eleventh Circuit Court of Appeals ruled that the statutes were unconstitutional. The Supreme Court affirmed this decision.[54] District Court Chief Judge William Brevard Hand had maintained jurisdiction with regard to the claims made by Smith and the other intervenors that the religion of secular humanism was unconstitutionally established in the public schools. Hand invited the parties to submit pleadings and subsequently reorganized the case. The original plaintiff, Jaffree, withdrew, and Smith and the other intervenors became the plaintiffs. (Pat Robertson's National Legal Foundation supported the plaintiffs; People For the American Way was called in to aid the defense.[55])

Smith and the other plaintiffs asserted that the religion of secular humanism was established in the Mobile County public schools and was being unconstitutionally advanced, and that the schools unconstitutionally inhibited Christianity and excluded from the curriculum "the existence, history, contributions and role of Christianity in the United States and the world."[56] These complaints focused on six home economics textbooks and thirty-nine history and social studies textbooks adopted by the Alabama State Board of Education and used by the Mobile County elementary and secondary schools.

Smith and other plaintiffs testified extensively, detailing their specific objections to the textbooks and to the overall educational philosophy of the public schools. Among their many objections was the complaint that secular humanism was being advanced in the schools by teaching values clarification, by teaching that there are no moral absolutes, by leaving God out of classroom discussions and instead focusing on man and the self as the basis of morality, and by specific antitheistic teaching. The plaintiffs submitted extensive exhibits of specific passages in textbooks to which they objected. These examples were categorized by plaintiffs as follows: "examples of anti-theistic teaching," "subjective and personal values without an external standard of right and wrong," "hedonistic, pleasure, need-satisfaction motivation," and "anti-parental, anti-family values."[57] Plaintiffs also claimed that their children were severely affected by repeated exposure to the textbooks and were upset about the obvious differences between the values advanced at school and those advanced at home. Parents testified that the school teaching had the effect of making their children turn outside the family for solutions to problems and that, each day, they had to reeducate their children after they returned home from school.

In response to plaintiffs' allegations, school board representatives contended that textbooks were selected by a textbook selection committee only after a lengthy process, during which some four thousand volumes were reviewed covering the various areas of education. Defendants maintained that the state had no antagonistic or ideological agenda against any religion in any of its textbooks, that the curriculum had a purely secular purpose, that the state had a compelling interest in educating the public in the least obtrusive manner, and, further, that nothing in the curriculum compelled students to believe the material presented to the exclusion of their fundamentalist Christian beliefs.

The school board representatives acknowledged that the textbooks did not appropriately reference the important contributions of religion to the development of the United States. They agreed that this omission should be corrected, but maintained that it did not create a burden on plantiff's free exercise right.

Defendants asserted that attempting to accommodate every objection on religious grounds would severely limit the state's ability to develop an educationally sound curriculum, and that the free exercise clause does not prohibit the state from using textbooks merely because they contain ideas that are contrary to someone's religious beliefs. Defendants also maintained that use of the textbooks met the *Lemon* test's criteria, and that therefore the school board had not violated the establishment clause.

Writing for the district court, Judge Hand concluded that secular humanism is a religion and that the challenged textbooks unconstitutionally advanced secular humanism in violation of the establishment clause. He granted an injunction to prohibit the further use of the books except for one text.[58]

In August 1987, the Eleventh Circuit Court, in a unanimous opinion, reversed Judge Hand's ruling. The court applied *Epperson*'s standard justifying court involvement in school matters when basic constitutional values are "directly and sharply implicate[d]." However, the court distinguished the facts at hand from *Epperson* (contrary to the district court's decision) in ruling on the issue of the omission from the texts of Christianity's role in history. The court reasoned that selecting a book that omits a topic for secular reasons, as the school had done in this case, was quite different from *requiring* the omission because it conflicts with a specific religious belief, as in *Epperson*.

Echoing the *Grove* decision, the Court cited *McCollum* in writing that the state does not have an interest in protecting religions from views that might offend them. It concluded that the district court had erred in ruling that the books advanced secular humanism and inhibited theistic religion, noting that governmental action must amount to an endorsement of religion in order to violate the First Amendment. The court thus concluded that the books did not violate the establishment clause, reasoning that this finding was proper because, even if secular humanism is a religion, the textbooks were religiously neutral and none of the books conveyed a message of governmental approval or disapproval of secular humanism, Christianity, or any other theistic religion. In 1988, the Supreme

Court refused to review the appellate court's decision. (It is interesting to note that notwithstanding the court's decision in this case, a textbook review undertaken by People For the American Way concluded that the texts too often ignored the contributions to history of Christianity and religious faith. See Chapter Four.)

In conclusion, the *Grove*, *Mozert*, and *Smith* cases were decided by the appellate courts on similar philosophical grounds. In applying the free exercise and establishment clause tests, each of these courts started with the assumption that state action is appropriately secular and therefore religiously neutral. This assumption had the effect of granting more weight to the actions of local school boards. The appellate court decisions in these cases made it clear that action by public school officials will have to amount to outright compulsion to declare religious beliefs, or blatant condemnation or endorsement of religion, to be considered unconstitutional.

The higher courts clearly oppose efforts to ban books—whether the banning is attempted by school boards or requested by parents. It can logically be concluded that the courts hold to a view of the public schools as places where students should virtually be required to explore and consider a multitude of opinions and ideas. The courts would no doubt take Brennan's argument in *Pico* one step further and grant public schools the same special status as libraries, viewing them as "the principal locus" of the freedom "to inquire, to study and to evaluate, to gain new maturity and understanding."[59]

These cases articulate the fundamental rights that the courts must balance: the right of local school boards to choose curricular materials versus the First Amendment liberties of public school students.

Appendix B

Resources

Organizations Supporting Intellectual Freedom

American Library Association (ALA)
Office for Intellectual Freedom
50 E. Huron Street
Chicago, IL 60611
(312) 944–6780

The ALA's Office for Intellectual Freedom publishes the *Newsletter on Intellectual Freedom* ($40/yr.). Each issue is an excellent, detailed summary of a wide variety of controversies around the country dealing with a range of intellectual freedom concerns—including student press, obscenity, and challenges in schools and libraries. Each issue of the newsletter also includes updates on relevant court cases.

The ALA also publishes the *Banned Books Resource Guide*. The 1995 issue of this annual publication lists 164 books that were challenged or banned between March 1994 and March 1995. It is an excellent resource, which also lists 1,184 books, textbooks, and plays that have been challenged or banned in schools and libraries around the country "throughout the ages." A majority of the resources listed have been challenged during the past ten to fifteen years.

Citizens Project
P.O. Box 2085
Colorado Springs, CO 80901
(719) 520–9899

Citizens Project describes itself as "a grassroots organization in the Pikes Peak region dedicated to upholding the traditional American values of pluralism, freedom of religion, and separation of church and state." It publishes *Freedom Watch*, a bimonthly newspaper that reports on issues and events related to the relationship between church and state, particularly those in the Colorado Springs area. Colorado Springs is home to Focus on the Family and a number of other active, conservative Christian organizations.

International Reading Association (IRA)
P.O. Box 8139
Newark, DE 19714–8139
(302) 731–1600

The IRA is a nonprofit organization dedicated to promoting literacy worldwide. It distributes a wealth of materials and position statements concerning protection of the freedom to read and learn.

National Coalition Against Censorship (NCAC)
275 7th Avenue
New York, NY 10001
(212) 807-NCAC

True to its name, NCAC is a coalition of forty-five educational, religious, and community organizations including the American Association of School Administrators, the American Federation of Teachers, the American Jewish Congress, the American Society of Journalists and Authors, and the National Council of Teachers of English.

National Council of Teachers of English (NCTE) and
Support for the Learning and Teaching of English (SLATE)
1111 W. Kenyon Road
Urbana, IL 61801–1096

Like other professional organizations, NCTE and SLATE have a wide variety of helpful resources. One noteworthy publication is *The Students' Right to Read* (1982), which offers guidelines for developing reconsideration policies in schools.

People For the American Way (PFAW)
National Headquarters
2000 M Street, Suite 400
Washington, D.C. 20036
(202) 467–4999

PFAW is the most active national organization involved in countering attacks on public education. Offices are located in Los Angeles, California; Boulder, Colorado; Indian Rocks Beach, Florida; Raleigh, North Carolina; and New York, New York. PFAW publishes numerous materials dealing with intellectual freedom and First Amendment liberties. Among these are *Protecting the Freedom to Learn: A Citizen's Guide* and an annual state-by-state report called *Attacks on the Freedom to Learn*, which documents challenges to educational materials and practices across the country each academic year.

For Information on Teaching About Religion

The Association for Supervision and Curriculum Development (ASCD)
1250 North Pitt Street
Alexandria, VA 22314

See in particular its volume, *Religion in the Curriculum*, 1987.

The California Three R's Project
Nicholas Piediscalzi, Project Director
777 Camino Pescadero
Isla Vista, CA 93117

The Three R's Project works to build consensus within school districts and communities on religious diversity in schools. The project is rooted in the three R's of the First Amendment (often called "civic ground rules"): rights, responsibilities, and respect.

The Freedom Forum First Amendment Center
Vanderbilt University
Charles Haynes, Visiting Professional Scholar
1207 18th Avenue South
Nashville, TN 37212

Haynes and the center are widely acknowledged as leaders in helping educators understand and implement the First Amendment's religious liberty principles. A number of resource materials are available on how to teach about religion while honoring diverse expressions of religion in the classroom. Among these materials are *Finding Common Ground: A First Amendment Guide to Religion and Public Education*, edited by Charles Haynes, and *Living with Our Deepest Differences: Religious Liberty in a Pluralistic Society*, a social studies curriculum. To order, contact John Leach. The Freedom Forum is one of the organizations that coauthored the statement *Religious Liberty, Public Education, and the Future of American Democracy: A Statement of Principles*.

For more than two decades, the National Council on Religion and Public Education (NCRPE) addressed the issue of religion and public education. When NCRPE dissolved in 1994, much of its responsibilities were taken over by three entities:

Religion and Public Education Resource Center
Robert Benoit
Butte County Office of Education
5 County Center Drive
Oroville, CA 95965
(916) 538–7847

The NCRPE's rich resources relevant to teaching about religion can now be accessed by contacting the Religion and Public Education Resource Center. A list of materials and their prices is available. Those who have developed curricular materials they would like to share can contact Bruce Grelle, the resource center's director, at the Department of Religious Studies, California State University at Chico, Chico, CA 95929–0740; (916) 898–4739.

ASCD Religion and Public Education Network
c/o Dr. Austin Creel
Department of Religion
University of Florida
P.O. Box 117410
Gainesville, FL 32611–7410

Creel, who serves as facilitator of the network, is a former president of NCRPE. The network is concerned with teaching about religion as well as with the broader range of issues involved in religion and public education. According to Creel, the *Network Newsletter* (formerly the NCRPE newsletter) is a way for teachers to exchange news and reports on experiences in teaching, the use of materials, and course projects.

Religion and Education
c/o Webster University
470 E. Lockwood
St. Louis, MO 63119–3194

The *Religion and Education* journal (formerly NCRPE's *Religion and Public Education* journal) is based at Webster University. The journal is published three times a year.

Character Education Resources

Character Education Partnership (CEP)
809 Franklin St.
Alexandria, VA 22314–4105
(703) 739–9515

According to its literature, CEP "is dedicated to developing civic virtue and moral character in our nation's youth as one means of creating a more compassionate and responsible society."

How to Establish a Values Education Program in Your School: A Handbook for School Administrators

This handbook may be ordered from Phyllis A. Bailey, Office of Planning, Baltimore County Public Schools, 6901 N. Charles Street, Towson, MD 21204.

Teaching Values and Ethics: Problems and Solutions

This is a critical issues report by Kristen J. Amundson (1991), available from the American Association of School Administrators, Publication Sales, 1801 North Moore Street, Arlington, VA 22209–9988.

Personal Responsibility Education Process Handbook and *Resources for Educators and Communities*

These volumes are available from PREP, The Network for Educational Development, 13157 Olive Spur Road, St. Louis, MO 63141

For the Conservative Christian World View

Although there are other organizations active in school issues, the groups listed here represent the range of concerns most often voiced by school critics.

National Association of Christian Educators/Citizens for Excellence in Education (NACE/CEE)
Dr. Robert L. Simonds, President
Box 3200
Costa Mesa, CA 92628
(714) 251–9333

NACE/CEE publishes a monthly *President's Report* as well as the quarterly *Education Newsline*. It has also published a number of books, including *Reinventing America's Schools*, vols. 1–3; *A Guide to the Public Schools*; and *How to Elect Christians to Public Office*. NACE/CEE is perhaps the most active, self-proclaimed "traditionalist" Christian group involved in challenges to books and educational techniques across the country.

The Eagle Forum
Box 618
Alton, IL 62002
(618) 462–5415

The Eagle Forum and its related organization, the Eagle Forum Education and Legal Defense Fund, publish the monthly *Education Reporter* and *The Phyllis Schlafly Report*. Phyllis Schlafly and the Eagle Forum are involved in a variety of national issues related to the family, including perceived problems in schools.

Focus on the Family
James Dobson, President
Colorado Springs, CO 80995–0351
(719) 531–3400

Focus on the Family, "dedicated to strengthening the home," is one of the most visible conservative Christian organizations in the country. It publishes *Teachers in Focus* and *Citizen* magazines and has resources available on a wide range of topics that affect the family.

The Mel Gablers
Educational Research Analysts
P.O. Box 7518
Longview, TX 75607–9986
(903) 753–5993

The Gablers claim to have "the world's largest textbook review library." Their work is a vital resource for many religiously conservative groups. The Gablers are the authors, with J. Hefley, of *What Are They Teaching Our Children?* (1985), a widely touted book that is highly critical of the alleged secular humanistic influence on American public education.

Content Learning Goals

Geography learning goals can be found in *Geography for Life: National Geography Standards* (1994), authored by the Geography Education Standards Project and available from National Geographic Research and Exploration, Washington, D.C.

History learning goals can be found in *National Standards for History for Grades K–4: Expanding Children's World in Time and Space* (1994); *National Standards for United States History: Exploring the American Experience* (1994); and *National Standards for World History: Exploring Paths to the Present* (1994). All three of these documents are authored and published by the National Center for History in Schools, Los Angeles, California.

Civic learning goals can be found in *National Standards for Civics and Government* (1994), authored and published by the Center for Civics Education, Calahasas, California.

Language arts learning goals can be found in the *Incomplete Work of the Task Forces of the Standards Project for English Language Arts* (draft, February 1994), authored by the Standards Project for the English Language Arts and available from the National Council of Teachers of English, Urbana, Illinois.

Physical education learning goals can be found in *Content Standards and Assessment Guide for School Physical Education* (draft, 1994), authored by the Standards and Assessment Task Force and available from the National Association for Sports and Physical Education, Boston, Virginia.

Science learning goals can be found in *Benchmarks for Science Literacy* (1993), authored by project 2061, American Association for the Advancement of Science, and published by Oxford University Press, New York; and in *Scope, Sequence, and Coordination of Secondary School Science, Vol. 1. The Content Core: A Guide for Curriculum Designers* (1993), authored and published by the National Science Teachers Association, Washington, D.C.

Social studies learning goals can be found in *Expectations for Excellence: Curriculum Standards for Social Studies* (1994), authored and published by the National Council for Social Studies, Washington, D.C.

Learning outcomes in dance, music, theater, and the visual arts can be found in *Dance, Music, Theatre, Visual Arts: What Every Young American Should Know and Be Able to Do in the Arts* (1994), authored by the National Standards for Arts Education and published by the Music Educators National Conference, Reston, Virginia.

Finally, for a comprehensive discussion of national efforts to set learning goals in the various content areas, see "Struggling for Standards," a special issue of *Education Week*, April 12, 1995.

Notes

Chapter One

1. People For the American Way, *Attacks*, 1994, p. 5.
2. People For the American Way, "If We Take Our Freedoms for Granted," n.d.; People For the American Way, *Attacks*, 1991, p. 2.
3. People For the American Way, *Attacks*, 1993, p. 26. For example, PFAW participated in the 1987 *Mozert* v. *Hawkins County Board of Education* case and in the *Smith* v. *Board of School Commissioners of Mobile County* case, both of which are discussed in Appendix A of this book.
4. See for example, Hulsizer, *Protecting the Freedom to Learn*, p. 4; Podesta, "Foreword," pp. vii–xiv.
5. Harrington-Lueker, "Book Battles," p. 19.
6. Plato, *Republic*, 2:323.
7. See Yerby, "Toward Religious Neutrality," p. 899; Bryson and Detty, *Legal Aspects of Censorship*, pp. 35–36.
8. See Rippa, *Education in a Free Society*, p. 88.
9. Rippa, *Education in a Free Society*, p. 92.
10. Rippa, *Education in a Free Society*, pp. 91–93. Rippa quotes from Emerson, "Man the Reformer" (lecture read before the Mechanics' Apprentices' Library Association, Boston, Jan. 25, 1841), in *Nature, Addresses, and Lectures* (Boston: Houghton Mifflin, 1855), vol. 1, p. 237.

11. Rippa, *Education in a Free Society*, pp. 98–99.

12. Larson, "Constitutional Challenges," p. 72, quoting from Horace Mann's annual report to the Massachusetts Board of Education in 1848.

13. Rippa, *Education in a Free Society*, pp. 104–105.

14. Larson, "Constitutional Challenges," pp. 72–73; Yerby, "Toward Religious Neutrality," p. 899.

15. Rippa, *Education in a Free Society*, p. 159.

16. See Rippa, *Education in a Free Society*, pp. 159–160.

17. See Rippa's discussion of Dewey's background and philosophy in *Education in a Free Society*, pp. 183–191.

18. See Rippa, *Education in a Free Society*, pp. 88–93.

19. Lee, "*Smith* v. *Board of School Commissioners*," p. 592, note 5, citing D. Purpel and K. Ryan, "Moral Education: What Is It and Where Are We?" in D. Purpel and K. Ryan (eds.), *Moral Education . . . It Comes with the Territory* (Berkeley, Calif.: McCutchan, 1976), p. 4, note 3, and Hafen, "Developing Student Expression Through Institutional Authority: Public Schools as Mediating Structures," *Ohio State Law Journal*, 1987, 48, p. 688, note 21.

20. Bryson and Detty, *Legal Aspects of Censorship*, p. 48; see also Provenzo, *Religious Fundamentalism*, p. 14.

21. Bryson and Detty, *Legal Aspects of Censorship*, pp. 51–53.

22. *Engel* v. *Vitale; Abington School District* v. *Schempp; Epperson* v. *Arkansas*.

Chapter Two

1. Simonds, *How to Elect Christians to Public Office*, p. 65.

2. Simonds, *How to Elect Christians to Public Office*, p. 7.

3. Simonds, *President's Report*, Apr. 1995, p. 3; Simonds, *How to Elect Christians to Public Office*, p. 7.

4. Citizens for Excellence in Education, Public School Awareness Committee, Audio Tape Series, 1990, Tape 1: "What a PSA Committee Is and Can Do," side 2.

5. See Simonds, *President's Report*, Mar. 1991, Jan. 1992, Jan. 1995.
6. Simonds, *How to Elect Christians to Public Office*, p. 34.
7. J. Green, *The Encyclopedia of Censorship*, p. 84.
8. Eagle Trust Fund, Introductory Letter, n.d. [1994].
9. See Schlafly, *Child Abuse*, p. 4.
10. P. Robertson, *The New Millennium*, jacket flap.
11. See Boston, *Out of Bondage*, p. 4.
12. Park, "Religious Right," pp. 5–11; Ostling, "Power, Glory and Politics," pp. 62–69.
13. People For the American Way, *Attacks*, 1992, p. 15.
14. See Christian Coalition, *Contract*, p. 4.
15. Dart, "Atmosphere of Alienation," pp. 212–213, citing *The Los Angeles Times*, March 4, 1988.
16. Gabler and Gabler, *What Are They Teaching Our Children?* p. 189.
17. Gabler and Gabler, "A Parent's Guide," p. 1; Gabler and Gabler, "How to Object to Textbooks."
18. Gabler and Gabler, Educational Research Analysts, Order Blank.
19. J. Green, *The Encyclopedia of Censorship*, p. 102.
20. As quoted in J. Green, *Encyclopedia of Censorship*, pp. 191–192.
21. Hadden and Swann, *Prime Time Preachers*, pp. 28–29.
22. *Focus on the Family* magazine, back cover, Oct. 1995; "The Chuck Baker Show."
23. *Focus on the Family* magazine, back cover, Oct. 1995; "The Chuck Baker Show."
24. *Focus on the Family* magazine, back cover, Oct. 1995; "The Chuck Baker Show."
25. See Castrone, "Focus on Family Founder."
26. See People For the American Way, "Focus on the Family"; People For the American Way, *Attacks*, 1994, p. 23; People For the American Way, "Coming to a Church Near You," pp. 2–3.
27. See Herrick, "Critic Calls."
28. Minnery, "'Watchdog' American Way"; Focus on the Family, Press Release, Apr. 30, 1993.

29. See Pelikan, "Fundamentalism and/or Orthodoxy?" p. 3.
30. Wilcox, *God's Warriors*, p. 3.
31. See Hadden and Shupe, *Televangelism*, p. 108; Pelikan, "Fundamentalism and/or Orthodoxy?" p. 3; Marsden, *Fundamentalism and American Culture*, pp. 118–123.
32. Cole, *History of Fundamentalism*, p. 34.
33. See Provenzo, *Religious Fundamentalism*, p. 1; Hadden and Shupe, *Televangelism*, p. 108; Wilcox, *God's Warriors*, p. 5.
34. *Scopes* v. *State of Tennessee*.
35. Larson, "Constitutional Challenges," pp. 73–74.
36. See Larson, "Constitutional Challenges," pp. 74–75; Marsden, *Fundamentalism and American Culture*, pp. 184–191.
37. See Marsden, *Fundamentalism and American Culture*, p. 188; Hadden and Shupe, *Televangelism*, pp. 110–113.
38. Wilcox, *God's Warriors*, pp. 9–10.
39. Wilcox, *God's Warriors*, p. 11.
40. See Jenkinson, *Censors in the Classroom*, pp. 1–27.
41. Jenkinson, *Censors in the Classroom*, p. 29, citing two 1978 newspaper articles.
42. See Wilcox, *God's Warriors*, pp. 11–12, citing Wald, *Religion and Politics in the United States* (New York: St. Martin's Press, 1987).

Chapter Three

1. See for example, Gabler and Gabler, *What Are They Teaching Our Children?* pp. 116–121; Simonds, *How to Elect Christians to Public Office*, pp. 34–35; and Buehrer, *New Age Masquerade*, pp. 70–82.
2. Simonds, *A Guide to the Public Schools*, p. 5.
3. P. Robertson, *The New Millennium*, p. 163.
4. Provenzo, *Religious Fundamentalism*, p. 34, citing J. C. Hefley, *Are Textbooks Harming Your Children? Norma and Mel Gabler Take Action and Show You How!* (Milford, Mich.: Mott Media, 1979), p. 42.

5. *Mozert* v. *Hawkins County Board of Education (Public Schools)*.
6. Sommer, *Schools in Crisis*, p. 250.
7. Gabler and Gabler, *What Are They Teaching Our Children?* p. 33.
8. Baer, *Inside the New Age Nightmare*, p. 84.
9. Groothuis, *Unmasking the New Age*, p. 40.
10. Provenzo, *Religious Fundamentalism*, pp. xii–xiii, citing K. Woodward with E. Saholz, "The Right's New Bogeyman," *Newsweek*, July 6, 1981, p. 48.
11. Rogers, *Banned!* p. 86, quoting Michael Farris, attorney for the plaintiffs in *Grove* v. *Mead School District;* Bryson and Detty, *Legal Aspects of Censorship*, p. 66, quoting Mel and Norma Gabler.
12. Gabler and Gabler, *What Are They Teaching Our Children?* p. 44.
13. Provenzo, *Religious Fundamentalism*, p. xiii, citing T. LaHaye, *The Battle for the Mind* (Old Tappan, N.J.: Fleming H. Revell, 1980), p. 19.
14. Bryson and Detty, *Legal Aspects of Censorship*, p. 67, citing *Torcaso* v. *Watkins; Smith* v. *Board of School Commissioners of Mobile County*, 655 F. Supp. 939, 944–955 (S.D. Ala. 1987); Bryson and Detty, p. 69, citing R. T. Rhode, "Is Secular Humanism the Religion of the Public Schools?" in *Dealing with Censorship*, ed. J. E. Davis (Urbana, Ill.: National Council of Teachers of English, 1979), pp. 122–123.
15. Provenzo, *Religious Fundamentalism*, p. xiii, quoting H. Duncan, *Secular Humanism: The Most Dangerous Religion in America* (Lubbock, Tex.: Missionary Crusader, 1980), p. 4.
16. See Simonds, *How to Elect Christians to Public Office*, p. 34.
17. P. Robertson, *The New Millennium*, pp. 163, 158, 162.
18. Gabler and Gabler, *What Are They Teaching Our Children?* p. 28.
19. Gabler and Gabler, *What Are They Teaching Our Children?* p. 26.
20. P. Robertson, *The New Millennium*, p. 167.
21. Quoted in Hadden and Shupe, *Televangelism*, p. 22.
22. P. Robertson, *The New Millennium*, pp. 166–169; see also pp. 170–175.

23. P. Robertson, *The New Millennium*, p. 74.

24. Marrs, *Dark Secrets*, p. viii.

25. See Hunt, *Peace, Prosperity*, pp. 64–72, specifically pp. 64 and 72.

26. Hunt, *Peace, Prosperity*, p. 66.

27. Hunt, *Peace, Prosperity*, p. 96.

28. Marrs, *Dark Secrets*, p. 262.

29. Cumbey, *Hidden Dangers*, p. 20.

30. Cumbey, *Hidden Dangers*, p. 20.

31. See Michaelsen, *Like Lambs to the Slaughter*, foreword by Hal Lindsey.

32. See Michaelsen, *Like Lambs to the Slaughter*, pp. 33–48; quote is from p. 34.

33. See for example, P. Robertson, *The New Millennium*, pp. 173–175; Citizens for Excellence in Education, Public School Awareness Committee, Audio Tape Series, Tape 2: "What Are They Teaching Our Children?"; and Simonds, *President's Report*, Mar. 1995.

34. Citizens for Excellence in Education, Public School Awareness Committee, "Questions People or Media Ask," in *PSA Committee Workbook*, 1990, p. D7.

35. See Gabler and Gabler, *What Are They Teaching Our Children?* pp. 115–128.

36. P. Robertson, *The New Millennium*, pp. 174–175.

37. Simonds, Fund-Raising Letter, May 6, 1991.

38. Gabler and Gabler, *What Are They Teaching Our Children?* pp. 110, 185.

39. Schlafly, *Child Abuse*, p. 12.

40. Buehrer, *New Age Masquerade*, p. 107.

41. Groothuis, *Unmasking the New Age*, p. 33.

42. Groothuis, *Unmasking the New Age*, p. 33.

43. Groothuis, *Unmasking the New Age*, p. 35.

Chapter Four

1. See "In Their Own Words."
2. Pliska and McQuaide, "Pennsylvania's Battle," p. 66.
3. Jones, "Stretching the Meaning of the Hatch Amendment," p. 27.
4. The Protection of Pupil Rights Amendment, 20 U.S. Code, section 1232h, is reprinted in Schlafly, *Child Abuse*.
5. Jones, p. 27.
6. Citizens for Excellence in Education, Public School Awareness Committee, *PSA Committee Workbook*, p. 2.
7. Simonds, *How to Elect Christians to Public Office*; Gabler and Gabler, *What Are They Teaching Our Children?*
8. Simonds, *How to Elect Christians to Public Office*, p. i.
9. Simonds, *How to Elect Christians to Public Office*, pp. iv, 4, 15.
10. Simonds, *How to Elect Christians to Public Office*, p. 8.
11. Simonds, *How to Elect Christians to Public Office*, p. 11.
12. Simonds, *How to Elect Christians to Public Office*, p. 4.
13. Citizens for Excellence in Education, Public School Awareness Committee, Audio Tape Series, Tape 1: "What a PSA Committee Is and Can Do."
14. Citizens for Excellence in Education, Public School Awareness Committee, *PSA Committee Workbook*, pp. 25–28.
15. Citizens for Excellence in Education, Public School Awareness Committee, *PSA Committee Workbook*, p. 29.
16. Citizens for Excellence in Education, Public School Awareness Committee, *PSA Committee Workbook*, p. 31.
17. Citizens for Excellence in Education, Public School Awareness Committee, *PSA Committee Workbook*, pp. 42–43.
18. Simonds, *How to Elect Christians to Public Office*, p. 8.
19. Simonds, *How to Elect Christians to Public Office*, pp. 30–31.
20. Simonds, *President's Report*, Dec. 1993, p. 2; Simonds, *President's Report*, Apr. 1994, p. 4.

21. "Christian Coalition Starts School Board Seminars," p. 2.
22. See People For the American Way, "If We Take Our Freedoms for Granted," n.d.; Hulsizer, *Protecting the Freedom to Learn*; People For the American Way, *Attacks*, 1993, p. 8; People For the American Way, *Attacks*, 1994, pp. 26–28.
23. As quoted in Provenzo, *Religious Fundamentalism*, p. 18.
24. Marty, "Profile of Norman Lear," p. 55.
25. Lear, "Search for Stable Values," pp. 41–45.
26. Hadden and Shupe, *Televangelism*, p. 67.
27. Hulsizer, *Protecting the Freedom to Learn*, p. 14.
28. Collins, "People For Action Fund," p. 3.
29. "Fighting Dragons in Jeffco," p. 40A; "A School Race Blows Smoke," p. 44A.
30. Morson, "'Religious Right' Claim," p. 21A.

Chapter Five

1. Simonds, "A Plea for the Children," pp. 12–15.
2. "SAT Scores Plunge Again," p. 1.
3. Berliner, "Educational Reform in an Era of Disinformation," p. 55, citing *Education Week*, Feb. 27, 1991.
4. Dow, *Schoolhouse Politics*, p. 243.
5. Quoted in Bennett, *The De-Valuing of America*, p. 42.
6. Carson, Huelskamp, and Woodall, *Perspectives on Education*.
7. Berliner, "Educational Reform in an Era of Disinformation," p. 7.
8. Berliner and Biddle, *The Manufactured Crisis*, p. 43, citing J. R. Flynn, "Massive IQ Gains in 14 Nations: What IQ Tests Really Measure," *Psychological Bulletin*, 1987, *101*, 171–191.
9. Berliner and Biddle, *The Manufactured Crisis*, pp. 43–44.
10. Berliner, "Educational Reform in an Era of Disinformation," p. 11.
11. Ravitch and Finn, *What Do Our 17-Year-Olds Know?* p. 7.
12. Hirsch, *Cultural Literacy*, p. 4.

13. Bennett, *De-Valuing of America*, p. 311.

14. Berliner, "Educational Reform in an Era of Disinformation," p. 12.

15. Carson, Huelskamp, and Woodall, *Perspectives on Education*, p. 44.

16. Carson, Huelskamp, and Woodall, *Perspectives on Education*, p. 46.

17. Carson, Huelskamp, and Woodall, *Perspectives on Education*, pp. 46–47.

18. Ravitch and Finn, *What Do Our 17-Year-Olds Know?* pp. 263–277.

19. Ravitch and Finn, *What Do Our 17-Year-Olds Know?* p. 1.

20. Whittington, "What Have 17-Year-Olds Known?" p. 763.

21. Berliner, "Educational Reform in an Era of Disinformation," p. 19.

22. Berliner, "Educational Reform in an Era of Disinformation," p. 17.

23. National Education Goals Panel, *Promises to Keep*, p. C(L)-5.

24. "National Educational Goals," *Noteworthy*, p. i.

25. For a description of the efforts in specific content areas, see Kendall and Marzano, *Systematic Identification*.

26. National Council of Teachers of Mathematics, *Curriculum and Evaluation Standards*, p. iv.

27. J. Anderson, *Cognitive Psychology and Its Implications*.

28. See Good, "How Teachers' Expectations Affect Results," pp. 25–32; Good and Brophy, "Behavioral Expression," pp. 616–624; Carkhuff, *Art of Helping*.

29. Hunter, *Rx*; Kerman, Kimball, and Martin, *Teacher Expectation*; L. Anderson, Evertson, and Emmer, "Dimensions in Classroom Management," pp. 343–356.

30. For example, J. Anderson, *Architecture of Cognition*, 1983; J. Anderson, *Cognitive Psychology and Its Implications*.

31. See Sheikh, *Imagery*.

32. C. A. Anderson and Bowman, "Education and Economic Modernization," pp. 37–58.

33. See Marzano and Paynter, *New Approaches to Literacy*.

34. Pearson and Stephens, "Learning About Literacy," p. 4.

35. Gough, "One Second of Reading," pp. 331–358.
36. Goodman, "Reading," p. 2.
37. Pearson and Stephens, "Learning About Literacy," p. 8.
38. Goodman, *What's Whole in Whole Language?* p. 26.
39. Calkins, *Art of Teaching Writing*; Atwell, *In the Middle*; Graves, *Writing*; Hansen, *When Writers Read*.
40. For a review of the research on whole language versus skills instruction, see *Educational Psychologist*, 1994, *29*(4), entire issue.
41. Mullis, Owen, and Phillips, *America's Challenge*, p. 16.
42. National Center for Education Statistics, *Can Students Do Mathematical Problem Solving?* p. 116.
43. National Center for Education Statistics, *Can Students Do Mathematical Problem Solving?* p. 121.
44. For a review, see Costa, "Teacher Behaviors."
45. Dewey, *Democracy and Education*, p. 6.
46. Education Policies Commission, *Central Purpose of American Education*, pp. 14–15.
47. See Resnick, *Education and Learning to Think*.
48. For a discussion see Sternberg, "Nothing Fails Like Success," pp. 142–155; Sternberg, *Understanding and Increasing Intelligence*; Sternberg, *Beyond IQ*, 1984; Sternberg, *Beyond IQ*, 1985.
49. Marzano, "Lessons from the Field," pp. 44–50.

Chapter Six

1. O'Neil, "Aiming for New Outcomes," p. 6.
2. Quoted in O'Neil, "Aiming for New Outcomes," pp. 6–7.
3. Spady, "Organizing for Results," pp. 4–8.
4. For a discussion of the problem with Spady's transformational approach, see Manno, *Outcomes-Based Education*.
5. LaHaye, "Radical Redefinition," pp. 28–29.
6. "What's Wrong with Outcome-Based Education?" pp. 1–3.

7. Chion-Kenney, "What's in a Name?" p. 14.
8. Metz, "Mother's Cry for Help," p. 1.
9. For a discussion of the differences between whole language and the "look-say" method, see M. J. Adams, *Beginning to Read*.
10. *Phyllis Schlafly Report*, Aug. 1991, p. 3.
11. Gabler and Gabler, *What Are They Teaching Our Children?* pp. 108–112.
12. P. Robertson, *The New Millennium*, p. 171.
13. Hudson, *Reinventing America's Schools*, vol. 2, pp. 16–18.
14. People For the American Way, *Attacks*, 1991, p. 8.
15. People For the American Way, "Challenges to the *Impressions* Series."
16. See *Brown* v. *Woodland Joint Unified School District*, CA 92–15772.
17. Harrington-Lueker, "Books from Hell," p. 20; Simonds, *President's Report*, Apr. 1991, p. 1. For other, similar criticisms of *Impressions*, see also Winn, "What's New in School?"; Harrington-Lueker, "Book Battles"; and Mendenhall, "Nightmarish Textbooks," pp. 1–7. See also People For the American Way, "Controversy over the *Impressions* Reading Series," pp. 1–3.
18. People For the American Way, "Controversy over the Impressions Reading Series," p. 4.
19. Simonds, *President's Report*, Apr. 1991; Provenzo, *Religious Fundamentalism*, p. 40.
20. Marzano, "History and Foundations of the *Tactics* Program."
21. Georges, "School Board Presentation." See also Caldemeyer, *The Trust Me Express*, and Collier, "Schools 'Alter' Children." For similar attacks on the *Tactics* program, see Viadero, "Parents in S.C. Attack," p. 8; Sponhour, "Thinking-Skills Program," p. 1B.
22. Georges, "School Board Presentation," p. 6.
23. Georges, "School Board Presentation," pp. 1–8.
24. Caldemeyer, *Trust Me Express*, pp. 24–27.

25. Gabler and Gabler, "Drugging of Students."
26. Simonds, *President's Report*, Oct. 1993, p. 3.
27. Torrance, "Teaching Creative and Gifted Learners," pp. 630–647.
28. Crabbe, "Creating a Brighter Future," pp. 2–11.
29. Gourley, "Adapting the Varsity Sports Model," pp. 164–166.
30. Michaelsen, *Like Lambs to the Slaughter*, p. 49.
31. Michaelsen, *Like Lambs to the Slaughter*, pp. 58–59.
32. Michaelsen, *Like Lambs to the Slaughter*, p. 51.
33. Michaelsen, *Like Lambs to the Slaughter*, p. 53.
34. Marrs, *Dark Secrets*, p. 100.
35. Edens, *Demystification*. Much of this research has been summarized by Kosslyn, "Stalking the Mental Image," pp. 22–28.
36. Edens, *Demystification*, p. 3.
37. J. Anderson, *Cognitive Psychology and Its Implications*; Holley and Dansereau, "Networking," pp. 81–108; Shepard, "Mental Image," pp. 125–137.
38. Shepard, "Mental Image," p. 126.
39. Marzano and Arredondo, *Tactics for Thinking*.
40. Buehrer, *New Age Masquerade*, pp. 89–90.
41. Buehrer, *New Age Masquerade*, p. 93.
42. Zimmerman, "Self-Regulated Learning," p. 3.
43. Buehrer, "Self-Esteem and Mediocrity," p. 3.
44. Adams, *The Biblical View of Self-Esteem*, pp. 29–31.
45. Adams, *The Biblical View of Self-Esteem*, p. 57.
46. Adams, *The Biblical View of Self-Esteem*, p. 88.
47. Adams, *The Biblical View of Self-Esteem*, p. 108.
48. "Censoring a Dragon," p. 6.
49. "Children Hypnotized at School," p. 12.
50. "Children Hypnotized at School," p. 12.
51. See "What is *Quest?*"

52. Ebert, "One Man's Bonfire," pp. 12–13.
53. Ebert, "Parents Split," p. 1.
54. Ebert, "Parents Split," p. 2.

Chapter Seven

1. Rogers, *Banned!* p. 15, articulated many of the controversies over public school materials in this way.
2. Doyle, *Banned Books Resource Guide*.
3. People For the American Way, *Attacks*, 1994, p. 10.
4. Krug, *Newsletter on Intellectual Freedom*, Sept. 1994, pp. 148–149.
5. Krug, Letter, 1995.
6. Doyle, *Banned Books Resource Guide*, p. 5.
7. S. Smith, "More Info on Dr. Seuss," p. 7.
8. Hentoff, "Texas Town," p. 42A.
9. Dobson, Monthly Letter, Apr. 1994, p. 2.
10. Dobson, Monthly Letter, Apr. 1994, p. 2.
11. Piepenburg, "How to 'Create' Science," p. 10.
12. Chong, Ham, and Morris, *What **Really** Happened to the Dinosaurs?* p. 19.
13. Quoted in Provenzo, *Religious Fundamentalism*, p. 56.
14. Quote from Gilkey, *Creationism on Trial*, p. 139. See also Geisler, *Creator in the Courtroom;* LaFollette, *Creationism, Science, and the Law*.
15. See Irons, *Brennan vs. Rehnquist*, p. 132.
16. Simonds, *President's Report*, Feb. 1991, p. 1.
17. Simonds, *President's Report*, Feb. 1991, p. 1, quoting *New York Times* article, Jan. 3, 1991.
18. "Evolution Under Fire," p. 2.
19. See "Creationism in the Springs," p. 1.
20. "Teacher Stands up Against Censorship," p. 1; see also Carter, *Culture of Disbelief*, p. 157.

GOVERNORS STATE UNIVERSITY
UNIVERSITY PARK
IL 60466

21. See "Creationism in Public Schools," p. 2.
22. J. Anderson, *Cognitive Psychology and Its Implications*.
23. Tye, "Introduction," p. 5.
24. Buehrer, *New Age Masquerade*, p. 29.
25. Buehrer, *New Age Masquerade*, p. 46.
26. See Buehrer, *New Age Masquerade*, p. 47, citing James M. Becker (ed.), *Schooling for a Global Age*, (New York: McGraw Hill, 1979). p. 45.
27. See Buehrer, *New Age Masquerade*, p. 47.
28. Groothuis, *Unmasking the New Age*, pp. 126–128.
29. Hudson, *Reinventing America's Schools*, Vol. 1, p. 18.
30. See Kalantzis and Cope, "Multiculturalism," p. B3, referencing D. Ravitch, *Point of View*, Oct. 24, 1990.
31. See Hudson, *Reinventing America's Schools*, vol. 1, p. 20; and Gabler and Gabler, *What Are They Teaching Our Children?* p. 48.
32. "Concerns About Public Education," n.d..
33. "FOCUS," p. 3.
34. Hudson, *Reinventing America's Schools*, vol. 1, p. 22, citing Shanker, "The Pitfalls of Multicultural Education," *Education Digest*, Dec. 1991, condensed from *The International Educator*, Apr. 1991.
35. Simonds, *President's Report*, Nov. 1993, p. 2; Simonds, *President's Report*, Mar. 1993, p. 3.
36. See Riechers, "Homosexuals Target Your Child."
37. "In Defense of a Little Virginity"; see, for example, "Surprise Results of Sex Education" and "'Safe Sex' Isn't Safe After All."
38. Citizens for Excellence in Education, Public School Awareness Committee, Audio Tape Series, Tape 2: "What Are They Teaching Our Children?" For similar allegations, see also Gabler and Gabler, *What Are They Teaching Our Children?* pp. 65–79.
39. Harrington-Lueker, "Book Battles," p. 19.
40. "HLI Conference on Sex Education," p. 4.
41. Citizens for Excellence in Education, Public School Awareness

Committee, "Anti-Family Sex Ed Guidelines Distributed." See also Gabler and Gabler, *What Are They Teaching Our Children?* p. 72; P. Robertson, *The New Millennium*, p. 166.

42. Citizens for Excellence in Education, Public School Awareness Committee, "Anti-Family Sex Ed Guidelines Distributed."
43. See Simonds, *President's Report*, July 1, 1991, p. 3; Simonds, *President's Report*, Aug. 1991, p. 1.
44. People For the American Way, *Attacks*, 1993, p. 22.
45. People For the American Way, *Attacks*, 1994, p. 24; People For the American Way, *Attacks*, 1991, p. 117.
46. People For the American Way, *Attacks*, 1993, p. 22–23.
47. "Publisher Pulls Textbook from Texas," p. 1.

Chapter Eight

1. Buehrer, *New Age Masquerade*, pp. 90, 92.
2. Kuhn, *Structure of Scientific Revolutions*, pp. 16–17. One writer, Constance Cumbey, has asserted that the term *paradigm* is a New Age "buzz word." (See Cumbey, *Hidden Dangers of the Rainbow*, p. 27.) Such a claim is based on the belief that prominent philosophers, psychologists, scientists, and theologians who use that term are all New Age advocates. That accusation cannot be taken seriously.
3. F. Smith, *Understanding Reading*, p. 57.
4. Tracey, *Plurality and Ambiguity*, pp. 48, 84.
5. Patton, *Utilization-Focused Evaluation*, p. 203.
6. Sathe, "Implications of Corporate Culture," pp. 73–84.
7. United Methodist Church, *Book of Discipline*.
8. Spong, *Rescuing the Bible from Fundamentalism*, p. 31.
9. See especially American philosopher William James's essays on pragmatism, published in many anthologies of his writings, for example, James, *Essays in Pragmatism*.
10. R. Niebuhr, *An Interpretation of Christian Ethics*, p. 67.

11. See Tillich, *Shaking of the Foundations*, chap. 19.
12. See, for example, Fox, *Original Blessing*. Fox argues against the "fall-redemption" theme and for "creation spirituality." Hence, he believes that original sin is a doctrine counter to the major themes of a positive faith of the Bible.
13. Emerson, "The Over Soul," pp. 190, 192.
14. This point of view is developed by H. R. Niebuhr in his book *The Responsible Self*, chap. 1. Niebuhr argues that moral people will ask the question "What is fitting?" in making value decisions.
15. Potthoff, *God and the Celebration of Life*, chap. 20.
16. This position can be identified with Reinhold Niebuhr in his essays published in D. B. Robertson (ed.), *Love and Justice*.
17. See for example, Fletcher, *Situation Ethics*.
18. Hunt, *Peace, Prosperity*, p. 83; see also "Origin of a Most Seductive Lie," in Hunt, *Peace, Prosperity*, pp. 242–244.
19. See, for example, Brightman, *Philosophy of Religion*.
20. Cobb, *God and the World*, p. 96.
21. Ogden, *Reality of God*, pp. 51, 59.
22. Whitehead, *Dialogues of Alfred North Whitehead*, p. 297.
23. See Sathe, "Implications of Corporate Culture."
24. Dewey, *School and Society*, p. 62.
25. Dewey, *School and Society*, p. 26.
26. Dewey, *Child and the Curriculum*. See especially pp. 14–15.
27. Dewey, *Child and the Curriculum*, p. 11.
28. Dewey, *School and Society*, pp. 54–56.
29. For more on Dewey's views, see his essay "The School and Social Progress," in *School and Society*, pp. 6–29, specifically p. 7. For Thomas Jefferson's views, see Dewey, *The Living Thoughts of Thomas Jefferson*, pp. 112, 118–120, 125–126. See also Rippa, *Education in a Free Society*, pp. 106–107, 184.
30. Dewey, *School and Society*, p. 16.

31. Dewey, *School and Society*.
32. Dewey, *School and Society*.
33. Dewey, *School and Society*, p. 29.
34. Dewey, *How We Think*, p. iii.
35. Dewey, *How We Think*, pp. 1–13.
36. Dewey, *A Common Faith*, pp. 3, 25, 27.
37. Jackson, *Handbook of Research on Curriculum;* Wittrock, *Handbook of Research on Teaching*.
38. See for example, Gabler and Gabler, *What Are They Teaching Our Children?* pp. 26–27.
39. Hitchcock, *What Is Secular Humanism?* p. 13.

Chapter Nine

1. See Albanese, *America*, p. 20.
2. Albanese, *America*, p. 21.
3. Albanese, *America*, p. 22.
4. *Random House College Dictionary*, rev. ed., 1988.
5. Gilkey, *Creationism on Trial*, p. 100.
6. Gilkey, *Creationism on Trial*, p. 99.
7. H. Smith, *World's Religions*, pp. 92–93.
8. Hall, Pilgrim, and Cavanagh, *Religion*, pp. 16–17.
9. H. Smith, *World's Religions*, p. 317.
10. Clebsch, *Christianity in European History*, p. 39.
11. R. M. Brown, *The Spirit of Protestantism*, p. 24.
12. These "family" categories are proposed by Melton in *Encyclopedia of American Religions*.
13. H. R. Niebuhr, *Social Sources of Denominationalism*, [1929] 1957.
14. G. C. Bedell, Sandon, and Wellborn, *Religion in America*, p. 204.
15. Both documents are available from the Baptist Joint Committee, 200 Maryland Ave. N.E., Washington, D.C. 20002.

16. "A New Coalition Emerges," p. 599.
17. "A New Coalition Emerges," p. 599.
18. See Herberg, *Protestant, Catholic and Jew*.
19. These characteristics of Judaism are discussed in detail in Albanese, *America*, pp. 45–47.
20. Yutter, "How to Bridge the Gap," pp. 37–39.
21. See Hall, Pilgrim, and Cavanagh, *Religion*, pp. 166–178.
22. Layman, *Buddhism in America*, p. 32.
23. Layman, *Buddhism in America*, p. xiv.
24. Haddad and Smith, *Muslim Communities in North America*, p. xx.
25. Moghrabi, personal communication at Denver, Colorado, reception, 1995.
26. See Cross, *The Burned-Over District*.
27. Barkun, *Crucible of the Millennium*, pp. 153–160.
28. See James, *Varieties of Religious Experience*, lectures 16, 17.
29. Lash, *Seeker's Handbook*, pp. 58–63.
30. See Lash, *Seeker's Handbook*, pp. 47–68.
31. Campbell, *Hero with a Thousand Faces*, p. 3.
32. Frankel and Hewitt, "Religion and Well-Being," pp. 62–71.
33. Burris and others, "What a Friend," pp. 326–333.

Chapter Ten

1. Garraty and Gay, *Columbia History of the World*, p. 503. See also Lamont, *Philosophy of Humanism*.
2. Bewkes, Keene, and others, *The Western Heritage of Faith and Reason*, p. 498.
3. Bewkes, Keene, and others, p. 495.
4. See Huxley, *Humanist Frame*, especially p. 151.
5. Hemming, "Moral Education," p. 118.
6. Gould, "Spiritual and Ethical Beliefs of Humanists," pp. 571–574.
7. Gould, "Spiritual and Ethical Beliefs of Humanists," p. 572.

8. *Random House College Dictionary*, rev. ed., 1988.
9. See Pfeffer, "Unity of the First Amendment," p. 134.
10. *Random House College Dictionary*, rev. ed., 1988.
11. Tarnas, *Passion of the Western Mind*, p. 282.
12. Tarnas, *Passion of the Western Mind*, p. 319.
13. See Carter, *Culture of Disbelief*, pp. 35–39.
14. Wood, *First Freedom*, p. 10.
15. K. B. Bedell, *Yearbook of American and Canadian Churches, 1995*, pp. 261–272; Carter, *Culture of Disbelief*, p. 4, citing Gallup poll figures.
16. Lamont, *Philosophy of Humanism*, p. 13.
17. Hitchcock, *What is Secular Humanism?* p. 10.
18. Lamont, *Philosophy of Humanism*, p. 77, quoting Carl Sandburg, *The People, Yes* (Orlando, Fla.: Harcourt Brace & Company, 1936). Renewed in 1964 by Carl Sandburg. Reprinted by permission of the publisher.
19. Humanist Manifesto I first appeared in *The New Humanist*, May-June 1933, 6(3). Humanist Manifesto II first appeared in *The Humanist*, Sept.-Oct. 1973, *33*(5). See Kurtz, *Humanist Manifestos I and II*, for a complete text of both of these manifestos.
20. Kurtz, *Humanist Manifestos I and II*, p. 7.
21. Kurtz, *Humanist Manifestos I and II*, p. 8.
22. Kurtz, *Humanist Manifestos I and II*, p. 20.
23. Kurtz, *Humanist Manifestos I and II*, pp. 15–16.
24. Kurtz, *Humanist Manifestos I and II*, p. 16.
25. Lee, "*Smith* v. *Board of School Commissioners*," p. 616.
26. Lee, "*Smith* v. *Board of School Commissioners*," p. 618.
27. Babbitt, "Humanism," p. 43.
28. Hartt, "Theism and Humanism," p. 83.
29. See Lee, "*Smith* v. *Board of School Commissioners*," p. 612, citing in part "The Myth of Religious Neutrality by Separation in Education," *Virginia Law Review*, 1985, *71*, 127–172.

Chapter Eleven

1. See Carter, *Culture of Disbelief*, p. 106, citing Thomas Jefferson, "Freedom of Religion at the University of Virginia," in S. K. Padover, ed., *The Complete Jefferson* (New York: Duell, Sloan & Pierce, 1943), p. 958.
2. U.S. Constitution, First Amendment.
3. For a partial text of Jefferson's letter, see Dewey, *Living Thoughts of Thomas Jefferson*, pp. 102–103.
4. Quoted in Irons, *Brennan vs. Rehnquist*, p. 116.
5. *Everson* v. *Board of Education*, p. 18.
6. *Everson* v. *Board of Education*, p. 15.
7. *Everson* v. *Board of Education*, p. 19.
8. *Lemon* v. *Kurtzman*, p. 612.
9. Lee, "*Smith* v. *Board of School Commissioners*," p. 601, quoting *School District of Grand Rapids* v. *Ball*, 473 U.S. 373, p. 383 (1985).
10. *Lemon* v. *Kurtzman*, pp. 612–613, citing *Walz* v. *Tax Commission*, 397 U.S. 664, p. 674 (1970); *Lemon* v. *Kurtzman*, pp. 616–617. An example of a state action that passed the *Lemon* test is a university policy allowing groups of students, including religious groups, to meet on school grounds. McGhehey, "The Public School Curriculum," p. 385, note 38, cites *Widmar* v. *Vincent*, 454 U.S. 263 (1981).
11. *Lemon* v. *Kurtzman*, p. 614.
12. These examples are cited by Justice Rehnquist in his dissenting opinion in the Supreme Court's *Wallace* v. *Jaffree* decision, 472 U.S. 38 (1985), pp. 110–111.
13. See *Wallace* v. *Jaffree*, p. 110.
14. See McClosky and Brill, *Dimensions of Tolerance*, pp. 103–104; McGhehey, "The Public School Curriculum," pp. 382–384.
15. *Davis* v. *Beason*, p. 342.
16. *Torcaso* v. *Watkins*, p. 495, note 11.
17. The statute was 50 App. U.S.C.A., Sec. 456 (j) 1951. See *United States* v. *Seeger*, 380 U.S. 163 (1965), p. 176.
18. The provision read: "Religious training and belief does not include

essentially political, sociological or philosophical views, or a merely personal moral code." As quoted in Abraham, *Freedom and the Court*, p. 217.

19. *Sherbert* v. *Verner*, pp. 403–406.
20. Quoted in Haynes, *Religion in American History*, p. 141.
21. See Lee, "*Smith* v. *Board of School Commissioners*," p. 598.
22. Quoted in S. K. Green, Presentation to Colorado Springs Conference, p. 3.
23. *Lee* v. *Weisman*, pp. 2659–2660.
24. Berson, "A Values-Affirming Moment of Silence," p. 1.
25. Berson, "A Values-Affirming Moment of Silence," p. 1.
26. Dobson, Monthly Letter, May 1995.
27. Dobson, Monthly Letter, May 1995, p. 2, quoting Newt Gingrich, *Religion and Politics: The Legitimate Role*, Heritage Foundation Lecture Series, Oct. 5, 1994.
28. Dobson, Monthly Letter, May 1995, p. 3, quoting Newt Gingrich, *Religion and Politics: The Legitimate Role*, Heritage Foundation Lecture Series, Oct. 5, 1994.
29. Quoted in "A Plain-Talking Citizens Guide to Public School Prayer," p. 2.
30. Quoted in "A Plain-Talking Citizens Guide to Public School Prayer," p. 2.
31. Dobson, Monthly Letter, May 1995, p. 4.
32. Dobson, Monthly Letter, May 1995, p. 7.
33. See, for example, Dobson, Monthly Letter, May 1995, p. 1.
34. Dobson, Monthly Letter, May 1995, pp. 4–5, quoting in part Dr. Vernon Grounds, president emeritus of Denver Conservative Baptist Seminary.
35. Haynes and Thomas, "Beyond the School Prayer Debate."

Chapter Twelve

1. See *Everson* v. *Board of Education*, specifically pp. 15, 16.
2. Haynes, *Religion in American History*, p. 169, quoting *Abington School District* v. *Schempp*.

3. Sebaly, *Teacher Education and Religion*.

4. Vitz, "A Study of Religion." See also Podesta, "American Way," p. 2.

5. Included in Haynes, *Religion in American History*, p. 168. Part of this statement was taken from W. E. Collie and L. H. Smith, "Teaching About Religion in the Schools: The Continuing Challenge," *Social Education*, Jan. 1981, *45*(1), 16.

6. Haynes, *Religion in American History*, pp. 169–170. Copyright by Association for Supervision and Curriculum Development. Used with permission.

7. See "Religion in the Public School Curriculum: Questions and Answers," in Haynes, *Religion in American History*, pp. 163–167.

8. "Williamsburg Charter," p. 2–8.

9. "Williamsburg Charter," p. 2–4.

10. Haynes, "Beyond the Culture Wars," p. 33.

11. This statement of principles was reprinted in California Three R's Project's newsletter, *Rights, Responsibilities & Respect*, Winter-Spring 1995, *2*(1), 9–10.

12. Haynes, "Beyond the Culture Wars," p. 33.

13. See for example, Lee, "*Smith* v. *Board of School Commissioners*," pp. 591–592, citing D. Purpel and K. Ryan, "Moral Education: What Is It and Where Are We?" in D. Purpel and K. Ryan (eds.), *Moral Education . . . It Comes with the Territory*, vol. 9 (Berkeley, Calif.: McCutchan, 1976); See also Yerby, "Toward Religious Neutrality," pp. 905–906.

14. See Lee, "*Smith* v. *Board of School Commissioners*," pp. 591–592, citing D. Purpel and K. Ryan, "Moral Education: What Is It and Where Are We?" in D. Purpel and K. Ryan (eds.), *Moral Education . . . It Comes with the Territory*, vol. 9 (Berkeley, Calif.: McCutchan, 1976).

15. See *Ambach, Commissioner of Education of the State of New York* v. *Norwick*, pp. 78–79.

16. Yerby, "Toward Religious Neutrality," p. 920, citing D. Purpel and K. Ryan, "Moral Education: What Is It and Where Are We?" in

D. Purpel and K. Ryan (eds.), *Moral Education . . . It Comes with the Territory*, vol. 9 (Berkeley, Calif.: McCutchan, 1976), p. 57, note 48.

17. Lickona, *Educating for Character*, p. 20.
18. See *Ambach*, pp. 76–77, citing a long list of Supreme Court cases supporting this view and referencing John Dewey and other authorities.
19. See *West Virginia State Board of Education* v. *Barnette*.
20. See Yerby, "Toward Religious Neutrality," pp. 908–909; see also Kemper, "Freedom of Religion," p. 423, citing numerous books and the Supreme Court case *FCC* v. *Pacifica* (1978) regarding the impressionability and vulnerability of children in general and especially in the school setting where attendance is mandatory.
21. Podesta, "American Way," p. 3.
22. Gordis, "Value of Pluralism," p. 63.
23. See Brubacher, *Public Schools and Spiritual Values*, chap. 2.
24. Yerby, "Toward Religious Neutrality," p. 921.
25. See *Mozert* v. *Hawkins County Board of Education (Public Schools)*, 827 F.2d 1058 (6th Cir. 1987), for Judge Lively's opinion; see *Board of Education, Island Trees Union Free School District No. 26* v. *Pico*, for both Justice Brennan's and Justice Rehnquist's opinions.
26. See Justice Rehnquist's comments in *Pico*.
27. Lickona, Schaps, and Lewis, *Eleven Principles*, p. 1.
28. Amundson, *Teaching Values and Ethics*.
29. Character Education Partnership, *Character Education*, citing *Phi Delta Kappan*, Oct. 1993, p. 145.

Chapter Thirteen

1. Brown and Stephens, "Rationales for Teaching Challenged Books."
2. Brown and Stephens, "Rationales for Teaching Challenged Books," p. 1.

Chapter Fourteen

1. See People For the American Way, *Attacks*, 1993, p. 120.
2. See People For the American Way, *Attacks*, 1992, p. 125; People For the American Way, *Attacks*, 1993, pp. 120–121.

3. Reported in Freedom to Learn Network, *The Freedom to Learn Network Newsletter,* Winter 1994, 2(2), 2.
4. Spady, Letter, Winter 1994, p. 2.
5. Simonds, *President's Report,* June 1995, p. 2.
6. Willis, "Conservative Christians Speak Out," p. 7.
7. See Barkun, *Religion and the Racist Right.*
8. People For the American Way, *Attacks,* 1994, p. 14.
9. Leo, "Hijacking of American History."
10. See Bates, "Cyberspace."
11. "Cyberspirit," pp. 19–20.
12. See Carter, *The Culture of Disbelief.*
13. McClosky and Brill, *Dimensions of Tolerance,* p. 5, citing José Ortega y Gasset, *The Revolt of the Masses* (New York: Norton, 1932) p. 83.
14. McClosky and Brill, *Dimensions of Tolerance,* p. 9, citing in part John Pearson Roche, "American Liberty: An Examination of the 'Tradition' of Freedom," in *Aspects of Liberty,* ed. Milton Konvitz and Clinton L. Rossiter (Ithaca, N.Y.: Cornell University Press, 1958), pp. 8, 11.
15. McClosky and Brill, *Dimensions of Tolerance,* p. 9, citing in part John Pearson Roche, "American Liberty: An Examination of the 'Tradition' of Freedom," in *Aspects of Liberty,* ed. Milton Konvitz and Clinton L. Rossiter (Ithaca, N.Y.: Cornell University Press, 1958), p. 15.
16. See, for example, Friends of Peace Pilgrim, *Peace Pilgrim,* p. 8.
17. Milton, "Areopagitica," p. 50.

Appendix A

1. Jenkinson, *Censors in the Classroom,* pp. 17–22.
2. Jenkinson, *Censors in the Classroom,* p. 22.
3. Provenzo, *Religious Fundamentalism,* pp. 23–24.
4. Jenkinson, *Censors in the Classroom,* pp. 2–8.
5. Jenkinson, *Censors in the Classroom,* pp. 10–11.

6. Rogers, *Banned!* pp. 55–58; see also Jenkinson, *Censors in the Classroom*, p. 15.
7. Rogers, *Banned!* pp. 59–60, citing *Zykan* v. *Warsaw Community School Corp*.
8. *West Virginia State Board of Education* v. *Barnette*, p. 640, quoting *Minersville School District* v. *Gobitis*, p. 595.
9. *Barnette*, p. 626, note 1, citing Section 1734, West Virginia Code (1941 Supp.).
10. *Barnette*, p. 626.
11. *Barnette*, p. 629, note 5, citing Section 1851 (1), West Virginia Code (1941 Supp.).
12. *Barnette*, p. 629. The Witnesses believed in a literal reading of Exodus, chap. 20, verses 4 and 5, which says: "Thou shalt not make unto thee any graven image, or any likeness of anything that is in heaven above, or that is in the earth beneath, or that is in the water under the earth; thou shalt not bow down thyself to them nor serve them."
13. *Barnette*, p. 628.
14. *Barnette*, pp. 631; see also p. 642.
15. *Barnette*, p. 637.
16. *Barnette*, p. 642.
17. See Justice Brennan's statement in *Board of Education, Island Trees Union Free School District No. 26* v. *Pico*, p. 1727, referencing *Tinker* v. *Des Moines School District*. Brennan notes that "later cases have consistently followed this rationale."
18. As reprinted in *Epperson* v. *Arkansas*, p. 100. The chancery court's opinion was not officially recorded.
19. 242 Ark. 922, 416 S.W. 2d 322 (1967), as quoted in Epperson, p. 101, note 7.
20. *Epperson*, pp. 104–105, quoting *Shelton* v. *Tucker*, 364 U.S. 479 (1960), p. 487, and *Keyishian* v. *Board of Regents*, 385 U.S. 589 (1967), p. 603.
21. *Epperson*, p. 106.

22. *Tinker* v. *Des Moines Independent Community School District*, p. 507.
23. *Tinker*, p. 511.
24. *Tinker*, p. 506.
25. "Litigation Epidemic," p. 45.
26. *Board of Education, Island Trees Union Free School District No. 26* v. *Pico*, p. 1723.
27. *Pico*, p. 1729.
28. *Pico*, p. 1729.
29. *Pico*, quoting from the *Keyishian* case.
30. *Pico*, pp. 1728–1729.
31. *Pico*, pp. 1727–1728.
32. *Pico*, p. 1745.
33. *Pico*, pp. 1735–1748.
34. *Pico*, p. 1737.
35. *Pico*, pp. 1735–1737. See in particular Justice Rehnquist's dissent, sharply criticizing Justice Brennan's opinion for the Court, pp. 1740–1748.
36. *Grove* v. *Mead School District No. 354*, p. 1534.
37. *Grove*, p. 1535, note 4.
38. *Grove*, pp. 1539, 1543.
39. *Grove*, p. 1533, quoting *McCollum* v. *Board of Education*, p. 235.
40. *Grove*, p. 1534.
41. *Grove*, pp. 1535–1538.
42. *Grove*, pp. 1541–1543.
43. *Grove*, p. 1539.
44. *Grove*, p. 1540.
45. See the appellate court's decision, *Mozert* v. *Hawkins County Board of Education*, 827 F.2d 1058, p. 1061.
46. Frost's testimony is presented in *Mozert*, 827 F.2d 1058, p. 1061.
47. *Mozert*, 827 F.2d 1058, pp. 1061–1062.

48. *Mozert*, 827 F.2d 1058; Salter, "Imagination Puts Fear of God into Superstitious," p. 29.

49. See *Mozert*, 827 F.2d 1058, p. 1062.

50. *Mozert*, 827 F.2d 1058, pp. 1068–1069.

51. See the district court's opinion, *Mozert*, 647 F.Supp. 1194 (E.D. Tenn., 1986), p. 1199.

52. *Mozert*, 827 F.2d 1058, p. 1069.

53. See *Smith* v. *Board of School Commissioners of Mobile County*, 655 F.Supp. 939, pp. 942–943 (S.D. Ala. 1987).

54. See *Wallace* v. *Jaffree*, 472 U.S. 38 (1985).

55. See Hulsizer, *Protecting the Freedom to Learn*, pp. 20–21.

56. See the appellate court's decision, *Smith*, 827 F.2d 684, p. 688, referencing a position statement filed by plaintiffs.

57. See the district court's decision, *Smith*, 655 F. Supp 939 (S.D. Ala. 1987), pp. 999–1013.

58. See *Smith*, 655 F.Supp. 939 (S.D. Ala. 1987).

59. *Pico*, p. 1728, in part citing *Keyishian*, 385 U.S. 589 (1967).

References

Abraham, H. J. *Freedom and the Court: Civil Rights and Liberties in the United States* (2nd ed.). New York: Oxford University Press, 1972.

Adams, J. E. *The Biblical View of Self-Esteem, Self-Love, and Self-Image*. Eugene, Oreg: Harvest House, 1986.

Adams, M. J. *Beginning to Read: Thinking and Learning About Reading*. Cambridge, Mass.: MIT Press, 1990.

Albanese, C. L. *America: Religions and Religion*. Belmont, Calif.: Wadsworth, 1981.

Amundson, K. J. *Teaching Values and Ethics: Problems and Solutions*. A Critical Issues Report. Arlington, Va.: American Association of School Administrators, 1991.

Anderson, C. A., and Bowman, M. J. "Education and Economic Modernization in Historical Perspective." In L. Stone (ed.), *School and Society: Studies in the History of Education*. Baltimore, Md.: Johns Hopkins University Press, 1976.

Anderson, J. *The Architecture of Cognition*. Cambridge, Mass.: Harvard University Press, 1983.

Anderson, J. *Cognitive Psychology and Its Implications*. (2nd ed.) New York: W. H. Freeman, 1990.

Anderson, L., Evertson, C., and Emmer, E. "Dimensions in Classroom Management Derived from Recent Research." *Journal of Curriculum Studies*, 1980, *12*, 343–356.

Atwell, N. C. *In the Middle*. Portsmouth, N.H.: Heinemann, 1987.

Babbitt, I. "Humanism: An Essay at Definition." In N. Foerster (ed.), *Humanism and America*. New York: Farrar and Rinehart, 1930.

Baer, R. N. *Inside the New Age Nightmare*. Lafayette, La.: Huntington House, 1989.

Barkun, M. *Crucible of the Millennium: The Burned-Over District of New York in the 1840s*. Syracuse, N.Y.: Syracuse University Press, 1986.

Barkun, M. *Religion and the Racist Right*. Chapel Hill: University of North Carolina Press, 1994.

Bates, S. "Cyberspace." Education Life. *The New York Times*, Nov. 6, 1994, pp. 22–23.

Bedell, G. C., Sandon, L., Jr., and Wellborn, C. J. *Religion in America*. New York: Macmillan, 1975.

Bedell, K. B. (ed.). *Yearbook of American and Canadian Churches, 1995*. Nashville, Tenn.: Abingdon Press, 1995.

Bennett, W. J. *The De-Valuing of America: The Fight for Our Culture and Our Children*. New York: Summit Books, 1992.

Berliner, D. C. "Educational Reform in an Era of Disinformation." Paper presented at the meeting of the American Association of Colleges for Teacher Education, San Antonio, Tex., Feb. 1992.

Berliner, D. C., and Biddle, B. J. *The Manufactured Crisis: Myths, Fraud, and the Attack on America's Public Schools*. Reading, Mass.: Addison-Wesley, 1995.

Berson, D. "A Values-Affirming Moment of Silence." *Freedom Watch*, Citizens Project, May 1995, pp. 1–2.

Bewkes, E. G., and others. *The Western Heritage of Faith and Reason*. New York: HarperCollins, 1963.

Boston, R. "Out of Bondage." *Church and State*, 1991, *44*(8), 4–5.

Brightman, E. S. *A Philosophy of Religion*. New York: Prentice-Hall, 1940.

Brown, J. E., and Stephens, F. C. "Rationales for Teaching Challenged Books," SLATE Starter Sheet, April 1994. Urbana, Ill.: SLATE/National Council of Teachers of English, 1994.

Brown, R. M. *The Spirit of Protestantism*. New York: Oxford University Press, 1961.

Brubacher, J. S. (ed.). *The Public Schools and Spiritual Values*. New York: HarperCollins, 1944.

Bryson, J. E., and Detty, E. W. *The Legal Aspects of Censorship of Public School Library and Instructional Materials*. Charlottesville, Va.: Michie Co., 1982.

Buehrer, E. *The New Age Masquerade: The Hidden Agenda in Your Child's Classroom*. Brentwood, Tenn.: Wolgemuth & Hyatt, 1990.

Buehrer, E. "Self-Esteem and Mediocrity: Justifying Poor Work in the Name of Feeling Good." *Education Newsline*, Citizens for Excellence in Education, May-June 1991, p. 3.

Burris, C. T., and others. "What a Friend . . . Loneliness as a Motivator of Intrinsic Religion." *Journal for the Scientific Study of Religion*, Dec. 1994, *33*(4), 326–333.

Caldemeyer, C. *The Trust Me Express*. East Gibson, Ind.: Cecile Caldemeyer, July 1989.

California Three R's Project. *Rights, Responsibilities & Respect*, 1995, *2*(1).

Calkins, L. M. *The Art of Teaching Writing*. Portsmouth, N.H.: Heinemann, 1986.

Campbell, J. *Hero with a Thousand Faces*. New York: World, 1949.

Carkhuff, R. R. *The Art of Helping*. (6th ed.) Amherst, Mass.: Human Resource Development Press, 1987.

Carson, C. C., Huelskamp, R. M., and Woodall, T. D. "Perspectives on Education in America." Annotated briefing, 3rd draft. Albuquerque, N.M.: Systems Analysis Department, Sandia National Laboratories, May 10, 1991.

Carter, S. L. *The Culture of Disbelief: How American Law and Politics Trivialize Religious Devotion*. New York: Basic Books, 1993.

Castrone, L. "Focus on Family Founder Urged to 'Come Out of Closet.'" *Rocky Mountain News*, Apr. 29, 1993, p. 26A.

"Censoring a Dragon." In J. F. Krug (ed.), *Newsletter on Intellectual Freedom*, American Library Association, Office for Intellectual Freedom, Jan. 1994, pp. 6–7.

Character Education Partnership. *Character Education: Questions & Answers*. Alexandria, Va.: Character Education Partnership, n.d.

"Children Hypnotized at School: Alabama Psychiatrist Exposes Curriculum Dangers." *Physician*, [1992], p. 12.

Chion-Kenney, L. "What's in a Name? The Semantics of Outcome-Based Education." *The School Administrator*, 1994, *51*(14).

Chong, J., Ham, K., and Morris, J. D. *What **Really** Happened to the Dinosaurs?* El Cajon, Calif.: Master Books, 1990.

Christian Coalition, *Contract with the American Family*, 1995.

"Christian Coalition Starts School Board Seminars." *Freedom Watch*, Citizens Project, July 1995, p. 2.

"The Chuck Baker Show with Dr. James C. Dobson." Audio Tape of Interview. KVOR 1300 AM Radio, Colorado Springs, Colo., Apr. 22, 1993. Colorado Springs, Colo.: Focus on the Family, 1993.

Citizens for Excellence in Education, Public School Awareness Committee. Audio Tape Series, Tapes 1–6. Costa Mesa, Calif.: National Association of Christian Educators/Citizens for Excellence in Education, 1990.

Citizens for Excellence in Education, Public School Awareness Committee. *PSA Committee Workbook*. Costa Mesa, Calif.: Citizens for Excellence in Education, 1990.

Citizens for Excellence in Education, Public School Awareness Committee. "Anti-Family Sex Ed Guidelines Distributed." *Children's Public School*

Awareness Bulletin. Costa Mesa, Calif.: Citizens for Excellence in Education, Oct. 1991.

Clebsch, W. A. *Christianity in European History*. New York: Oxford University Press, 1979.

Cobb, J. *God and the World*. Philadelphia: Westminster Press, 1969.

Cole, S. G. *The History of Fundamentalism*. New York: R. R. Smith, 1931.

Collier, K. "Schools 'Alter' Children." *Spotlight*, Sept. 5, 1988.

Collins, M. J. "People For Action Fund Launches School Board Project." *People For the American Way News*, Fall 1994, *1*(1), 3.

"Concerns About Public Education." Colorado Springs, Colo.: Focus on the Family, n.d.

Costa, A. "Teacher Behaviors that Enable Student Thinking." In A. Costa (ed.), *Developing Minds: A Resource Book for Teaching Thinking*. Alexandria, Va.: Association for Supervision and Curriculum Development, 1985.

Crabbe, A. B. "Creating a Brighter Future: An Update on the Future Problem Solving Program." *Journal for the Education of the Gifted*, 1982, *5*, 2–11.

"Creationism in Public Schools." *Freedom Watch*, Citizens Project, Jan. 1995, p. 2.

"Creationism in the Springs." *Freedom Watch*, Citizens Project, Sept.-Oct. 1994, pp. 1–2.

Cross, W. R. *The Burned-Over District: The Social and Intellectual History of Enthusiastic Religion in Western New York, 1800–1850*. New York: Harper Torchbooks, 1965.

Cumbey, C. E. *The Hidden Dangers of the Rainbow: The New Age Movement and Our Coming Age of Barbarism*. Lafayette, La.: Huntington House, 1983.

"Cyberspirit: New On Line Services Embrace More Believers." *USA Weekend*, Nov. 18–20, 1994, pp. 19–20.

Dart, J. "An Atmosphere of Alienation." In M. Horton (ed.), *The Agony of Deceit*. Chicago: Moody Press, 1990.

Dewey, J. *The Child and the Curriculum*. Chicago: University of Chicago Press, 1902.

Dewey, J. *How We Think*. Lexington, Mass.: Heath, 1910.

Dewey, J. *Democracy and Education*. New York: Macmillan, 1916.

Dewey, J. *A Common Faith*. New Haven: Yale University Press, 1934.

Dewey, J. *The Living Thoughts of Thomas Jefferson: Presented by John Dewey*, ed. A. O. Mendel. White Plains, N.Y.: Longman, 1940. The selections are from H. A. Washington (ed.), *The Writings of Thomas Jefferson*. New York, 1853.

Dewey, J. *The School and Society*. (rev. ed.) Chicago: University of Chicago Press, 1943.

Dobson, J. Monthly Letter. Colorado Springs, Colo.: Focus on the Family, Apr. 1994.

Dobson, J. Monthly Letter. Colorado Springs, Colo.: Focus on the Family, May 1995.

Dow, P. *Schoolhouse Politics: Lessons from the Sputnik Era*. Cambridge, Mass.: Harvard University Press, 1991.

Doyle, R. P. *Banned Books Resource Guide*. Chicago: American Library Association, 1995.

Eagle Trust Fund. Introductory Letter. Alton, Ill.: Eagle Forum, n.d. [1994].

Ebert, M. "One Man's Bonfire Ignites *Quest* Debate." *Citizen*, Focus on the Family, July 20, 1992, 6(7), 12–13.

Ebert, M. "Parents Split Over *Quest*." *Citizen*, Focus on the Family, July 20, 1992, 6(7), 2.

Edens, K. M. "The Demystification of Visual Imagery, Visualization and Attention-Control Strategies." Unpublished paper, Department of Educational Psychology, University of South Carolina, 1991.

Education Policies Commission. *The Central Purpose of American Education*. Washington, D.C.: National Education Association, 1961.

Emerson, R. W. "The Over Soul." In *Emerson's Essays*. New York: HarperCollins, 1926.

"Evolution Under Fire." *Freedom Watch*, Citizens Project, Sept.-Oct. 1994, pp. 1–3.

"Fighting Dragons in Jeffco." *Rocky Mountain News*, Oct. 20, 1993, p. 40A.

Fletcher, J. F. *Situation Ethics: The New Morality*. Philadelphia: Westminster Press, 1966.

Focus on the Family. Press Release. Colorado Springs, Colo.: Focus on the Family, April 30, 1993.

Focus on the Family magazine. Back cover, Oct. 1995.

"FOCUS: What Happened to History?" *Education Reporter*, Eagle Forum Education and Legal Defense Fund, Apr. 1995, pp. 3–4.

Fox, M. *Original Blessing*. Santa Fe, N.M.: Bear & Co., 1983.

Frankel, B. G., and Hewitt, W. E. "Religion and Well-Being Among Canadian University Students: The Role of Faith Groups on Campus." *Journal for the Scientific Study of Religion*, Mar. 1994, 33(1), 62–71.

Freedom to Learn Network. *The Freedom to Learn Network Newsletter*, Winter 1994, 2(2).

Friends of Peace Pilgrim. *Peace Pilgrim: Her Life and Work in Her Own Words*. Santa Fe, N.M.: Ocean Tree Books, 1991.

Gabler, M., and Gabler, N. "A Parent's Guide to Textbook Review and Reform," Special Supplement to *Education Update*, The Heritage Foundation, Winter 1978.

Gabler, M., and Gabler, N., with Hefley, J. C. *What Are They Teaching Our Children?* Wheaton, Ill.: Victor Books, 1985.

Gabler, M., and Gabler, N. "The Drugging of Students." Flyer/pamphlet. Longview, Tex.: The Mel Gablers, n.d. [1994].

Gabler, M., and Gabler, N. "How to Object to Textbooks." Longview, Tex.: The Mel Gablers, [1995].

Gabler, M., and Gabler, N. Educational Research Analysts. Order Blank, rev. Apr. 28, 1995.

Garraty, J. A., and Gay, P. *The Columbia History of the World.* New York: HarperCollins, 1972.

Geisler, N. L. *The Creator in the Courtroom. "Scopes II": The 1981 Arkansas Creation-Evolution Trial.* Milford, Mich.: Mott Media, 1982.

Georges, J. "School Board Presentation." East Gibson, Ind.: unpublished, Nov. [1990?].

Gilkey, L. *Creationism on Trial: Evolution and God at Little Rock.* Minneapolis, Minn.: Winston Press, 1985.

Good, T. L. "How Teachers' Expectations Affect Results." *American Education,* 1982, *18*(10), 25–32.

Good, T. L., and Brophy, J. E. "Behavioral Expression of Teacher Attitudes." *Journal of Educational Psychology,* 1972, *63*(6), 616–624.

Goodman, K. S. "Reading: A Psycholinguistic Guessing Game." Paper presented at the annual meeting of the American Educational Research Association, New York, N.Y., Feb. 1967.

Goodman, K. S. *What's Whole in Whole Language?* Portsmouth, N.H.: Heineman, 1986.

Gordis, D. "The Value of Pluralism." In People For the American Way, *Values, Pluralism, and American Education.* Washington, D.C.: People For the American Way, 1987.

Gough, P. B. "One Second of Reading." In J. F. Kavana and I. G. Mattingly (eds.), *Language by Ear and by Eye.* Cambridge, Mass.: MIT Press, 1972.

Gould, N. "Spiritual and Ethical Beliefs of Humanists in the Counseling Profession." *Journal of Counseling and Development,* 1990, 68(5), 571–574.

Gourley, T. J. "Adapting the Varsity Sports Model to Non-Psychomotor Gifted Students." *Gifted Child Quarterly,* 1981, *25,* 164–166.

Graves, D. *Writing: Teachers and Children at Work.* Portsmouth, N.H.: Heinemann, 1983.

Green, J. *The Encyclopedia of Censorship.* New York: Facts on File, 1990.

Green, S. K. Presentation to Colorado Springs Conference, 1994.

Groothuis, D. R. *Unmasking the New Age.* Downers Grove, Ill.: InterVarsity Press, 1986.

Haddad, Y. Y., and Smith, J. I. (eds.). *Muslim Communities in North America*. Albany: State University of New York Press, 1994.

Hadden, J. K., and Shupe, A. *Televangelism: Power and Politics on God's Frontier*. Troy, Mo.: Holt, Rinehart and Winston, 1988.

Hadden, J. K., and Swann, C. E. *Prime Time Preachers: The Rising Power of Televangelism*. Reading, Mass.: Addison-Wesley, 1981.

Hall, T. W., Pilgrim, R. B., and Cavanagh, R. R. *Religion: An Introduction*. New York: HarperCollins, 1985.

Hansen, J. *When Writers Read*. Portsmouth, N.H.: Heinemann, 1987.

Harrington-Lueker, D. "Book Battles." *American School Board Journal*, Feb. 1991, pp. 18–21, 37.

Harrington-Lueker, D. "The Books from Hell." *American School Board Journal*, Feb. 1991, p. 20.

Hartt, J. "Theism and Humanism: Some Preliminary Observations." In J.A.C. Auer and J. Hartt, *Humanism Versus Theism*. Ames: Iowa State University Press, 1981, pp. 79–86.

Haynes, C. C. *Religion in American History: What to Teach and How*. Alexandria, Va.: Association for Supervision and Curriculum Development, 1990.

Haynes, C. C. "Beyond the Culture Wars." *Educational Leadership*, Dec. 1993-Jan. 1994, 5(4), 30–34.

Haynes, C. C., and Thomas, O. "Beyond the School Prayer Debate: Taking Religion Seriously in Public Schools." In *Rights, Responsibilities & Respect*, a newsletter from the California Three R's Project, Winter-Spring 1995, p. 8.

Hemming, J. "Moral Education." In A. J. Ayer (ed.), *The Humanist Outlook*. London: Pemberton, 1968, pp. 115–127.

Hentoff, N. "Texas Town Casts 'Satan' from Classroom." *Rocky Mountain News*, Nov. 22, 1993, p. 42A.

Herberg, W. *Protestant, Catholic and Jew: An Essay in American Religious Sociology*. New York: Doubleday, 1955.

Herrick, T. "Critic Calls 'Virginity' Ad a Jeffco Political Tool." *Rocky Mountain News*, July 8, 1993, p. 11A.

Hill, M., and Pechar, G. M. *Is OBE Working? A Report on Existing Outcomes-Based Programs*. Overland Park, Kans.: Blue Valley School District, 1994.

Hirsch, E. D., Jr. *Cultural Literacy: What Every American Needs to Know*. Boston: Houghton Mifflin, 1987.

Hitchcock, J. *What is Secular Humanism? Why Humanism Became Secular and How It Is Changing Our World*. Ann Arbor, Mich.: Servant Books, 1982.

"HLI Conference on Sex Education Held in St. Louis." *Education Reporter*, Eagle Forum Education and Legal Defense Fund., Nov. 1994, p. 4.

Holley, C. C., and Dansereau, D. F. "Networking: Techniques and Empirical Evidence." In C. C. Holley and D. F. Dansereau (eds.), *Spatial Learning Strategies*. San Diego, Calif.: Academic Press, 1984.

Hudson, K. *Reinventing America's Schools: A Practical Guide to Components of Restructuring and Non-Traditional Education*, vol. 1. Costa Mesa, Calif.: National Association of Christian Educators/Citizens for Excellence in Education, 1992.

Hudson, K. *Reinventing America's Schools: A Practical Guide to Components of Restructuring and Non-Traditional Education*, vol. 2. Costa Mesa, Calif.: National Association of Christian Educators/Citizens for Excellence in Education, 1992.

Hulsizer, D. *Protecting the Freedom to Learn: A Citizen's Guide*. Washington, D.C.: People For the American Way, 1989.

Hunt, D. *Peace, Prosperity, and the Coming Holocaust*. Eugene, Oreg.: Harvest House, 1983.

Hunter, M. *Rx: Improved Instruction*. El Segundo, Calif.: TIP Publications, 1976.

Huxley, J. (ed.). *The Humanist Frame*. New York: HarperCollins, 1961.

"In Defense of a Little Virginity: A Message from Focus on the Family." Colorado Springs, Colo.: Focus on the Family, [1992].

"In Their Own Words." *American School Board Journal*, April 1993, *180*(4), 25.

Irons, P. *Brennan vs. Rehnquist: The Battle for the Constitution*. New York: Knopf, 1994.

Jackson, P. W. (ed). *Handbook of Research on Curriculum*. New York: Macmillan, 1992.

James, W. *Essays in Pragmatism*, ed. A. Castell. New York: Hafner, 1948.

James, W. *The Varieties of Religious Experience*. New York: New American Library, 1958.

Jenkinson, E. B. *Censors in the Classroom: The Mind Benders*. Carbondale: Southern Illinois University Press, 1979.

Jones, J. L. "Stretching the Meaning of the Hatch Amendment." *American School Board Journal*, April 1993, *180*(4), 27.

Kalantzis, M., and Cope, W. "Multiculturalism May Prove to Be the Key Issue of Our Epoch." *Chronicle of Higher Education*, Nov. 4, 1992, p. B3.

Kemper, K. "Freedom of Religion vs. Public School Reading Curriculum." *Puget Sound Law Review*, 1989, *12*, 405–449.

Kendall, J. S., and Marzano, R. J. *The Systematic Identification and Articulation of Content Standards and Benchmarks*. Aurora, Colo.: Mid-Continent Regional Educational Laboratory, Mar. 1995.

Kerman, S., Kimball, T., and Martin, M. *Teacher Expectation and Student Achievement: Coordinator's Manual*. Bloomington, Ind.: Phi Delta Kappa, 1980.

Kosslyn, S. M. "Stalking the Mental Image." *Psychology Today*, 1985, pp. 22–28.

Krug, J. Letter. Chicago: American Library Association, Office for Intellectual Freedom, 1995.

Krug, J. F. (ed.). *Newsletter on Intellectual Freedom*, Jan. 1993. Chicago: American Library Association, Office for Intellectual Freedom, 1993.

Krug, J. F. (ed.). *Newsletter on Intellectual Freedom*, Mar. 1993. Chicago: American Library Association, Office for Intellectual Freedom, 1993.

Krug, J. F. (ed.). *Newsletter on Intellectual Freedom*, May 1993. Chicago: American Library Association, Office for Intellectual Freedom, 1993.

Krug, J. F. (ed.). *Newsletter on Intellectual Freedom*, July 1993. Chicago: American Library Association, Office for Intellectual Freedom, 1993.

Krug, J. F. (ed.). *Newsletter on Intellectual Freedom*, Sept. 1993. Chicago: American Library Association, Office for Intellectual Freedom, 1993.

Krug, J. F. (ed.). *Newsletter on Intellectual Freedom*, Nov. 1993. Chicago: American Library Association, Office for Intellectual Freedom, 1993.

Krug, J. F. (ed.). *Newsletter on Intellectual Freedom*, Jan. 1994. Chicago: American Library Association, Office for Intellectual Freedom, 1994.

Krug, J. F. (ed.). *Newsletter on Intellectual Freedom*, Mar. 1994. Chicago: American Library Association, Office for Intellectual Freedom, 1994.

Krug, J. F. (ed.). *Newsletter on Intellectual Freedom*, May 1994. Chicago: American Library Association, Office for Intellectual Freedom, 1994.

Krug, J. F. (ed.). *Newsletter on Intellectual Freedom*, July 1994. Chicago: American Library Association, Office for Intellectual Freedom.

Krug, J. F. (ed.). *Newsletter on Intellectual Freedom*, Sept. 1994. Chicago: American Library Association, Office for Intellectual Freedom, 1994.

Krug, J. F. (ed.). *Newsletter on Intellectual Freedom*, Nov. 1994. Chicago: American Library Association, Office for Intellectual Freedom, 1994.

Krug, J. F. (ed.). *Newsletter on Intellectual Freedom*, Jan. 1995. Chicago: American Library Association, Office for Intellectual Freedom, 1995.

Krug, J. F. (ed.). *Newsletter on Intellectual Freedom*, Mar. 1995. Chicago: American Library Association, Office for Intellectual Freedom, 1995.

Krug, J. F. (ed.). *Newsletter on Intellectual Freedom*, May 1995. Chicago: American Library Association, Office for Intellectual Freedom, 1995.

Kuhn, T. S. *The Structure of Scientific Revolutions*. (2nd ed., enlarged) Chicago: University of Chicago Press, 1970.

Kurtz, P. (ed.). *Humanist Manifestos I and II*. Buffalo, N.Y.: Prometheus Books, 1973.

LaFollette, M. C. *Creationism, Science, and the Law: The Arkansas Case*. Cambridge, Mass: MIT Press, 1983.

LaHaye, B. "A Radical Redefinition of Schooling." *The School Administrator*, Sept. 1994, *51*(8), 28–29.

Lamont, C. *The Philosophy of Humanism*. (6th ed.) New York: Frederick Ungar, 1982.

Larson, E. J. "Constitutional Challenges to Textbooks." In P. G. Altbach, G. P. Kelly, H. G. Petrie, and L. Weis (eds.), *Textbooks in American Society: Politics, Policy, and Pedagogy*. Albany: State University of New York Press, 1991.

Lash, J. *The Seeker's Handbook: The Complete Guide to Spiritual Pathfinding*. New York: Harmony Books, 1990.

Layman, E. M. *Buddhism in America*. Chicago: Nelson-Hall, 1976.

Lear, N. "The Search for Stable Values." In *Values, Pluralism, and Public Education, A National Conference*. Washington, D.C.: People For the American Way, Apr. 3, 1987, pp. 41–45.

Lee, S. M. "*Smith* v. *Board of School Commissioners*: The Religion of Secular Humanism in Public Education." *Notre Dame Journal of Law, Ethics & Public Policy*, Winter 1988, *3*, 591–627.

Leo, J. "The Hijacking of American History." *U.S. News and World Report*, Nov. 14, 1994, p. 36.

Lickona, T. *Educating for Character: How Our Schools Can Teach Respect and Responsibility*. New York: Bantam Books, 1991.

Lickona, T., Schaps, E., and Lewis, C. *Eleven Principles of Effective Character Education*. Alexandria, Va.: Character Education Partnership, n.d. [1995].

"Litigation Epidemic," *Christianity Today*, Feb. 17, 1989, p. 45.

McClosky, H., and Brill, A. *Dimensions of Tolerance: What Americans Believe About Civil Liberties*. New York: Russell Sage Foundation, 1983.

McGhehey, K. S. "The Public School Curriculum, Secular Humanism, and the Religion Clauses." *Washburn Law Journal*, Spring 1989, *28*, 380–399.

Manno, B. V. *Outcomes-Based Education: Has it Become More Affliction than Cure?* Minneapolis, Minn.: Center for the American Experiment, 1994.

Marrs, T. *Dark Secrets of the New Age: Satan's Plan for a One World Religion*. Wheaton, Ill.: Crossway Books, 1987.

Marrs, T. *Texe Marrs Book of New Age Cults and Religions*. Austin, Tex.: Living Truth Publishers, 1990.

Marsden, G. M. *Fundamentalism and American Culture: The Shaping of Twentieth-Century Evangelicalism: 1870–1925*. New York: Oxford University Press, 1980.

Marty, M. E. "A Profile of Norman Lear: Another Pilgrim's Progress." *Christian Century*, Jan. 21, 1987, pp. 55–58.

Marzano, R. J. "History and Foundations of the *Tactics* Program." Handout. Aurora, Colo.: Mid-Continent Regional Educational Laboratory, [1989].

Marzano, R. J. "Lessons from the Field About Outcomes-Based Performance Tasks." *Educational Leadership*, 1994, *51*(6), 44–50.

Marzano, R. J., and Arredondo, D. E. *Tactics for Thinking: Teacher's Manual*. Alexandria, Va.: Association for Supervision and Curriculum Development, 1986.

Marzano, R. J., and Paynter, D. E. *New Approaches to Literacy: Helping Students Develop Reading and Writing Skills*. Washington, D.C.: American Psychological Association, 1994.

Marzano, R. J., Pickering, D., and McTighe, J. *Assessing Student Outcomes: Performance Assessment Using the Dimensions of Learning Model*. Alexandria, Va.: Association for Supervision and Curriculum Development, 1993.

Melton, J. G. (ed.). *The Encyclopedia of American Religions: Religious Creeds*. (1st ed.) Detroit: Gale Research, 1988.

Mendenhall, D. "Nightmarish Textbooks Await Your Kids." *Citizen*, Focus on the Family, Sept. 17, 1990, pp. 1–7.

Metz, G. "A Mother's Cry for Help." *Education Newsline*, Citizens for Excellence in Education, Jan.-Feb. 1991, p. 1.

Michaelsen, J. *Like Lambs to the Slaughter*. Eugene, Oreg.: Harvest House, 1989.

Milton, J. "Areopagitica." In G. Sabine (ed.), *Areopagitica and Of Education*. New York: Appleton-Century-Crofts, 1951.

Minnery, T. "'Watchdog' American Way Lobs Mudballs Wide of the Mark." *Gazette Telegraph*, 1993.

Morson, B. "'Religious Right' Claim Irks Trustee." *Rocky Mountain News*, Dec. 29, 1993, p. 21A.

Mullis, I.V.S., Owen, E. H., and Phillips, G. W. *America's Challenge: Accelerating Academic Achievement: A Summary of Findings from 20 Years of NAEP*. Princeton, N. J.: Educational Testing Service, 1990.

National Center for Education Statistics. *Can Students Do Mathematical Problem Solving?* Washington, D.C.: National Center for Educational Statistics, 1993.

National Council of Teachers of Mathematics. *Curriculum and Evaluation Standards for School Mathematics*. Reston, Va.: National Council of Teachers of Mathematics, 1989.

National Education Goals Panel. *Handbook for Local Goals Reports: Building a Community of Learners*. Washington, D.C.: National Education Goals Panel, Jan. 1993.

National Education Goals Panel. *Promises to Keep: Creating High Standards for American Students*. Washington D.C.: National Education Goals Panel, Nov. 15, 1993.

"National Educational Goals: Can They Lead Schools to Real Reform?" *Noteworthy*. Aurora, Colo.: Mid-Continent Regional Educational Laboratory, Fall 1990.

"A New Coalition Emerges." *Christian Century*, June 7–14, 1995, pp. 599–600.

"A New Statement of Principles." *Rights, Responsibilities & Respect*, a newsletter from the California Three Rs Project, Winter-Spring 1995, 2(1), 9–10.

Niebuhr, H. R. *The Social Sources of Denominationalism*. New York: Living Age Books, Meridian Books, 1957. (Originally published 1929.)

Niebuhr, H. R. *The Responsible Self*. New York: HarperCollins, 1978.

Niebuhr, R. *An Interpretation of Christian Ethics*. New York: Living Age Books, Meridian Books, 1956. (Originally published 1935.)

Ogden, S. *The Reality of God*. New York: HarperCollins, 1966.

O'Neil, J. "Aiming for New Outcomes: The Promise and the Reality." *Educational Leadership*, 1994, *51*(6), 6–10.

Ostling, R. N. "Power, Glory and Politics." *Time*, Feb. 1986, pp. 62–69.

Park, C. J. "The Religious Right and Public Education." *Educational Leadership*, 1987, *44*(8), 5–11.

Patton, M. Q. *Utilization-Focused Evaluation*. Newbury Park, Calif.: Sage, 1978.

Pearson, P. D., and Stephens, D. "Learning About Literacy: A 30-Year Journey." In C. J. Gordon, G. D. Labercane, and W. R. McEachern (eds.), *Elementary Reading Instruction*. Needham Heights, Mass.: Ginn Press, 1992.

Pelikan, J. "Fundamentalism and/or Orthodoxy? Toward an Understanding of the Fundamentalist Phenomenon." In N. J. Cohen (ed.), *The Fundamentalist Phenomenon*. Grand Rapids, Mich.: William B. Eerdmans, 1990.

People For the American Way. "If We Take Our Freedoms for Granted, Others Will Take Our Freedoms Away." Pamphlet. Washington, D.C.: People For the American Way, n.d.

People For the American Way. *Attacks on the Freedom to Learn: 1990–1991 Report*. Washington, D.C.: People For the American Way, 1991.

People For the American Way. "The Controversy over the *Impressions* Reading Series." Washington, D.C.: People For the American Way, [1991].

People For the American Way. "Challenges to the *Impressions* Series." Washington, D.C.: People For the American Way, Aug. 26, 1991.

People For the American Way. *Attacks on the Freedom to Learn: 1991–1992 Report*. Washington, D.C.: People For the American Way, 1992.

People For the American Way. "Focus on the Family; Extremism Cloaked in the Rhetoric of Family Values." Washington, D.C.: People For the American Way, n.d. [1993].

People For the American Way. *Attacks on the Freedom to Learn: 1992–1993 Report*. Washington, D.C.: People For the American Way, 1993.

People For the American Way. *Attacks on the Freedom to Learn: 1993–1994 Report*. Washington, D.C.: People For the American Way, 1994.

People For the American Way. "Coming to a Church Near You . . ." *Right-Wing Watch*, May 1994, *4*(7).

Pfeffer, L. "The Unity of the First Amendment Religion Clauses." In J. Wood (ed.), *The First Freedom: Freedom and the Bill of Rights*. Waco, Tex.: J. M. Dawson Institute of Church-State Studies at Baylor University, 1990.

The Phyllis Schlafly Report, Eagle Trust Fund, Aug. 1991, *25*(1), sect. 1.

Piepenburg, E. "How to 'Create' Science Out of Religion." *People For the American Way News*, Spring 1995, p. 10.

"A Plain-Talking Citizens Guide to Public School Prayer." *Freedom Watch*, Citizens Project, Feb. 1995, *4*(2), 1.

Plato. *The Republic, The Dialogues of Plato*. (B. Jowett, trans.) New York: Oxford University Press, 1892.

Pliska, A.-M., and McQuaide, J. "Pennsylvania's Battle for Student Learning Outcomes." *Educational Leadership*, Mar. 1994, *51*(6), 66–69.

Podesta, A. T. "The American Way." In People For the American Way, *Values, Pluralism, and American Education*. Washington, D.C.: People For the American Way, 1987.

Podesta, A. T. "Foreword." In West, M. I. *Trust Your Children: Voices Against Censorship in Children's Literature*. New York: Neal-Schuman, 1988.

Potthoff, H. H. *God and the Celebration of Life*. Skokie, Ill.: Rand McNally, 1969.

Provenzo, E. F., Jr. *Religious Fundamentalism and American Education: The Battle for the Public Schools*. Albany: State University of New York Press, 1990.

"Publisher Pulls Textbook from Texas." In J. F. Krug (ed.), *Newsletter on Intellectual Freedom*, American Library Association, Office for Intellectual Freedom, July 1994, p. 1.

Random House College Dictionary, rev. ed. New York: Random House, 1988.

Ravitch, D., and Finn, C. E., Jr. *What Do Our 17-Year-Olds Know?* New York: HarperCollins, 1987.

Redding, N. "Assessing the Big Outcomes." *Educational Leadership*, 1991, *49*(8), 49–53.

"Religion in the Public Schools: A Joint Statement of Current Law." New York, N.Y., 1995.

"Religious Liberty, Public Education, and the Future of American Democracy: A Statement of Principles." Sponsored by the Freedom Forum First Amendment Center, Vanderbilt University, and others. Nashville, Tenn.: The Freedom Forum First Amendment Center, Vanderbilt University, 1995.

Resnick, L. B. *Education and Learning to Think*. Washington, D.C.: National Academy Press, 1987.

Riechers, A. "Homosexuals Target Your Child: Curriculum Writers Press for 'Gay' Literature." *Education Newsline*, Citizens for Excellence in Education, 1991.

Rippa, S. A. *Education in a Free Society: An American History*. (6th ed.) White Plains, N.Y.: Longman, 1988.

Robertson, D. B. (ed.). *Love and Justice: Selections from the Shorter Writings of Reinhold Niebuhr*. Philadelphia: Westminster Press, 1957.

Robertson, P. *The New Millennium: 10 Trends That Will Impact You and Your Family by the Year 2000*. Dallas, Tex.: Word Publishing, 1990.

Rogers, D. J. *Banned! Book Censorship in the Schools*. New York: Julian Messner, 1988.

"'Safe Sex' Isn't Safe After All." *Phyllis Schlafly Report*, Eagle Trust Fund, 1994, 28(4).

Salter, S. "Imagination Puts Fear of God into Superstitious." *Rocky Mountain News*, July 28, 1986, p. 29.

"SAT Scores Plunge Again," *Education Reporter*, Sept. 1991, p. 1.

Sathe, V. "Implications of Corporate Culture: A Manager's Guide to Action." *Organizational Dynamics*, 1983, 5, 73–84.

Schlafly, P. (ed.). *Child Abuse in the Classroom*. (3rd ed.) Alton, Ill.: Pere Marquette Press, Aug. 1993.

"A School Race Blows Smoke." *Rocky Mountain News*, Oct. 1993, p. 44A.

Sebaly, A. L. (ed.). *Teacher Education and Religion*. Oneonta, N.Y.: American Association of Colleges for Teacher Education, 1959.

"A Shared Vision: Religious Liberty in the 21st Century." Statement published by the the American Jewish Committee, the Baptist Joint Committee, and the National Council of Churches, and signed by others, 1995.

Sheikh, A. A. *Imagery: Current Theory, Research, and Application*. New York: Wiley, 1983.

Shepard, R. N. "The Mental Image." *American Psychologist*, 1978, *25*, 125–137.

Simonds, R. L. *How to Elect Christians to Public Office*. Costa Mesa, Calif.: National Association of Christian Educators/Citizens for Excellence in Education, 1985.

Simonds, R. L. *President's Report*. Costa Mesa, Calif.: National Association of Christian Educators/Citizens for Excellence in Education, Feb. 1991.

Simonds, R. L. *President's Report*. Costa Mesa, Calif.: National Association of Christian Educators/Citizens for Excellence in Education, Mar. 1991.

Simonds, R. L. *President's Report*. Costa Mesa, Calif.: National Association of Christian Educators/Citizens for Excellence in Education, Apr. 1991.

Simonds, R. L. Fund-Raising Letter. National Association of Christian Educators/Citizens for Excellence in Education, May 6, 1991.

Simonds, R. L. *President's Report*. Costa Mesa, Calif.: National Association of Christian Educators/Citizens for Excellence in Education, July 1, 1991.

Simonds, R. L. *President's Report*. Costa Mesa, Calif.: National Association of Christian Educators/Citizens for Excellence in Education, Aug. 1991.

Simonds, R. L. *President's Report*. Costa Mesa, Calif.: National Association of Christian Educators/Citizens for Excellence in Education, Jan. 1992.

Simonds, R. L. *A Guide to the Public Schools: For Christian Parents and Teachers, and* Especially *for Pastors*. Costa Mesa, Calif.: National Association of Christian Educators/Citizens for Excellence in Education, 1993.

Simonds, R. L. *President's Report*. Costa Mesa, Calif.: National Association of Christian Educators/Citizens for Excellence in Education, Mar. 1993.

Simonds, R. L. *President's Report*. Costa Mesa, Calif.: National Association of Christian Educators/Citizens for Excellence in Education, Oct. 1993.

Simonds, R. L. *President's Report*. Costa Mesa, Calif.: National Association of Christian Educators/Citizens for Excellence in Education, Nov. 1993.

Simonds, R. L. *President's Report*. Costa Mesa, Calif.: National Association of Christian Educators/Citizens for Excellence in Education, Dec. 1993.

Simonds, R. L. "A Plea for the Children." *Educational Leadership*, Dec. 1993–Jan. 1994, *51*(4), 12–15.

Simonds, R. L. *President's Report*. Costa Mesa, Calif.: National Association of Christian Educators/Citizens for Excellence in Education, Apr. 1994.

Simonds, R. L. *President's Report*. Costa Mesa, Calif.: National Association of Christian Educators/Citizens for Excellence in Education, Jan. 1995.

Simonds, R. L. *President's Report*. Costa Mesa, Calif.: National Association of Christian Educators/Citizens for Excellence in Education, Mar. 1995.

Simonds, R. L. *President's Report*. Costa Mesa, Calif.: National Association of Christian Educators/Citizens for Excellence in Education, Apr. 1995.

Simonds, R. L. *President's Report*. Costa Mesa, Calif.: National Association of Christian Educators/Citizens for Excellence in Education, June 1995.

Smith, F. *Understanding Reading*. Troy, Mo.: Holt, Rinehart and Winston, 1982.

Smith, H. *The World's Religions: A Completely Revised and Updated Edition of* The Religions of Man. San Francisco: Harper San Francisco, 1991; original copyright 1958.

Smith, S. "More Info on Dr. Seuss." *The Forum*, Colorado Eagle Forum, Winter 1992, p. 7.

Sommer, C. *Schools in Crisis: Training for Success or Failure?* Houston, Tex.: Cahill, 1984.

Spady, W. G. "Organizing for Results: The Basis of Authentic Restructuring and Reform." *Educational Leadership*, 1988, 46(2), 4–8.

Spady, W. G. Letter to Freedom to Learn Network. Reported in *The Freedom to Learn Network Newsletter*, Winter 1994, 2(2).

Spong, J. S. *Rescuing the Bible from Fundamentalism: A Bishop Rethinks the Meaning of Scripture*. San Francisco: Harper San Francisco, 1991.

Sponhour, M. "Thinking-Skills Program Dogged by 'New Age' Jitters." *The State*, Sept. 27, 1991, p. 1B.

Sternberg, R. J. "Nothing Fails Like Success: The Search for an Intelligent Paradigm for Studying Intelligence." *Journal of Educational Psychology*, 1981, *73*, 142–155.

Sternberg, R. J. *Understanding and Increasing Intelligence*. Orlando, Fla.: Harcourt Brace Jovanovich, 1983.

Sternberg, R. J. *Beyond IQ: A Triarchic Theory of Human Intelligence*. New York: Cambridge University Press, 1984.

Sternberg, R. J. *Beyond IQ*. London: Cambridge University Press, 1985.

"Struggling for Standards." An *Education Week* Special Report, April 12, 1995.

"Surprise Results of Sex Education." *The Phyllis Schlafly Report*, Eagle Trust Fund, Nov. 1994, 28(4).

Tarnas, R. *The Passion of the Western Mind: Understanding the Ideas That Have Shaped Our World View*. New York: Ballantine Books, 1991.

"Teacher Stands Up Against Censorship." *Education Newsline*, Citizens for Excellence in Education, May-June 1991, p. 1.

Tillich, P. *The Shaking of the Foundations*. New York: Charles Scribner's Sons, 1948.

Torrance, E. P. "Teaching Creative and Gifted Learners." In M. C. Wittrock (ed.), *Handbook of Research on Teaching*. (3rd ed.) New York: Macmillan, 1986.

Tracey, D. *Plurality and Ambiguity: Hermeneutics, Religion, Hope*. New York: HarperCollins, 1987.

Tye, K. A. "Introduction: The World at a Crossroads." In K. A. Tye (ed.), *Global Education: From Thought to Action*. Alexandria, Va.: Association for Supervision and Curriculum Development, 1991.

United Methodist Church. *The Book of Discipline of the United Methodist Church, 1972*. Nashville, Tenn.: United Methodist Publishing House, 1973.

Viadero, D. "Parents in S.C. Attack Alleged 'New Age' Program." *Education Week*, Jan. 30, 1991, p. 8.

Vitz, P. C. "A Study of Religion and Traditional Values in Public School Textbooks." In R. J. Neuhaus (ed.), *Democracy and the Renewal of Public Education*. Grand Rapids, Mich.: William B. Eerdmans, 1983.

"What is *Quest?*" *Citizen*, Focus on the Family, 1992, 6(7), 4.

"What's Wrong with Outcome-Based Education?" In *The Phyllis Schlafly Report*, Eagle Trust Fund, May 1993, *26*(10), 1–3.

Whitehead, A. N. *Dialogues of Alfred North Whitehead*. New York: A Mentor Book, 1954.

Whittington, D. "What Have 17-Year-Olds Known in the Past?" *American Educational Research Journal*, 1991, *28*(4), 759–780.

Wilcox, C. *God's Warriors: The Christian Right in Twentieth-Century America*. Baltimore, Md.: Johns Hopkins University Press, 1992.

"The Williamsburg Charter: Summary of Principles." Fairfax, Va.: First Liberty Institute, George Mason University, 1989.

Willis, S. "Conservative Christians Speak Out." *Education Update*, May 1995, *37*(4), 7.

Winn, P. "What's New in School? Lesbians and Wizards." *Citizen*, Focus on the Family, June 18, 1990, pp. 10–11.

Wittrock. M. C. (ed.). *Handbook of Research on Teaching*. (3rd ed.) New York: Macmillan, 1986.

Wood, J. E., Jr. (ed.). *The First Freedom: Religion and the Bill of Rights*. Waco, Tex.: J. M. Dawson Institute of Church-State Studies, Baylor University, 1990.

Yerby W. E., III. "Toward Religious Neutrality in the Public School Curriculum." *University of Chicago Law Review*, 1989, *56*, 899–934.

Yutter, A. J. "How to Bridge the Gap Between Liberal and Orthodox Jews." *Jewish Spectator*, Winter 1994–95.

Zimmerman, B. J. "Self-Regulated Learning and Academic Achievement: An Overview." *Educational Psychologist*, 1990, *25*(1), 3–17.

Legal Cases Cited

Abington School District v. *Schempp*, 374 U.S. 203 (1963).

Ambach, Commissioner of Education of the State of New York v. *Norwick*, 441 U.S. 68 (1978).

Board of Education, Island Trees Union Free School District No. 26 v. *Pico*, 8 Med.L.Rptr. 1721 (1982).

Brown v. *Woodland Joint Unified School District*, No. Civ. S-91–0032 (E.D. Ca. April 2, 1992), CA 92–15772.

Davis v. *Beason*, 133 U.S. 333 (1890).

Engel v. *Vitale*, 370 U.S. 421 (1962).

Epperson v. *Arkansas*, 393 U.S. 97 (1968).

Everson v. *Board of Education*, 330 U.S. 1 (1947).

Grove v. *Mead School District No. 354*, 753 F.2d 1528 (9th Cir. 1985), cert. denied, 106 S.Ct. 85 (1985).

Harris v. *Joint School District No. 241*, 821 F. Supp. 638 (D. Idaho 1993), 41 F. 3rd 447 (9th Cir. 1994).

Jones v. *Clear Creek Independent School District*, 977 F.2d 963 (5th Cir. 1992), cert. denied, 113 S.Ct. 2950 (1993).

Lee v. *Weisman*, 112 S.Ct. 2649 (1992).

Lemon v. *Kurtzman*, 403 U.S. 602 (1971).

McCollum v. *Board of Education*, 333 U.S. 203 (1948).

Mozert v. *Hawkins County Board of Education (Public Schools)*, 647 F.Supp. 1194 (E.D. Tenn. 1986), rev'd, 827 F.2d 1058 (6th Cir. 1987), cert. denied, 108 S.Ct. 1029 (1988).

Scopes v. *State of Tennessee*, 154 Tenn. 105 (1927).

Sherbert v. *Verner*, 374 U.S. 398 (1963).

Smith v. *Board of School Commissioners of Mobile County*, 655 F.Supp. 939 (S.D. Ala. 1987) (on remand), rev'd, 827 F.2d 684 (11th Cir. 1987).

Tinker v. *Des Moines Independent Community School District*, 393 U.S. 503 (1969).

Torcaso v. *Watkins*, 367 U.S. 488 (1961).

United States v. *Seeger*, 380 U.S. 163 (1965).

Wallace v. *Jaffree*, 472 U.S. 38 (1985).

West Virginia State Board of Education v. *Barnette*, 319 U.S. 624, 63 S.Ct. 1178, 87 L.Ed. 1628 (1943).

Zykan v. *Warsaw Community School Corp.*, 631 F.2d 1300 (7th Cir. 1980).

Index